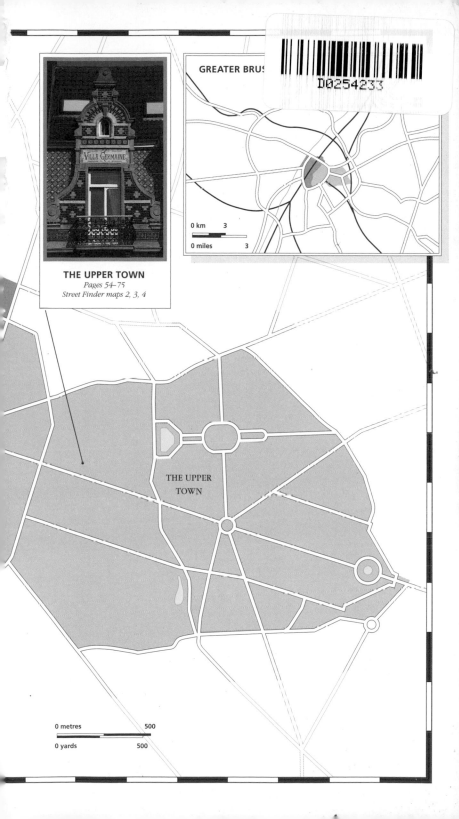

GREATER BRUS

0 km 3

0 miles 3

THE UPPER TOWN
Pages 54–75
Street Finder maps 2, 3, 4

THE UPPER
TOWN

0 metres 500

0 yards 500

EYEWITNESS TRAVEL

BRUSSELS

BRUGES, GHENT & ANTWERP

EYEWITNESS TRAVEL

BRUSSELS

BRUGES, GHENT & ANTWERP

LONDON, NEW YORK,
MELBOURNE, MUNICH AND DELHI
www.dk.com

PRODUCED BY Duncan Baird Publishers
London, England

MANAGING EDITOR Rebecca Miles
MANAGING ART EDITOR Vanessa Marsh
EDITORS Georgina Harris, Michelle de Larrabeiti
DESIGNERS Dawn Davies-Cook, Ian Midson
DESIGN ASSISTANTS Rosie Laing, Kelvin Mullins
VISUALIZER Gary Cross
PICTURE RESEARCH Victoria Peel, Ellen Root
DTP DESIGNER Sarah Williams

Dorling Kindersley Limited
PROJECT EDITOR Paul Hines
ART EDITOR Jane Ewart
MAP CO-ORDINATOR David Pugh

CONTRIBUTORS
Zoë Hewetson, Philip Lee, Zoë Ross,
Sarah Wolff, Timothy Wright, Julia Zyrianova

PHOTOGRAPHERS
Demetrio Carrasco, Paul Kenward

ILLUSTRATORS
Gary Cross, Richard Draper, Eugene Fleury, Paul Guest, Claire Littlejohn,
Robbie Polley, Kevin Robinson, John Woodcock

Printed and bound by South China Printing Co. Ltd., China

First American Edition, 2000

13 14 15 16 10 9 8 7 6 5 4 3 2 1

Published in the United States by DK Publishing,
375 Hudson Street, New York, New York, 10014

Reprinted with revisions 2003, 2005, 2007, 2009, 2011, 2013

Copyright 2000, 2013 © Dorling Kindersley Limited, London

Published in the UK by Dorling Kindersley Limited.
A catalog record for this book is available from the Library of Congress.

ISSN 1542-1554
ISBN 978-0-7369-472-2

FLOORS ARE REFERRED TO THROUGHOUT IN ACCORDANCE WITH EUROPEAN
USAGE; I. E., THE "FIRST FLOOR" IS THE FLOOR ABOVE GROUND LEVEL

Front cover main image: The Grand Place, Brussels

MIX
Paper from
responsible sources
FSC
www.fsc.org   FSC™ C018179

**The information in this
DK Eyewitness Travel Guide is checked regularly.**
Every effort has been made to ensure that this book is as
up-to-date as possible at the time of going to press. Some details,
however, such as telephone numbers, opening hours, prices, gallery
hanging arrangements and travel information are liable to change.
The publishers cannot accept responsibility for any
consequences arising from the use of this book, nor for any material
on third party websites, and cannot guarantee that any website address
in this book will be a suitable source of travel information. We value
the views and suggestions of our readers very highly. Please write to:
Publisher, DK Eyewitness Travel Guides, Dorling Kindersley, 80 Strand,
London WC2R 0RL, UK, or email: travelguides@dk.com.

◁ **The Grand Place, centre of the Lower Town, at night**

CONTENTS

INTRODUCING BRUSSELS

FOUR GREAT DAYS
8

Belgian heroes Tintin and Snowy

Revellers in colourful costume at a festival in the Grand Place

Vista of a tree-lined path in the Parc du Cinquantenaire

Basilique National du Sacré-Coeur

Gilt statue on façade of a
Guildhouse in Antwerp

Belgian chocolates

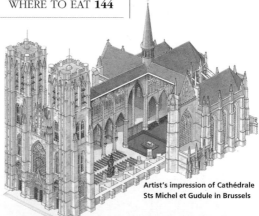
Artist's impression of Cathédrale
Sts Michel et Gudule in Brussels

INTRODUCING
BRUSSELS

FOUR GREAT DAYS

The charms of Brussels, Antwerp, Ghent and Bruges are always agreeably understated. All are small enough to make walking the best means to get around. The pleasures lie in wandering, happening upon hospitable places to eat and drink, and visiting some of their

Notre Dame du Sablon, Brussels

rich and diverse collections of museums, galleries and churches. In best Belgian tradition, the way to approach such days is first and foremost to be unhurried. Be warned that almost all Belgian museums are closed on Monday. Prices shown include admission but not travel or food.

BRUSSELS IN A NUTSHELL

- **The Grand Place, the city's magnificent centrepiece**
- **The Manneken Pis in all his glory**
- **Belgian art: wonderful and weird**
- **The historic sound of music**

TWO ADULTS allow at least €80

Morning
The **Grand Place** *(see pp42–3)* is one of Europe's finest historic squares, and is a "must-see" sight. You could spend an hour just looking at the guildhouses, or dwell longer by settling into one of the bar-cafés on the square. Then walk along the Rue de l'Étuve to visit that famous icon of Brussels, the **Manneken Pis** *(see pp44–5)*.

Return to the Grand Place and the **Musée de la Ville de Bruxelles** to see its surreal collection of costumes and interesting exhibits on the history of the city. There are many places to find lunch in and around the Grand

Place, but choose carefully to avoid disappointment *(see pp152–55)*, especially around Rue des Bouchers.

Afternoon
The afternoon can be spent in Brussels' best museums, which are in the Upper Town. It is not far to walk, or you can take a bus to the **Place Royale** *(see p59)*. This is the location of Belgium's great national art collection, the **Musées Royaux des Beaux-Art de Belgique** and the **Musée Magritte** *(see pp62–7)*, which includes unmissable work by Rubens, plus the wonderful alternative art of the Belgian Symbolists. Also nearby is the excellent **Musée des Instruments de Musique** *(see p60)*, which has fine views over Brussels from its top-floor Café Du Mim. You could instead continue by tram or bus to the unique shrine to Art Nouveau, the **Musée Horta** *(see p82)*, stopping perhaps on the way back for some shopping in the upmarket boutiques of the Avenue Louise and **Avenue de la Toison d'Or** *(see pp168–71)*.

ANTWERP: FASHION, NEW AND OLD

- **Rubens' home, 17th-century seat of fashion**
- **High art from the age of Rubens**
- **A dynamic museum of modern fashion**
- **High-class boutiques**

TWO ADULTS allow at least €80

Het Modepaleis, the principal boutique of Dries van Noten

Morning
First, get a glimpse of Antwerp's 17th-century golden age at the **Rubenshuis** *(see pp102–103)*. Then take a short walk, or a hop on a tram, to Antwerp's fine-art collection, currently at the **Museum Aan De Stroom** *(see p95)*. Followers of fashion will want to see Ann Demeulemeester's shop, which shares Leopold de Waelplaats with the museum. From here it is just a short walk along the river to the **Koninklijk Museum voor Schone Kunsten** *(see pp100–101)*, and also the excellent **FotoMuseum** *(see p99)*.

The gabled buildings of the Grand Place in Brussels

◁ *The Archduchess Isabella Shooting Down a Bird at the Grand Serment, Sablon 1615 (studio of Antoon Sallaert)*

Afternoon

After lunch in one of the pleasant cafés located in the Grote Markt and the nearby streets *(see p164)*, visit Antwerp's museum of fashion, the **ModeMuseum** or **MoMu** *(see p98)*. Nearby is Het Modepaleis, the shop of designer **Dries van Noten** (Nationalestraat 16), and there are other good fashion-hunting grounds in the area. To seek refuge from all this high-octane fashion, head for the more stately charms of Antwerp's great cathedral, the **Onze Lieve Vrouwe Kathedraal** *(see p95)* and the old city square, the **Grote Markt** *(see p94)*.

The Korenlei on the bank of the River Leie in Ghent

GHENT: SACRED AND PROFANE

- Jan van Eyck's outstanding masterpiece
- One of Europe's best design museums
- Cutting-edge modern art

TWO ADULTS allow at least €80

Morning

First, make a pilgrimage to Jan (and Hubert) van Eyck's exquisite panel painting, *The Adoration of the Mystic Lamb* in **St Baafskathedraal** *(see p114)*. Then walk to the Graslei and Korenlei *(see p115)*, stopping to admire the views from the St Michiels-brug bridge over the canal. Continue to **Design Museum Ghent** *(see p115)*, a superb museum tracing the history of interiors, furniture and furnishings. You could now take a 40-minute canal trip from the Korenlei, which gives an insight into the importance of the waterways in the city's medieval life. For lunch, there is a good choice of restaurants in the area *(see pp160–61)*.

Afternoon

Take a tram from the Korenmarkt to Charles de

Detail from *The Adoration of the Mystic Lamb*, Ghent

Kerchovelaan and walk across the Citadelpark to the **Stedelijk Museum voor Actuele Kunst**, or **SMAK** *(see p117)*. This great collection of contemporary art is bound to leave an impression on you. Returning to the historic centre of the town, try an aperitif of *jenever* gin in one of the bars by the canal or in the Vrijdagmarkt.

BRUGES: MEDIEVAL GLORY

- A view of medieval Bruges
- Supreme art from its Golden Age
- A relaxing canal trip
- Beer "academies"

TWO ADULTS allow at least €100

Morning

Start the day with an energetic climb up the 366 steps of the **Belfort** *(see p121)*, the city bell-tower, for some exhilarating views across Bruges. Now walk the short distance to the **Burg** *(see p120)*, a delightful square lined with historic buildings, including the **Stadhuis** *(see p120)*, and the double church of the **Heilig Bloed Basiliek** *(see p120)*. It is a short and pretty walk from here, along the canals, to the **Groeningemuseum** *(see pp124–25)*, celebrated for its small but fabulous collection of late-medieval painting. There are plenty of places to eat nearby, especially around the Vismarkt back near the Burg, or by heading further west to Gruuthusestraat, Mariastraat and Walplein.

Afternoon

Start with a restful canal trip; tours last about 30 minutes and most start from landing stages near the Burg. Next, walk back along the canal called the Dijver to **Onze Lieve Vrouwekerk** *(see p121)*, one of Bruges' most attractive churches. On the other side of Mariastraat is the **Memling in Sint-Jan Hospitaalmuseum** *(see p123)*, a museum that combines a medieval hospital with a collection of late medieval paintings by Hans Memling. From here you could take a short walk to the **Gruuthuse Museum** *(see p122)* for a taste of medieval life.

The view of Bruges from the top of the Belfort

Putting Brussels on the Map

Brussels is the capital of Belgium and the centre of government for the European Union. Although one of Europe's smallest countries, covering 30,500 sq km (11,580 sq miles), Belgium has one of the highest population densities, with 11 million inhabitants (360 people for every square kilometre). Belgium is a trilingual country (Dutch, French and German). Although Brussels falls geographically in the Flemish (Dutch-speaking) half, it is largely French-speaking, and is Belgium's largest city, with more than one million inhabiting the region. Brussels is also the most visited, with around six million visitors a year, although 70 per cent of these come for business. Brussels' excellent communications make it an ideal place from which to explore Antwerp, Ghent and Bruges.

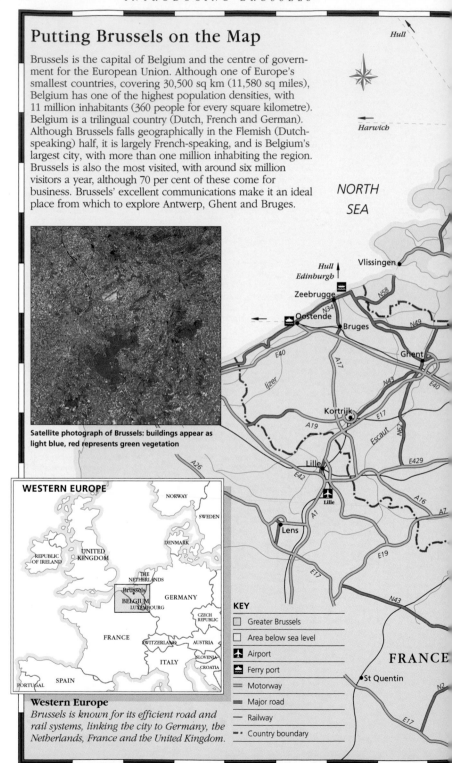

Satellite photograph of Brussels: buildings appear as light blue, red represents green vegetation

WESTERN EUROPE

Western Europe

Brussels is known for its efficient road and rail systems, linking the city to Germany, the Netherlands, France and the United Kingdom.

KEY

☐ Greater Brussels

☐ Area below sea level

✈ Airport

⛴ Ferry port

═ Motorway

▬ Major road

— Railway

▬•▬ Country boundary

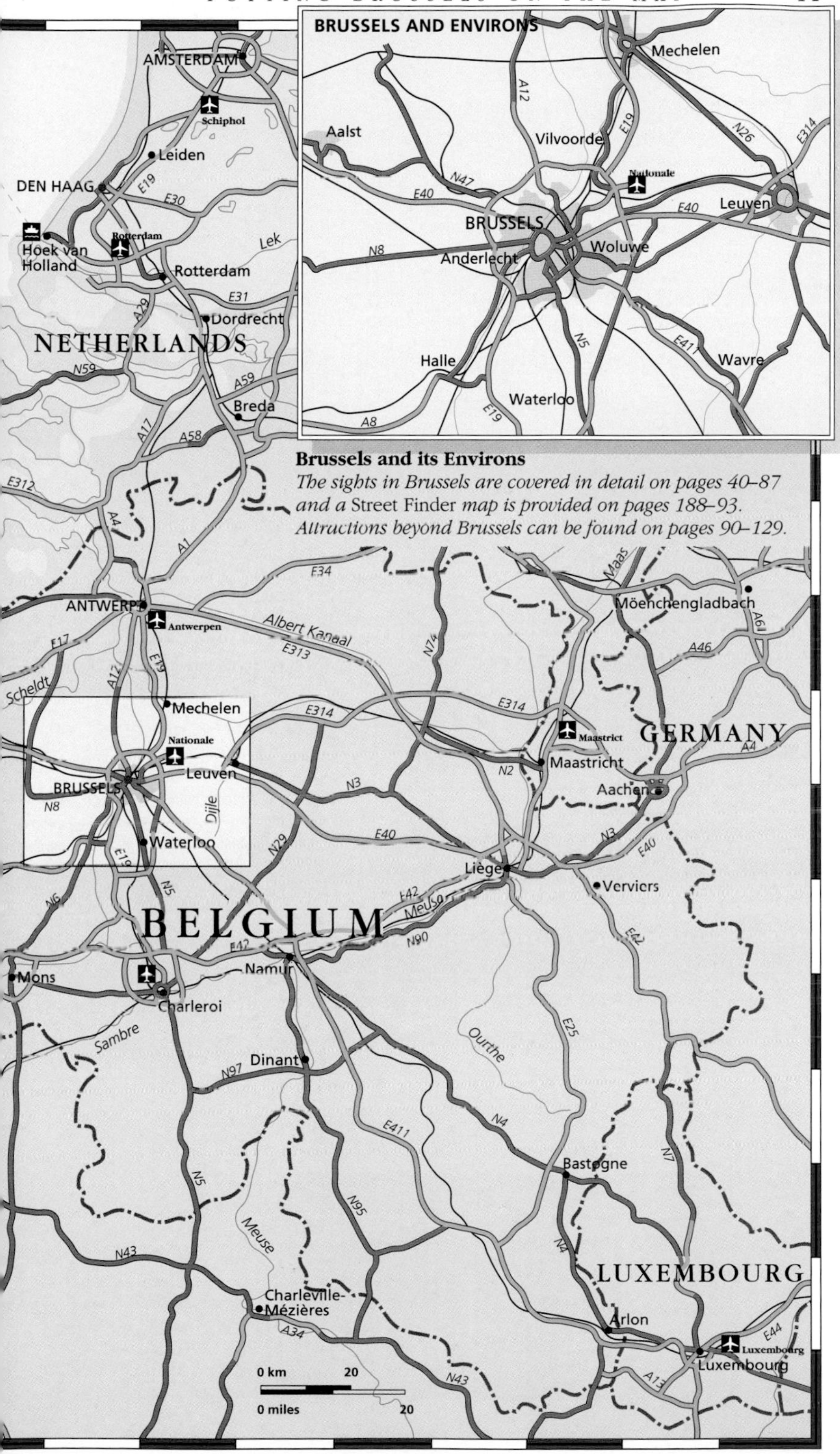

BRUSSELS AND ENVIRONS

Mechelen

Aalst

Vilvoorde

Nationale

BRUSSELS

Leuven

Anderlecht

Woluwe

Halle

Wavre

Waterloo

Brussels and its Environs

*The sights in Brussels are covered in detail on pages 40–87
and a Street Finder map is provided on pages 188–93.
Attractions beyond Brussels can be found on pages 90–129.*

AMSTERDAM

Schiphol

Leiden

DEN HAAG

Rotterdam

Hoek van
Holland

Rotterdam

Lek

Dordrecht

NETHERLANDS

Breda

Möenchengladbach

ANTWERPEN

Albert Kanaal

Antwerpen

Scheldt

Mechelen

Maastrict

GERMANY

Nationale

Maastricht

BRUSSELS

Leuven

Dijle

Aachen

Waterloo

BELGIUM

Liège

Verviers

Mons

Namur

Meuse

Charleroi

Sambre

Ourthe

Dinant

Bastogne

Charleville-
Mézières

LUXEMBOURG

Arlon

Luxembourg
Luxembourg

0 km   20

0 miles   20

Central Brussels

Central Brussels is divided into two main areas, each of which has its own chapter in the guide. Historically the poorer area where workers and immigrants lived, the Lower Town contains the exceptional 17th-century heart of the city, the Grand Place, as well as the cosmopolitan Place de Brouckère, and the historic workers' district, the Marolles. The Upper Town, traditional home of the aristocracy, is an elegant area which encircles the city's green oasis, the Parc de Bruxelles. Running up through the area is Rue Royale, which ends in the 18th-century Place Royale, home to the city's finest art museums, including the Musée Magritte.

Hôtel de Ville
The focus of the Grand Place, Brussels' historic Town Hall dates from the early 15th century. Its Gothic tracery façade features the famous needle-like crooked spire (see pp44–5).

KEY

- Major sight
- Parking
- Tourist information
- Police station
- Hospital
- Bus terminus
- Tram stop
- Railway station
- Metro station
- Church

La Bourse Façade
Just behind the Grand Place on busy Boulevard Anspach in the Lower Town, Brussels' Stock Exchange was built in 1873 in ornate style (see p47).

Place du Petit Sablon
This square is a jewel of the Upper Town. Originally a horse market, the central area became a flower garden in 1890, surrounded by wrought-iron railings decorated with stone statuettes. Each figure represents a medieval trade or craft that brought prosperity to the capital (see pp68–9).

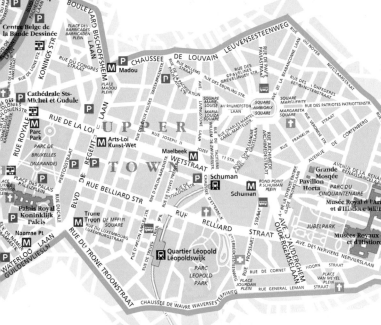

Palais Royal
The official work place of the Belgian monarch, this is one of the finest 18th-century buildings in the Upper Town. A highlight of Neo-Classical architecture, it overlooks Parc de Bruxelles (see pp58–9).

0 metres 500

0 yards 500

Brussels' Best: Architecture

Reflecting Brussels' importance in the history of northern Europe, the city's architecture ranges from grand medieval towers to the glittering post-modern structures of European institutions. With a few examples of medieval Brabant Gothic still on show, the capital of Europe has the best Flemish Renaissance architecture in the world in the Baroque splendour of the Grand Place, as well as elegant Neo-Classical churches and houses. The quantity and quality of Art Nouveau *(see pp18–19)*, with its exquisite interiors and handmade features, are highlights of 19th- and 20th-century residential building. The cutting-edge designs in the Parliament Quarter, planned by committees of European architects, take the tour up to date.

Basilique du Sacré-Coeur
Begun in 1905 and only completed in 1970, this huge Art Deco edifice is the world's fifth-largest church (see p85).

BASILIQUE DU SACRÉ-COEUR

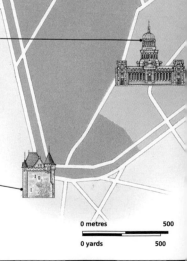

Grand Place
Almost entirely rebuilt by merchants after French bombardment in 1695, this cobbled square is one of the world's best Baroque ensembles (see pp42–3).

Palais de Justice
Bigger in area than St Peter's in Rome, the city's law courts were built in Neo-Classical style using the profits of colonialism, and completed in 1883 (see p69).

Lower Town

Porte de Hal
This imposing 14th-century tower is the only remaining trace of the city's solid, thick second perimeter wall. It owes its survival to its use as an 18th-century prison and latterly as a museum (see p83).

| 0 metres | | 500 |
| 0 yards | | 500 |

Cathédrale Sts Michel et Gudule
The white stone façade from 1250 is an outstanding example of Brabant Gothic style (see pp70–71).

Palais de la Nation
The home of the Belgian Parliament since the country's independence in 1830, this magnificent building was constructed in the late 18th century by the French Neo-Classical architect Guimard, who also designed the expansive stone façade and many of the surrounding state buildings.

Upper Town

Palais d'Egmont
This ducal mansion bears the name of a Flemish count executed for defending his countrymen's civil rights in 1568 (see p69).

European Parliament
Nicknamed "Caprice des Dieux" ("Whim of the Gods"), this postmodern building serves more than 700 politicians.

Belgian Artists

Belgian art rose to the fore when the region came under Burgundian rule in the 15th century. Renaissance painters produced strong works in oil, characterized by intricate detail and lifelike, unidealized portraiture. The quest for realism and clarity of light was heavily influenced by the new Dutch schools of art. Yet, in contrast, Belgium's second golden artistic age, in the 20th century, abandoned reality for surrealism in the challenging work of artists such as René Magritte.

Belgium is justifiably proud of its long artistic tradition. Rubenshuis in Antwerp *(see pp102–103)*, Brussels' Musée Wiertz *(see p72)*, Musées Royaux des Beaux-Arts de Belgique and Musée Magritte *(see pp62–7)* are fine examples of the respect Belgium shows to its artists' homes and their works.

Portrait of Laurent Froimont
by Rogier van der Weyden

THE FLEMISH PRIMITIVES

Art in Brussels and Flanders first attracted European attention at the end of the Middle Ages. **Jan van Eyck** (c.1395–41) is considered to be responsible for the major revolution in Flemish art. Widely credited as the creator of oil painting, van Eyck was the first artist to use the oil medium to fix longer-lasting glazes and to mix colour pigments for wood and canvas. As works could now be rendered more permanent, the innovation spread the Renaissance fashion for panel paintings. However, van Eyck was more than just a practical innovator, and can be seen as the forefather of the Flemish Primitive school

with his lively depictions of human existence in an animated manner. Van Eyck is also responsible, with his brother, for the striking polyptych altarpiece *Adoration of the Mystic Lamb*, displayed in Ghent Cathedral *(see p114)*.

The trademarks of the Flemish Primitives are a lifelike vitality, enhanced by realism in portraiture, texture of clothes and furnishings and a clarity of light. The greatest interpreter of the style was Rogier de la Pasture (c.1400–64), better known as **Rogier van der Weyden**, the town painter of Brussels, who combined van Eyck's light and realism with work of religious intensity, as in *Lamentation (see p66)*.

Many in Belgium and across Europe were schooled and inspired by his work, continuing and expanding the new techniques. **Dirk Bouts** (1415–75) extended

the style. With his studies of bustling 15th-century Bruges, **Hans Memling** (c.1430–94) is considered the last Flemish Primitive. Moving towards the 16th century, landscape artist **Joachim Patinir** (c.1480–1524) produced the first European industrial scenes.

THE BRUEGHEL DYNASTY

In the early years of the 16th century, Belgian art was strongly influenced by the Italians. Trained in Rome, **Jan Gossaert** (c.1478–1532) brought mythological themes to the art commissioned by the ruling Dukes of Brabant.

But it was the prolific Brueghel family who had the most influence on Flemish art throughout the 16th and 17th centuries. **Pieter Brueghel the Elder** (c.1525–69), one of the greatest Flemish artists, settled in Brussels in 1563. His earthy rustic landscapes of village life, peopled with comic peasants, are a social study of medieval life and remain his best-known work. **Pieter Brueghel the Younger** (1564–1636) produced religious works such as *The Enrolment of Bethlehem* (1610). In contrast, **Jan Brueghel the Elder** (1568–1625) painted intricate floral still lifes with a draped velvet backdrop, becoming known as "Velvet Brueghel". His son, **Jan Brueghel the Younger** (1601–78) also became a court painter in Brussels and a fine landscape artist of note.

The Fall of Icarus by Pieter Brueghel the Elder

Self-portrait by Rubens, one of many from his lifetime

THE ANTWERP ARTISTS

In the 17th century, the main centre of Belgian art moved from the social capital, Brussels, to Antwerp, in the heart of Flanders. This move was largely influenced by **Pieter Paul Rubens** (1577–1640), who lived in Antwerp. He was one of the first Flemish artists to become known through Europe and Russia. A court painter, Rubens was also an accomplished landscape artist and interpreter of mythology, but is best known for his depiction of plump women, proud of their figures. Rubens was so popular in his own time that his bold and large-scale works were translated by Flemish weavers into series of tapestries.

Anthony van Dyck (1599–1641), a pupil of Rubens and court portraitist, was the second Antwerp artist to gain world renown. The Brueghel dynasty continued to produce notable figures. Jan Brueghel the Elder eventually settled in Antwerp to produce art with Rubens, while his son-in-law, **David Teniers II** (1610–90) founded the Antwerp Academy of Art in 1665.

THE EUROPEAN INFLUENCE

The influence of Rubens was so great that little innovation took place in the Flemish art scene in the 18th century. In the early years of the 19th

century, Belgian art was largely dominated by the influence of other European schools. **François-Joseph Navez** (1787–1869) introduced Neo-Classicism to Flemish art. Realism took off with **Constantin Meunier** (1831–1905) and Impressionism with **Guillaume Vogels** (1836–96). The Brussels-based **Antoine Wiertz** (1806–65) was considered a Romantic, but his distorted and occasionally disturbing works, such as *Inhumation précipitée* (c.1830) seem to have early Surrealist leanings. **Fernand Khnopff** (1858–1921) was influenced by the German Romantic Gustav Klimt. An early exponent of Belgian Symbolism, Khnopff's work is notable for his portraits of menacing and ambiguous women. Also on a journey from Naturalism to Surrealism, **James Ensor** (1860–1949) often used eerie skeletons in his work, reminiscent of Bosch. Between 1884 and 1894, the artists' cooperative **Les XX (Les Vingt)** reinvigorated the Brussels art scene with exhibitions of famous foreign and Avant Garde painters.

SURREALISM

The 20th century began with the emergence of Fauvism led by **Rik Wouters** (1882–1916), whose bright sun-filled landscapes show the influence of Cézanne.

Surrealism began in Brussels in the mid-1920s, dominated from the start by **René Magritte** (1898–1967). The movement had its roots back in the 16th century, with the phantasmagoria of Bosch and Pieter Brueghel the Elder. Fuelled by the chaos of World War I, much of which took place on Flemish battlefields, Magritte defined his disorientating Surrealism as "[restoring] the familiar to the strange". More ostentatious and emotional, **Paul Delvaux** (1897–1994) produced elegant, freakish interiors occupied by ghostly figures. In 1948 the **COBRA Movement** promoted abstract art, which gave way in the 1960s to conceptual art, led by installationist **Marcel Broodthaers** (1924–76), who used daily objects, such as a casserole dish full of mussels, for his own interpretation.

Sculpture by Rik Wouters

UNDERGROUND ART

Notre Temps (1976) by Expressionist Roger Somville at Hankar station

Some 58 Brussels metro stations have been decorated with a combination of murals, sculptures and architecture by 54 Belgian artists. Although none but the most devoted visitor to the city is likely to see them all, there are several notable examples. **Annessens** was decorated by the Belgian COBRA artists, Dotremont and Alechinsky. In the **Bourse**, surrealist Paul Delvaux's *Nos Vieux Trams Bruxellois* is still on show with *Moving Ceiling*, a series of 75 tubes that move in the breeze by sculptor Pol Bury. At **Horta** station, Art Nouveau wrought ironwork from Victor Horta's now destroyed People's Palace is displayed, and **Stockel** is a tribute to Hergé and his boy hero, Tintin *(see pp20–1)*.

Brussels' Best: Art Nouveau

Among Europe's most important architectural move-
ments at the start of the 20th century, Art Nouveau in
Belgium was led by Brussels architect Victor Horta
(1861–1947) and the Antwerp-born interior designer
Henry van de Velde (1863–1957). The style evolved
from the Arts and Crafts Movement in England and the
fashion for Japanese simplicity, and is characterized
by its sinuous decorative lines, stained glass, carved
stone curves, floral frescoes and elaborately curled
and twisted metalwork. As new suburbs rose up in
the 1890s, over 2,000 new houses were built in the
style. Although many were demolished, details can
still be seen in almost every Brussels street.

Hôtel Métropole
*The high-vaulted lobby and
bar of this luxurious 1894
hotel recall the city's fin-de-
siècle heyday* (see p49).

Old England
*This former department
store uses glass and steel
rather than brick, with
large windows and
twisted metal turrets*
(see p60).

Hôtel Ciamberlani
*Architect Paul Hankar
designed this redbrick
house in rue Defacqz
for the* sgraffiti *artist
Albert Ciamberlani,
with whom he worked.*

The Lower Town

Musée Horta
*Curved window frames
and elaborate metal
balconies mark this out
as the home and studio of
Art Nouveau's best-known
architect* (see p82).

Hôtel Hannon
*This stylish 1902 townhouse
was built by Jules Brunfaut
(1852–1942). One of its metal-
framed windows has striking
stained-glass panes* (see p83).

Maison Cauchie

Restored in 1989, architect Paul Cauchie's home in rue des Francs has examples of sgraffiti, a technique in which designs are incised onto wet plaster to reveal another colour beneath.

Maison Saint Cyr

Horta's disciple Gustave Strauven was keen to out-do his mentor with this intricate façade, only 4 m (14 ft) wide (see p72).

The Upper Town

Hôtel Solvay

An early Horta creation of 1894, this home was built for a wealthy family. Horta designed every element of the building, from the ochre and yellow cast-iron façade columns and glass front door to the decorative but functional doorknobs (see p83).

| 0 metres | 500 |
| 0 yards | 500 |

Belgian Comic Strip Art

Tintin's dog Snowy

Belgian comic strip art is as famous a part of Belgian culture as chocolates and beer. The seeds of this great passion were sown when the US comic strip Little Nemo was published in French in 1908 to huge popular acclaim in Belgium. The country's reputation for producing some of the best comic strip art in Europe was established after World War II. Before the war, Europe was awash with American comics, but the Nazis called a halt to the supply. Local artists took over, and found that there was a large audience who preferred homegrown comic heroes. This explosion in comic strip art was led by perhaps the most famous Belgian creation ever, Tintin, who, with his dog Snowy, is as recognizable across Europe as Mickey Mouse.

demonstrated by his work before and during the war, where he expressed a strong sense of justice in such stories as *King Ottakar's Sceptre*, where a fascist army attempts to seize control of a central European state. Hergé took great care in researching his stories; for *Le Lotus Bleu* in 1934, which was set in China, he wrote: "I started… showing a real interest in the people and countries I was sending Tintin off to, concerned by a sense of honesty to my readers."

Spirou cover

Hergé at work in his studio

HERGÉ AND TINTIN

Tintin's creator, Hergé, was born Georges Remi in Brussels in 1907. He began using his pen name (a phonetic spelling of his initials in reverse) in 1924. At the young age of 15, his drawings were published in the *Boy Scout Journal*. He became the protégé of a priest, Abbot Norbert Wallez, who also managed the Catholic journal *Le XXe Siècle*, and was swiftly given the

responsibility of the children's supplement, *Le petit Vingtième*. Eager to invent an original comic strip, Hergé came up with the character of Tintin the reporter, who first appeared in the story *Tintin au Pays des Soviets* on 10 January 1929. Over the next 10 years the character developed and grew in popularity. Book-length stories began to appear from 1930.

During the Nazi occupation in the 1940s *Tintin* continued to be published, with political references carefully omitted, in an approved paper *Le Soir*. This led to Hergé being accused of collaboration at the end of the war. He was called in for questioning but released later the same day without charge. Hergé's innocence was amply

Statue of Tintin and Snowy

POST-WAR BOOM

Belgium's oldest comic strip journal *Spirou* was launched in April 1938 and, alongside the weekly *Journal de Tintin* begun in 1946, became a hothouse for the artistic talent that was to flourish after the war. Artists such as Morris, Jijé, Peyo and Roba worked on the journal. Morris (1923–2001) introduced the cowboy parody, *Lucky Luke* in *Spirou* in 1947, a character who went on to feature in live-action films and US television cartoons. Marc Sleen, another celebrated Belgian cartoonist, created the popular character *Nibbs* (or *Nero* in Flemish).

COMIC STRIP CHARACTERS

Some of the world's best-loved comic strip characters originated in Belgium. *Tintin* is the most famous, but *Lucky Luke* the cowboy, the cheeky children *Suske en Wiske* and *The Smurfs* have also been published worldwide, while modern artists such as Schueten break new ground.

Tintin by Hergé

Lucky Luke by Morris

During the 1960s, the idea of the comic strip being the Ninth Art (after the seventh and eighth, film and television) expanded to include adult themes in the form of the comic-strip graphic novel.

PEYO AND THE SMURFS

Best known for *The Smurfs*, Peyo (1928–92) was also a member of the team behind the *Spirou* journal which published his poetic medieval series *Johan et Pirlouit*, in 1952. *The Smurfs* first appeared as characters here – tiny blue people whose humorous foibles soon eclipsed any interest in the strip's supposed main characters. Reacting to their popularity, Peyo created a strip solely about them. Set in the Smurf village, the stories were infused with satirical social comment. *The Smurfs* were a popular craze between 1983 and 1985, featuring in advertising and merchandising of every type. They spawned a feature length film, TV cartoons and popular music, and had several hit records in the 1980s.

Modern cover by Marvano

WILLY VANDERSTEEN

While *Spirou* and *Tintin* were French-language journals, Willy Vandersteen (1913–90) dominated the Flemish market. His popular creation, *Suske en Wiske* has

been translated into English and appears as *Bob and Bobette* in the UK, and *Willy and Wanda* in the US. The main characters are a pair of "ordinary" kids aged between 10 and 14 years who have extraordinary adventures all over the world, as well as travelling back and forth in time. Today, Vandersteen's books sell in their millions.

COMIC STRIP ART TODAY

Comic strips, known as *bandes dessinées* or *beeldverhaal*, continue to be published in Belgium in all their forms. In newspapers, children's comics and graphic novels the Ninth Art remains one of the country's biggest exports. The high standards and imaginative scope of a new generation of artists, such as Schueten and Marvano, have fed growing consumer demand for comic books. Both French and Flemish publishers issue

Contemporary comic-strip artists at work in their studio

over 22 million comic books each year. Today, Belgian cartoons are sold in more than 30 countries, including the US.

Larger-than-life cartoon by Frank Pé adorning a Brussels building

STREET ART

There are currently 18 large comic strip images decorating the sides of buildings around Brussels' city centre. This outdoor exhibition is known as the Comic Strip Route and is organized by the Centre Belge de la Bande Dessineé (the Belgian Comics Strip Centre) (*see pp50–51*) and the city of Brussels. Begun in 1991 as a tribute to Belgium's talent for comic strip art, this street art project continues to grow. A free map of the route is available from tourist information offices, as well as from the comic museum itself.

Suske en Wiske by Vandersteen

The Smurfs by Peyo

Contemporary cartoon strip by Schueten

Tapestry and Lace

Lacemaker's studio sign

For over six centuries, Belgian lace and tapestry have been highly prized luxury crafts. Originating in Flanders in the 12th century, tapestry has since been handmade in the centres of Tournai, Brussels, Arras, Mechelen and Oudenaarde, while the lace trade was practised from the 1500s onwards in all the Belgian provinces, with Bruges and Brussels particularly renowned for their delicate work. The makers often had aristocratic patrons; intricate lace and fine tapestries were status symbols of the nobility and staple exports throughout Europe from the 15th to 18th centuries. Today Belgium remains home to the very best tapestry and lace studios in the world.

Tapestry weavers *numbered over 50,000 in Flanders from 1450–1550. With the ruling Dukes of Burgundy as patrons, weavers prospered, and hangings grew more elaborate.*

Tapestry designs *involve weaver and artist working closely together. Painters, including Rubens, produced drawings for a series of weavings of six or more on grand themes (detail shown).*

The texture of the weave was the finest ever achieved; often 12 threads to the inch (5 per cm).

Weavers working today *still use medieval techniques to produce contemporary tapestry, woven in Mechelen and Tournai to modern designs.*

TAPESTRY

By 1200, the Flemish towns of Arras (now in France) and Tournai were Europe-wide known centres of weaving. Prized by the nobility, tapestries were portable and could be moved with the court as rulers travelled their estates. As trade grew, techniques were refined; real gold and silver were threaded into the fine wool, again increasing the value. Blending Italian idealism with Flemish realism, Bernard van Orley (1492–1542) revolutionized tapestry designs, as seen above in *The Battle of Pavia 1525*, the first of a series. Flemish weavers were eventually lured across Europe, where ironically their skill led to the success of the Gobelins factory in Paris that finally stole Flanders' crown in the late 1700s.

The lace trade *rose to the fore during the early Renaissance. Emperor Charles V decreed that lace-making should be a compulsory skill for girls in convents and béguinages (see p53) throughout Flanders. Lace became fashionable on collars and cuffs for both sexes. Trade reached a peak in the 18th century.*

Battles and classical myths were popular themes for tapestry series.

Lace makers *are traditionally women. Although their numbers are dwindling, many craftswomen still work in Bruges and Brussels, centres of bobbin lace, creating intricate work by hand.*

Victorian lace *heralded a revival of the craft after its decline in the austere Neo-Classical period. Although men no longer wore it, the growth of the status of lace as a ladies' accessory and its use in soft furnishing led to its renewed popularity.*

Belgian lace *is bought today mainly as a souvenir, but despite the rise in machine-made lace from other countries, the quality here still remains as fine as it was in the Renaissance.*

BRUSSELS THROUGH THE YEAR

The temperate climate of Brussels is typical of Northern Europe and means that a range of activities throughout the year take place both inside and out. Mild damp winters and gentle summers allow the city's strong artistic life to flourish in historic buildings and modern stadiums alike. The Belgians make the most of their seasonal changes. Theatre, dance and film start their season in January, with evening venues

Revellers at Ommegang

that range from ancient abbeys lit by the setting sun to drive-in cinemas. The city's flower festival launches the summer in highly colourful style, with the Grand Place literally carpeted in millions of blooms every other August. Through the year, festivals in Brussels range from energetic, exuberant historic processions that have taken place yearly since medieval times, to innovative European experimental art.

SPRING

Brussels' lively cultural life takes off as the crisp spring days lengthen and visitors begin to arrive in the city. Music festivals take place in a wide variety of open-air venues. As the city's parks burst into bloom, the world-famous tropical greenhouses at Laeken are opened to the public and Brussels' chocolatiers produce delicious creations for Easter.

The Royal Glasshouse at Laeken, famed for its rare exotic orchids

MARCH

Ars Musica *(early Mar to early Apr)*. This celebration of modern music is one of Europe's finest festivals, boasting famous performers and beautiful venues, often the Musée d'art ancien *(see pp62–3)*. The festival is now a must for connoisseurs of the contemporary music world.
Eurantica *(mid-to end Mar)*. From archaeology to the modern arts, more than 150 antique dealers from all over Europe gather together for this large-scale fair.
Museum Night Fever *(early Mar)*. One night of exhibitions, music, dance, performances and DJs. Twenty museums take part.

APRIL

BIFFF (Brussels International Fantastic Film Festival) *(early to mid-Apr)*. Two weeks of

thrills, shivers and off-the-wall films. Over 150 cinemas open their doors for special festival screenings and a series of film-based discussions are held throughout the festival.
Sablon Baroque Spring *(third week)*. The Place du Grand Sablon hosts new classical ensembles in a gathering of young Belgian talent performing 17th-century music.
The Royal Greenhouses at Laeken *(late Apr to early May)*. The private greenhouses of the Belgian Royal family are opened to the public as their exotic plants and cacti start to flower. Breathtaking 19th-century glass and wrought ironwork shelters hundreds of rare species *(see pp86–7)*.
Flanders Festival *(mid-Apr to Oct)*. A celebration of all things musical, this

classical medley offers more than 120 performances by internationally renowned choirs and orchestras.
Scenes d'Ecran *(third weekend)*. Over 100 new European films draw crowds in cinemas across the city.

MAY

Europe Day Festivities *(7–9 May)*. As the capital of Europe, Brussels celebrates its role in the European Union – even Manneken

Runners taking part in the Brussels Twenty-Kilometre Race

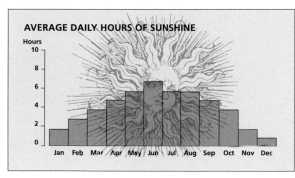

AVERAGE DAILY HOURS OF SUNSHINE

Hours
10
8
6
4
2
0
Jan Feb Mar Apr May Jun Jul Aug Sep Oct Nov Dec

Climate
Belgium has a fairly temperate Northern European climate. Although not often freezing, winters are chilly and a heavy coat is required. Summers are warmer and much brighter, though you will still need a jersey for the evenings. Rainwear is always a necessity.

Pis is dressed as a Euro-supporter, in a suit of blue, decorated with yellow stars.
Kunsten FESTIVAL des Arts *(early to end May)*. This innovative theatre and dance festival provides a platform for new talent to perform.
Les Nuits Botaniques *(mid–May)*. Held in the former green houses of the Botanical gardens, now the French cultural centre, this series of musical events is a delight.
Queen Elisabeth Music Contest *(all month)*. Classical fans will flock to the prestigious musical competition, now in its fifth decade. Young singers, violinists and pianists gather in front of well-known conductors and soloists to determine the champion among Europe's finest student players.
Brussels Twenty-Kilometre Race *(last Sunday)*. As many as 20,000 keen professional and amateur runners race round the city, taking in its major landmarks.
Jazz Marathon *(last weekend)*. Bistros and cafés are the venues for myriad small jazz bands, with some well-known artists playing anonymously.

SUMMER

The season of pageantry arrives with Ommegang in July, one of Europe's oldest and best-known processions, which takes place in the Grand Place and the surrounding streets. Multicultural music runs throughout the summer, with classical,

jazz and avant-garde US and European performers playing in venues ranging from tiny beer cafés to the great King Baudouin stadium in Heysel. Independence is celebrated on Belgian National Day. Families enjoy the Foire du Midi, the huge fairground over 2 km square (1 sq mile) covered with rides and stalls.

JUNE

Brussels Rollers *(mid-Jun to end Aug)*. Rollerskaters dominate the streets of Brussels every Friday evening as they follow an exclusive skate route around the city.
City of Brussels Summer Festival *(mid-Jun to end Aug)*. Classical concerts take place in some of the city's best-known ancient buildings.
Brussels European Film Festival *(late Jun)*. Premières and film stars are adding weight to this European film showcase. **Couleur Café Festival** *(last weekend)*. Spread over three summer evenings in the Tour et Taxis

African drummer performing at the Couleur Café Festival

renovated warehouse, the fashionable and funky programme includes salsa, African drummers, acid jazz and multicultural music.
Fête de la Musique *(last weekend)*. Two days of concerts and recitals featuring world music take place in the halls and museums of the city.

JULY

Ommegang *(first Thu in Jul and the Tue before)*. This festival has been celebrated in Brussels since 1549, and now draws crowds from around the world.

The Ommegang pausing in front of dignitaries in the Grand Place

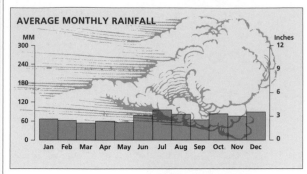

AVERAGE MONTHLY RAINFALL

Jan Feb Mar Apr May Jun Jul Aug Sep Oct Nov Dec

Rainfall chart
*On the whole
Belgium is rather
a rainy country,
with Brussels expe-
riencing constant
low rainfall
throughout the year.
Spring is the driest
season, but
summers can be
damp. In winter,
rain may turn to
snow and sleet.*

Translated as "a tour", the procession revolves around the Grand Place and the surrounding streets. Over 2,000 participants dress up and become members of a Renaissance town; jesters, courtiers, nobles and soldiers; they go on to parade before Belgian dignitaries. Tickets have to be booked months in advance.

Brosella Folk and Jazz Festival *(second weekend).*
Musicians from all over Europe play informal gigs in the Parc d'Osseghem in the shadow of the Atomium.

Festival d'Eté de Bruxelles *(Jul–Aug).* Classical concerts take place through the high summer in venues around the Upper and Lower Town.

Foire du Midi *(mid-Jul–mid-Aug).* Brussels' main station, Gare du Midi, is host to this month-long funfair, which attracts people in their thousands. Especially popular with children, it is one of the biggest fairs in Europe, and includes an enormous Ferris wheel.

Belgian National Day *(21 Jul).* The 1831 declaration of independence is com-memorated annually with a military parade followed by a firework display in the Parc de Bruxelles.

Palais Royal Open Days *(last week in Jul–second week of Sep).* The official residence of the Belgian Royal family, the opulent staterooms of the Palais Royal, including the huge throne room, are open to the public for six weeks during the summer *(see pp58–9).*

Costumed revellers at the Plantation of the Meiboom

AUGUST

Plantation du Meiboom *(9 Aug).* This traditional festival dates from 1213. Parading crowds dressed in huge puppet costumes parade around the Lower Town and finally reach the Grand Place where a maypole is planted as a celebration of summer.

Tapis des Fleurs *(mid-Aug,*

biennially, for four days). Taking place on even-num-bered years, this colourful celebration pays tribute to Brussels' long-established flower industry. The Grand Place is carpeted with millions of fresh flowers in patterns echoing historical scenes. The beautiful flower carpet meas-ures 2,000 sq m (21,000 sq ft).

AUTUMN

Fresh autumn days are the cue for many indoor events; innovative jazz is performed in the city's cafés and the French cultural centre in Le Botanique. Architecture is celebrated in the heritage weekend where the public can tour many private houses and personal art collections.

SEPTEMBER

The Birthday of Manneken Pis *(last weekend).* Brussels' celebrated mascot is clothed in a new suit by a chosen

The Grand Place, carpeted in millions of fresh flowers

AVERAGE MONTHLY TEMPERATURE

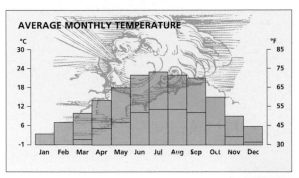

°C
30
24
18
12
6
-1

°F
85
75
65
55
45
30

Jan Feb Mar Apr May Jun Jul Aug Sep Oct Nov Dec

Temperature chart
This chart gives the average maximum and minimum temperatures for Brussels. Generally mild, Brussels' climate does produce chilly weather and cold winters from October to March. Spring sees milder temperatures and is followed by a warm summer.

dignitary from abroad.
Lucky Town Festival *(first weekend)*. Sixty concerts take place in over 30 of some of Brussels' best-known and atmospheric cafés.
Journées du Patrimoine/ Heritage Days *(second or third weekend)*. Private homes, listed buildings and art collections are opened for a rare public viewing to celebrate the city's architecture.

OCTOBER

Audi Jazz Festival *(early Oct–mid-Dec)*. All over Belgium informal jazz concerts bring autumnal cheer to country towns and the capital. Performers are mainly local, but some European stars fly in for performances in Brussels' Palais des Beaux-Arts. Ray Charles and Herbie Hancock have appeared in past years.

WINTER

Snow and rain typify Brussels' winter weather, and attractions move indoors. Art galleries launch world-class exhibitions and the Brussels Film Festival showcases new and established talent. As the festive season approaches, the ancient Lower Town is brightly lit and families gather for Christmas with traditional Belgian cuisine.

NOVEMBER

Nocturnes des Sablons *(last weekend)*. Shops and galleries stay open until

11pm around the Place du Grand Sablon. Horse-drawn carriages transport shoppers around the area, with mulled wine on offer in the festively decorated main square.

DECEMBER

Fête de Saint Nicolas *(6 Dec)*. The original Santa Claus, the patron saint of Christmas, is alleged to arrive in the city on this day. Children throughout the country are given their presents, sweetmeats and chocolate.
Reveillon/Fête de Noel *(24–25 Dec)*. In common with the rest of mainland Europe, Christmas is celebrated over a feast on the evening of 24 December. Gifts are given by adults on this day, and 25 December is traditionally for visiting extended family. The city's Christmas decorations provide a lively sight until 6 January.

JANUARY

Fête des Rois *(6 Jan)*. Epiphany is celebrated with almond cake, the *galette des rois*, and the search for the bean inside that declares its finder king for the night.

FEBRUARY

Antiques Fair *(middle fortnight)*. Brussels' cross-roads location is useful here as international dealers

Christmas market in the Grand Place around the traditional Christmas Pine

gather in the historic Palais des Beaux-Arts *(see p60)*.
International Comic strip and Cartoon Festival *(middle fortnight)*. Artists and authors, both new and established, arrive for lectures and screenings in this city with its comic strip heritage.

PUBLIC HOLIDAYS

New Year's Day (1 Jan)
Easter Sunday (variable)
Easter Monday (variable)
Labour Day (1 May)
Ascension Day (variable)
Whit Sunday (variable)
Whit Monday (variable)
Belgian National Day (21 July)
Assumption Day (15 Aug)
All Saints' Day (1 Nov)
Armistice Day (11 Nov)
Christmas Day (25 Dec)

THE HISTORY OF BRUSSELS

A *s the cultural and civic heart of Belgium since the Middle Ages, Brussels has been the focus of much political upheaval over the centuries. But, from the battles of the 17th century to the warfare of the 20th century, it has always managed to re-create itself with vigour. Now, at the start of a new millennium, Belgium's capital is prospering as the political and economic centre of Europe.*

When Julius Caesar set out to conquer the Gauls of northern Europe in 58 BC, he encountered a fierce tribe known as the Belgae (the origins of the 19th-century name "Belgium"). Roman victory led to the establishment of the region they called Gallia Belgica. The earliest mention of Brussels itself is as "Broucsella", or "settlement in the marshes" and dates from a 7th-century manuscript.

15th-century Flemish tapestry showing the stars

Following the collapse of the Roman Empire in the 5th century, a Germanic race known as the Franks came to rule the region and established the Merovingian dynasty of kings, based in their capital at Tournai. They were followed by the Carolingian dynasty, which produced one of the most important figures in the Middle Ages – Charlemagne (AD 768–814). His noted military expertise ensured that invaders such as the Northern Saxons and the Lombards of Italy were repelled. He was also credited with establishing Christianity as the major religion across western Europe. The pope rewarded him by crowning him Emperor of the West in AD 800; effectively he was the first Holy Roman Emperor, ruling a vast area extending from Denmark to Italy. By the 10th century, the inheritance laws of the Franks meant that the empire was divided up among Charlemagne's grandsons, Louis, Charles the Bald and Lothair. Lothair's fortress, founded in 977, marks the official founding of Brussels. The period had brought a measure of stability to the area's volatile feudal fiefdoms, leading to a trading boom in the new towns of the low countries.

INDUSTRIAL BEGINNINGS

At the start of the 12th century, commerce became the guiding force in western Europe and the centres of trade quickly grew into powerful cities. Rivers and canals were the key to the growth of the area's trading towns. Ghent, Ypres, Antwerp and Bruges became the focus of the cloth trade plied across the North Sea between France, Germany, Italy and England. Brussels, with its skilled craftsmen, became a trade centre, and buildings such as the Cathédrale Sts Michel et Gudule *(see pp70–71)*, started in 1225, demonstrated its stature.

TIMELINE

58–50 BC Gauls defeated by Julius Caesar and Roman occupation begins	**768** Charlemagne is born and goes on to rule most of Europe as the Holy Roman Emperor	*Charlemagne*	**1106** Dukes of Louvain become the Dukes of Brabant
600 AD	**750**	**900**	**1050**
695 First mention of Brussels as "Broucsella" in the Bishop of Cambrai's papers	**843** Emperor Otto II gives the region of Lower Lotharingia to Charlemagne's grandson, Lothair	**1000** Lotharingia now under the rule of the Holy Roman Emperor	**1005** Henry II, Count of Louvain, builds town walls around Brussels

◁ *Philip the Good,* **Duke of Burgundy (c.1500) by Rogier van der Weyden**

Nineteenth-century painting of the Battle of the Golden Spurs

THE CRAFTSMEN'S REBELLION

Over the next two hundred years Brussels became one of the foremost towns of the Duchy of Brabant. Trade here specialized in fine fabrics that were exported to lucrative markets in France, Italy and England. A handful of merchants became rich and exercised political power over the towns. However, conflict grew between the merchants, who wanted to maintain good relations with England, and their autocratic French rulers who relied upon tax revenue from the towns.

The 14th century witnessed a series of rebellions by the craftsmen of Bruges and Brussels against what they saw as the tyranny of the French lords. In May 1302, Flemish craftsmen, armed only with spears, defeated the French at the Battle of the Golden Spurs, named for the humiliating theft of the cavalry's spurs. Encouraged by this success, the Brussels craftsmen revolted against the aristocracy who controlled their trading economy in 1356. They were also angered by the Hundred Years' War between England and France, which began in 1337. The war threatened wool supplies from England which were crucial to their cloth-based

economy. The subsequent depression marked the beginning of decades of conflict between the craftsmen and merchant classes. In 1356, Jeanne, Duchess of Louvain, gained control over Brussels, and instituted the workers' Charter of Liberties. Craftsmen were finally given some political powers in the city. Trade resumed, attracting new people to Brussels. As the population grew, new streets were built outside the city walls to accommodate them. Between 1357 and 1379 a second town wall was constructed around these new districts.

THE HOUSE OF BURGUNDY

The new town walls were also built in reply to the invasion of Brussels by the Count of Flanders. However, in 1369 Philip, Duke of Burgundy, married the daughter of the Count of Flanders, and when the count died in 1384 the Low Countries and eastern France came under the couple's Burgundian rule.

In the 1430s Brussels became the capital of Burgundy, a situation that was to change the city forever. Brussels

Richly detailed Brussels tapestries such as this *Allegory of Hope* (1525) were prized commodities

TIMELINE

1225 Construction of Cathédrale Sts Michel et Gudule

Medieval helmet

1302 Battle of the Golden Spurs – Flemish defeat of French cavalry

1356 Craftsmen's leader Everard 't Serclaes expels Flemish from Brussels

1200	1250	1300	1350

St-Michel status

1229 Brussels granted its first charter, and relations between England and Flanders break down

1338 Flemish towns become allied to England for the Hundred Years' War

1356 Duchess Jeanne of Louvain grants Charter of Liberties

Painting of the family of the Hapsburg King of Austria, Maximillian I and Mary of Burgundy

was now an administrative and cultural centre, famous for its grand architecture, in the form of mansions and churches, and its luxury crafts trade.

THE HAPSBURG DYNASTY

In 1477 Mary of Burgundy, the last heir to the duchy, married Maximillian of Austria. Mary died in 1482, leaving Maximillian and the Hapsburg dynasty rulers of the city at a time when Brussels was experiencing serious economic depression. In 1488 Brussels and the rest of Flanders rebelled against this new power which had reinstated relations with France. The Austrians held on to power largely because of the plague of 1490 which halved Brussels' population. Maximillian passed his rule of the Low Countries to his son, Philip the Handsome in 1494 the year after he became Holy Roman Emperor. When

Portrait of Charles V,
Holy Roman Emperor

Maximillian died, his daughter, Regent Empress Margaret of Austria, moved the capital of Burgundy from Brussels to Mechelen, where she educated her nephew, the future emperor Charles V.

SPANISH RULE

In 1515, at the age of 15, Charles became Sovereign of Burgundy. The following year he inherited the Spanish throne and, in 1519, became the Holy Roman Emperor. As he was born in Ghent, and considered Flanders his real home, he restored Brussels as the capital of Burgundy. Dutch officials arrived to run the three government councils that were now based here.

For the first time the city had a court. Both aristocratic families and immigrants, eager to cash in on the city's expansion, were drawn to the heady mix of tolerance, intellectual sophistication and business. Brussels quickly emerged as the most powerful city in Flanders, overtaking its long-standing rivals Bruges and Antwerp.

However, the Reformation, begun in Germany by Martin Luther, was to usher in a period of religious conflict. When Charles V abdicated in 1555, he fractured the empire's unity by leaving the Holy Roman Empire to his brother Ferdinand and all other dominions to his devoutly Catholic son, Philip II of Spain. His persecution of the Protestant movement finally sparked the Revolt of the Netherlands led by the House of Orange. Brussels' Protestant rulers surrendered to Philip in 1585. His power ended when the English defeated the Spanish Armada in 1588, by which time 8,000 Protestants had been put to death.

1419 Philip the Good succeeds as Count of Burgundy	**1506** Margaret of Austria moves the Burgundian capital from Brussels to Mechelen	**1515** Charles Hapsburg becomes Sovereign of Burgundy	**1555** Catholic Philip II succeeds Charles V as religious reformation comes to Brussels
1400	1450	1500	1550
1430 Under Burgundian control, Brussels becomes the major administrative centre of the region	**1490** Plague decimates the city **1488** Civil war – Brussels joins Flanders against Maximillian of Austria	*Count Egmont*	**1566** Conseil des Troubles set up by Duke d'Alba. Prominent Counts Egmont and Hornes executed

The armies of Louis XIV, the Sun King, bombard Brussels' city walls

THE COUNTER-REFORMATION

From 1598 Archduchess Isabella and Archduke Albert were the Catholic rulers of the Spanish Netherlands, installing a Hapsburg governor in Brussels. They continued to persecute Protestants: all non-Catholics were barred from working. Thousands of skilled workers moved to the Netherlands. But new trades like lace-making, diamond-cutting and silk-weaving flourished. Isabella and Albert were great patrons of the arts, and supported Rubens in Antwerp *(see pp102–03)*.

Protestant prisoners paraded in Brussels during the Counter-Reformation under Albert and Isabella

INVASION OF THE SUN KING

The 17th century was a time of of religious and political struggle all over Europe. The Thirty Years War (1618–48) divided western Europe along Catholic and Protestant lines. After 1648, France's Sun King, Louis XIV, was determined to add Flanders to his territory.

By 1633 both Albert and Isabella were dead and Philip IV of Spain, passed control of the Spanish Netherlands to his weak brother, the Cardinal-Infant Ferdinand. Keen to pursue his ambitions, Louis XIV besieged Maastricht in the 1670s and took Luxembourg. Having failed to win the nearby enclave of Namur, the piqued Sun King moved his army to Brussels, whose defences were weaker.

On August 13, 1695, the French bombarded Brussels from a hill outside the city walls, destroying the Grand Place *(see pp42–3)* and much of its environs. The French withdrew, but their desire to rule the region was to cause conflict over subsequent decades.

A PHOENIX FROM THE ASHES

Despite the destruction incurred by the bombardment, Brussels was quick to recover. The guilds ensured that the Grand Place was rebuilt in a matter of years, with new guildhouses as a testament to the on-going success of the city's economic life and craftsmanship.

The building of the Willebroek canal during the 17th century gave Brussels access to the Rupel and Scheldt rivers, and thus to Antwerp and the North Sea. Large industries began to replace local market trading. Factories and mills grew up around the city's harbour, and Brussels became an export centre.

TIMELINE

1599 Artist Antony van Dyck born in Antwerp

1600 Antwerp becomes the centre of Flemish art

1621 Archduke Albert dies amid new bout of Protestant/Catholic fighting

1641 Van Dyck dies after glittering artistic career

Louis XIV of France in costume

1600	1625	1650	1675

1598 Isabella and Albert run strong Catholic, anti-Protestant regime

Manneken Pis

1619 Manneken Pis installed in Brussels

1640 Rubens dies after a 40-year career as painter of over 3,000 paintings

1633 Cardinal-Infant Ferdinand is new ruler

1670 Louis XIV beseiges Maastricht and Luxembourg; William of Orange goes on defensive

AUSTRIAN SUCCESSION

Subsequent decades were dogged by war as Austria and England sought to stave off French ambitions. When Philip of Anjou succeeded to the Spanish throne, it looked as if the combined threat of Spain and France would overwhelm the rest of Europe. Emperor Leopold I of Austria, together with England and many German states, declared war on France. The resulting 14-year War of the Spanish Succession ended with the Treaty of Utrecht in 1713, which ceded the Netherlands, including Brussels, to Austria.

Governor of Brussels, Duke Charles of Lorraine

The treaty did not end the conflict. Emperor Charles VI of Austria ruled after Leopold, but failed to produce a male heir. His death in 1731 sparked another 17 years of war – The War of the Austrian Succession over whether his daughter Maria Theresa should be allowed to inherit the crown. It was not until 1748, with the signing of the Treaty of Aix-la-Chapelle, that Maria Theresa gained control.

THE BOOM PERIOD

The endless fighting took its toll, and Brussels, along with the rest of Belgium, was impoverished. Despite the sophistication of the aristocratic elite, the majority of the population were still ruled by feudal laws: they could not change jobs or move home without permission; and only three per cent of the population was literate.

In the 1750s Empress Maria Theresa of Austria installed her brother, Charles of Lorraine, in Brussels. Under the influence of the Enlightenment, his court attracted European artists and intellectuals, and Brussels became the most glamorous city in Europe. Industry also boomed with the construction of new roads and waterways. Brussels was transformed as the Place Royale and Parc de Bruxelles were laid out.

THE WORKERS' REVOLT

While the aristocracy and new middle-classes flourished, Brussels' workers were suffering. As the city's population grew there were more workers than jobs: wages plummeted and factory conditions were harsh.

When Joseph II succeeded Maria Theresa in 1780, he enforced a series of reforms including freedom of religion. However, he also cancelled the 500-year-old Charter of Liberties.

Influenced by the ideas of the French Revolution of 1789, the Belgians now demanded reform. Their rebellion was to result in an independent state.

French prince Philip of Anjou became Philip V of Spain, sparking the War of the Spanish Succession

1695 French Bombardment of Brussels	1713–14 Treaties of Utrecht and Rastadt mark beginning of Austrian period	*Ceramic Delft plate*	1760s Brussels is cultural and artistic centre of Europe	1788 Joseph II cancels Charter of Liberties which results in liberal opposition
1700	**1725**		**1750**	**1775**
1697 Willebroek Canal completed, links Brussels to the sea via Antwerp	1731 Beginning of the 17-year-long war against Austrian rule	1748 Treaty of Aix-la-Chapelle restores the Netherlands to Austrian rule	1753 New roads and canals constructed, which boosts industry in Brussels	1789 Belgian revolt for independence fired by French Revolution

The Fight for Independence

Belgium was again occupied by foreign powers between 1794 and 1830. First, by the French Republican armies, then, after Napoleon's defeat at Waterloo in 1815, by the Dutch. French radical reforms included the abolition of the guild system and fairer taxation laws. Although French rule was unpopular, their liberal ideas were to influence the Belgian drive for independence. William I of Orange was appointed King of the Netherlands (which included Belgium) after 1815. His autocratic style, together with a series of anti-Catholic measures, bred discontent, especially in Brussels and among the French-speaking Walloons in the south. The south was also angered when William refused to introduce tariffs to protect their trade – it was the last straw. The uprising of 1830 began in Brussels and Léopold I became king of the newly independent nation.

King William I of Orange
William's rule as King of the Netherlands after 1815 was unpopular.

A Cultural Revolution in Brussels
French ideas not only influenced the revolution, but also Belgian culture. Under Napoleon the city walls were demolished and replaced by tree-lined boulevards.

Liberals joined workers already protesting in the square outside.

The Battle of Waterloo
Napoleon's influence came to an end after the battle of Waterloo on 18 June, 1815. A Prussian army came to Wellington's aid, and by 5:30pm Napoleon faced his final defeat. This led to Dutch rule over Belgium.

Agricultural Workers
Harsh weather in the winter of 1829 caused hardship for both farmers and agricultural labourers, who also joined the protest.

The Revolution in Industry
Unemployment, low wages and factory closures during the early decades of the 19th century sparked unrest in 1830.

Le Théâtre de la Monnaie
A patriotic song, L'Amour Sacré de la Patrie led the audience on the night of 25 August, 1830, to join demonstrators outside (see pp48–9).

BELGIAN REVOLUTION

High unemployment, poor wages and a bad winter in 1829 provoked protests about living and working conditions. The revolution was ignited by a patriotic and radical opera at the Brussels' opera house, and the largely liberal audience rushed out into the street, raising the Brabant flag. Ten thousand troops were sent by William to quash the rebels, but the Belgian soldiers deserted and the Dutch were finally driven out of Belgium.

The initial list of demands asked for administrative independence from the Dutch, and for freedom of press.

This symbolic illustration of the revolution shows both liberals and workers ready to die for their country.

King of Belgium, Léopold I
The crowning of German prince, Léopold of Saxe-Coburg, in Brussels in 1831 finally established Belgium's independence.

TIMELINE

1790 Republic of United Belgian States formed. Temporary end of Austrian rule	**1799** Emperor Napoleon rules France *Wellington*		**1815** Battle of Waterloo. Napoleon defeated by army led by the Duke of Wellington	**1830** Rebellion begins at the Théâtre de la Monnaie in Brussels
1790	**1800**	**1810**	**1820**	**1830**
	1794 Brussels loses its importance to The Hague	**1815** Belgium, allied with Holland under the United Kingdom of the Netherlands, is ruled by William I of Orange. Brussels becomes second capital	**1831** State of Belgium formed on 21 July. Treaty of London grants independence	
1790 War between France and Austria			**1835** Continental railway built from Brussels to Mechelen	

THE FLEMISH AND THE WALLOONS: THE BELGIAN COMPROMISE

Linguistically and culturally, Belgium is divided. In the north, the Flemish have their roots in the Netherlands and Germany. In the south are the Walloons, the French-speaking Belgians, culturally connected to France. The "Linguistic Divide" of 1962 officially sanctioned this situation, dividing Belgium into Flemish- and French-speaking zones. The exception is Brussels, an officially bilingual city since the formation of Bruxelles-Capitale in 1963, and a national region by 1989 when it came to comprise 19 outlying districts. Conflicts still erupt over the issue, but the majority of Belgians seem to be in favour of a united country.

Bilingual road signs

CONSOLIDATING THE NEW STATE

During its early days as an independent nation, Brussels was a haven for free-thinkers, including the libertarian poet Baudelaire, and a refuge for exiles, such as Karl Marx and Victor Hugo. Belgium's industries also continued to expand throughout the 19th century.

By 1870 there were no less than four main railway stations in Brussels able to export goods all over Europe. However, the population of Brussels had almost doubled, resulting in poor-quality housing and working conditions. Towards the end of the reign of Belgium's second monarch, Léopold II (r.1865–1909), industrial unrest led to new legislation which improved conditions, and all men over 25 gained the right to vote in 1893. But the king's principal concern was his colonialist policy in the Congo in Central Africa.

THE GERMAN OCCUPATIONS

Albert I succeeded Léopold II as Belgium's new king. He encouraged the nation's artists and architects, and was a keen supporter of Art Nouveau *(see pp18–19)*. All of this ended as the country entered its bleakest period.

Despite its neutral status, Belgium was invaded by the German army in the summer of 1914. All of the country, except for the northern De Panne region, was occupied by the Germans. Some of the bloodiest battles of World War I were staged on Belgian soil. Flanders was the scene of brutal trench warfare, including the introduction of poison gas at Ypres *(see p109)*. Today, Belgium contains several vast graveyards, which include the resting places of the tens of thousands of soldiers who died on the Western Front.

The Belgians conducted resistance from their stronghold in De Panne, cutting telephone wires and destroying train tracks. The Germans responded by confiscating property, deporting Belgians to German labour camps

King Léopold III visits a goldmine in the Congo in Africa

TIMELINE

The Belgian Congo

1840	1870	1900	1925
1847 Opening of Europe's first shopping mall, the Galéries St Hubert	**1871** Under Léopold II, the River Senne is reclaimed, and new districts built to cope with the growing city	**1898** Flemish language given equal status to French in law	**1914–18** World War I. Germany occupies Belgium
1839 Treaty of London grants neutrality to Belgium	**1884** Léopold II is granted sovereignty over the Congo	**1910** World Fair in Brussels promotes Belgium's industrial boom. Art Nouveau flourishes	**1929–31** Great Depression and reduction in foreign trade

German troops raising the flag of the Third Reich at the Royal Castle at Laeken, near Brussels

INTERNATIONAL STATUS

Belgium's history in the latter half of the 20th century has been dominated by the ongoing language debate between the Flemish and the French-speaking Walloons. From 1970 to 1994 the constitution was redrawn, creating a federal state with three separate regions; the Flemish north, the Walloon south and bilingual Brussels. While this smoothed over conflicts, cultural divisions run deep. Today, all parliamentary speeches have to be delivered in both French and Flemish.

Like most of Europe, Belgium went from economic boom in the 1960s to recession and retrenchment in the 1970s and 1980s. Throughout these decades Brussels' stature at the heart of Europe was consolidated. In 1958, the city became the headquarters for the European Economic Community (EEC), later the European Union. In 1967 NATO also moved to Brussels.

and murdering random hostages. Belgium remained under German occupation until the last day of the war, 11 November, 1918.

The 1919 Treaty of Versailles granted Belgium control of Eupen-Malmédy, the German-speaking area in the southeast. But by 1940 the country was again invaded by the Germans under Hitler. In May of that year, King Léopold III surrendered.

Despite national resistance to the Occupation, the King was interned at Laeken until 1944, after which he was moved to Germany until the end of the war. Rumours that Léopold had collaborated with the Nazis led to his abdication in 1951, in favour of his 20-year-old son, Baudouin.

THE EUROPEAN CAPITAL

Modern Brussels is a multilingual and cosmopolitan city at the forefront of Europe. This historically industrial city now prospers as a base for many large corporations such as ICI and Mitsubishi.

The European Parliament, Brussels

Despite its flourishing status, the city has had its fair share of disasters, including the deaths of 38 Italian football supporters at the Heysel stadium in 1985. Also, two tragic paedophile murder cases in the 1990s led many Belgians to protest against the apparent failures of the police system. However, Brussels' future as a city of world importance seems certain as it lies at the political centre of the European Union.

1939–45 World War II. Germany again occupies Belgium	1951 Abdication of Léopold III; Baudouin I succeeds	1962 The Belgian Congo is granted independence		1993 King Baudouin I dies; Albert II succeeds	2002 The euro becomes legal tender
	Baudouin I	*European flag*			
	1950		**1975**	**2000**	**2025**

1944 Benelux Unions with Holland and Luxembourg formed

1934 Albert I is killed in a climbing accident

1967 Brussels is new NATO HQ

1985 Heysel Stadium disaster

1989 Brussels is officially a bilingual city with 19 outlying districts

2001 Crown Prince Philippe and Princess Mathilde have a daughter, Elisabeth

Palais de la Nation seen from the fountain in Parc de Bruxelles ▷

BRUSSELS
AREA BY AREA

THE LOWER TOWN

Maison du Cygne, Grand Place

Most visits to Brussels begin with a stroll around the Lower Town, the ancient heart of the city and home to its most famous area, the Grand Place *(see pp42–3)*. The original settlement of the city was located here and most of the streets surrounding this market square date from the Middle Ages up to the 18th century. The architecture is an eclectic blend of Gothic, Baroque and Flemish Renaissance.

In and around the Place de Brouckère and the busy Boulevard Anspach are the more recent additions to the city's history. These appeared in the 19th century when the slums around the River Senne were cleared to make way for ornate constructions such as the financial centre, La Bourse, and Europe's first shopping arcade, Galeries St-Hubert. With its many restaurants and cafés, the Lower Town is also popular at night.

SIGHTS AT A GLANCE

Historic Buildings and Monuments
Hôtel de Ville pp44–45 **7**
Manneken Pis **3**
La Bourse **7**

Museums and Galleries
Musée du Costume et de la Dentelle **1**
Bruxella 1238 **8**
Centre Belge de la Bande Dessinée pp50–51 **14**
Maison de la Bellone **21**

Churches
Notre-Dame de la Chapelle **4**
Eglise St-Nicolas **9**
Eglise St-Jean-Baptiste **19**
Eglise Ste-Catherine **2**

Shopping
Galeries St-Hubert **10**
Rue Neuve **16**

Streets and Squares
Rue des Bouchers **11**
Place de Brouckère **18**

Theatres
Théâtre Marionnettes de Toone **12**
Théâtre Royal de la Monnaie **13**
Théâtre Royal Flamand **20**

Cultural Centres
Le Botanique **15**

Historic Districts
Quartier Marolles **5**
Halles St-Géry **6**

Hotels
Hôtel Métropole **17**

KEY

🚇	Train station
🚃	Tram stop
Ⓜ	Metro station
🚌	Bus terminus
ℹ	Tourist information

THE GRAND PLACE

GETTING AROUND

The area is well served by trams which encircle the old town. However, the tiny streets are often pedestrianized, and usually the quickest and most enjoyable means of transport for short distances is on foot. Otherwise metro stations are well placed.

0 metres	500
0 yards	500

◁ **Detail of the façade of the Hôtel de Ville in the Grand Place – centre of the Lower Town**

The Grand Place

The geographical, historical and commercial heart of the
city, the Grand Place is the first port of call for most
visitors to Brussels. The square remains the civic centre,
centuries after its creation, and offers the finest surviving
example in one area of Belgium's ornate 17th-century
architecture. Open-air markets took place on or near
this site as early as the 11th century, but by the end of
the 15th century Brussels' town hall, the Hôtel de Ville,
was built, and city traders added individual guildhouses
in a medley of styles. In 1695, however, three days of
cannon fire by the French destroyed all but the façades
of the town hall and some of the guildhouses. Trade
guilds were urged to rebuild their halls to styles
approved by the Town Council, producing the harmon-
ious unity of Flemish Baroque buildings here today.

The vibrant flower market in bloom
in the Grand Place

The Maison du Roi was first
built in 1536 but redesigned in
1873. Once used by the
ruling Spanish
monarchs, it is
now home to
the Musée de
la Ville, which
includes 16th-
century paint-
ings, tapestries,
and the many
tiny outfits of
Manneken Pis.

① NORTHEAST CORNER

② MAISON DU ROI

The Hôtel de Ville occupies the
entire southwest side of the
square. Still a functioning civic
building, Brussels' town hall is
the architectural masterpiece of
the Grand Place *(see pp44–5)*.

The spire
was built
by Jan van
Ruysbroeck
in 1449 and
stands 96 m
(315 ft) high;
it is slightly
crooked.

**Ornate
stone
carvings**

Everard 't Serclaes was murdered
defending Brussels in the 14th
century; touching the bronze
arm of his statue is said
to bring luck.

⑤ EVERARD 'T SERCLAES

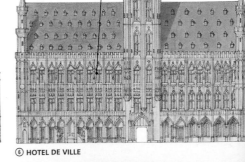

⑥ HOTEL DE VILLE

Le Pigeon was home to Victor Hugo, the exiled French novelist who chose the house as his Belgian residence in 1852. Some of the most complimentary comments about Brussels emerged later from his pen.

La Maison des Ducs de Brabant is a group of six guildhouses. Designed by the Controller of Public Works, Guillaume de Bruyn, the group looks like an Italian Baroque palazzo.

LOCATOR MAP
See Brussels Street Finder, map 2

Stone busts of the ducal line along the façade gave this group of houses their name.

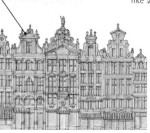

③ LE PIGEON

④ LA MAISON DES DUCS DE BRABANT

Le Renard was built in 1699 as the guild-house of the haber-dashers by the Flemish architects Marc de Vos and van Nerum. Façade details show St Nicolas, patron saint of merchants, and cherubs playing with haber-dashery ribbons.

La Maison des Boulangers, also known as "Le Roi d'Espagne", was a showpiece built by the wealthy and powerful guild of bakers. The 1697 octagonal copper dome is topped by a golden figure blowing a trumpet.

Le Cornet displays Italianate Flemish style. This Boatmen's Guildhouse (1697) is most notable for its gable, which is constructed in the form of a 17th-century frigate's bow.

Le Roi d'Espagne now houses the Grand Place's finest bar with a view of the bustling square and its splendours above ground level *(see p162)*. The gilt bust over the entrance represents Saint Aubert, patron saint of bakers. There is a vast bust of Charles II of Spain on the second floor.

⑦ LE RENARD, LE CORNET AND LE ROI D'ESPAGNE

Musée du Costume et de la Dentelle ❶

Rue de la Violette 12, 1000 BRU.
Map 2 D3. 🚌 27, 29, 38, 46, 48, 63, 86, 95. 🚊 3, 4, 31, 32, 33. **Tel** (02) 213 4450. Ⓜ Bourse, Gare Centrale. ◯ 10am–5pm Thu–Tue. ⬤ Wed, 1 May, 1 & 11 Nov, 25 Dec. 🌐 🚻 on request, call (02) 279 4355. www.musees.bruxelles.be

Found within two 17th-century gabled houses is the museum dedicated to one of Brussels' most successful exports, Belgian lace *(see pp20–21)*. The intricate skill employed by Belgian lace-makers has contributed a vital economic role in the city

A wedding dress at the Musée du Costume et de la Dentelle

since the 17th century, and the collection explains and displays the history of this delicate craft. The second floor houses a small collection

of antique lace, carefully stored in drawers and demonstrating the various schools of lacemaking in France, Flanders and Italy. The museum displays temporary exhibitions of contemporary textiles and fashion.

Manneken Pis ❸

Rues de l'Etuve & du Chêne, 1000 BRU. **Map** 1C3. 🚌 27, 29, 38, 46, 48, 63, 86, 95. 🚊 3, 4, 31, 32, 33. Ⓜ Bourse, Gare Centrale.

An unlikely attraction, this tiny statue of a young boy barely 61 cm (2 ft) high relieving himself into a small pool is as much a part of Brussels as the Trevi

Hôtel de Ville ❷

Stone gargoyle

The idea of having a town hall to reflect Brussels' growth as a major European trading centre had been under consideration since the end of the 13th century. It was not until 1401 that the first foundation stone was laid and the building was finally completed in 1455, emerging as the finest civic building in the country, a stature it still enjoys.

Jacques van Thienen was commissioned to design the left wing and belfry of the building, where he used ornate columns, sculptures, turrets and arcades. The tower and spire begun in 1449 by Jan van Ruysbroeck helped seal its reputation. In 1995, the 1455 statue of the city's patron saint, Michael, was restored and now resides inside the tower. A copy of the statue sits on top of the tower. Tours are available of the interior, which contains 18th-century tapestries and works of art.

A detail of the delicately carved façade with stone statues

137 statues adorn walls and many mullioned windows.

★ **Aldermen's Room**
Still in use today for the meetings of the aldermen and mayor of Brussels, this council chamber contains a series of 18th-century tapestries depicting the history of 6th-century King Clovis.

STAR SIGHTS

★ Conference Room Council Chamber

★ Aldermen's Room

Fountain is part of Rome or Trafalgar Square's proud lions are of London.

The current statue of Manneken Pis by Jérôme Duquesnoy the Elder has been in place since 1619. However, there is evidence to suggest that a stone fountain depicting the same figure stood there before it, possibly as early as 1451. In its long history the statuette has been the victim of several thefts. A particularly violent theft in 1965 left the statue broken in two pieces, leaving just the ankles and feet remaining. The

missing body of the statue reappeared a year later when it was found in a canal.

In 1698 the governor of the Netherlands, Maximilian Emmanuel, brought a gift to the city in the form of a blue woollen coat for the statue. This is a tradition that continues today, with visiting heads of state donating miniature versions of their national costume. The little boy has a collection of over 800 outfits which are housed in the Musée de la Ville de Bruxelles (*see p42*), where 100 are on display at any one time. Among the collection is a miniature Samurai, Santa Claus and Elvis suit.

THE LEGENDS OF MANNEKEN PIS

The charm of this famous statue comes from the many rumours and fables behind it. One theory claims that in the 12th century the son of a duke was caught urinating against a tree in the midst of a battle and was thus commemorated in bronze as a symbol of military courage. The inspiration for the statue has been revealed as Cupid.

The belfry was built by architect Jan van Ruysbroeck. A statue of St Michael tops the 96 m (315 ft) spire.

Aldermen's Room

Banqueting room

The gabled roof, like much of the town hall, was fully restored in 1837, and cleaned in the 1990s.

VISITORS' CHECKLIST

Grand Place, 1000 BRU. **Map** 2 D3. **Tel** (02) 279 4371. 27, 29, 38, 46, 48, 63, 86, 95. 3, 4, 31, 32, 33. Bourse, Gare Centrale. **Hôtel de Ville** for guided tours. pub hols, election days. (tickets at Hôtel de Ville or Grand Place tourist office). Mon am, Tue, Wed am, Thu pm. **www**.brucity.be

★ **Conference Room Council Chamber**
The most splendid of all the public rooms, ancient tapestries and gilt mirrors line the walls above an inlaid floor.

Wedding Room
A Neo-Gothic style dominates this civil marriage office, with its many ornate carved timbers, including ancient ebony and mahogany.

Notre-Dame de la Chapelle ❹

Place de la Chapelle 1, 1000 BRU. **Map**
1 C4. **Tel** (02) 512 0737. 🚌 27, 29,
38, 63. 🚊 3, 4, 31, 32, 33. Ⓜ
Anneessens, Centrale. ◯ 9am–7pm
daily; Mass 4pm Sat, 8am, 9:30am,
11am, 5:30pm Sun.

In 1134 King Godefroid I
decided to build a chapel
outside the city walls. It quickly
became a market church, serving the many craftsmen living
nearby. In 1210 its popularity
was such that it was made a
parish church, but it became
really famous in 1250, when a
royal donation of five pieces
of the True Cross turned the
church into a pilgrimage site.

Originally built in Romanesque style, the majority of the
church was destroyed by fire
in 1405. Rebuilding began in
1421 in a Gothic style typical
of 15th-century Brabant architecture, including gables decorated with finials and interior
capitals decorated with cab-
bage leaves at the base. The
Bishop of Cambrai consecrated
the new church in 1434.

One of the most striking
features of the exterior are the
monstrously lifelike gargoyles
– a representation of evil
outside the sacred interior.
The Baroque belltower was
added after the 1695 bombardment by the French *(see p32)*.
Another moving feature is the
carved stone memorial to the
16th-century Belgian artist
Pieter Brueghel the Elder
(see p16), who is buried here.

The elegant interior of
Notre-Dame de la Chapelle

Rue Haute in the Quartier Marolles, with old-style shops and cafés

Quartier Marolles ❺

Map 1 C5. 🚌 27, 48. 🚊 3, 4, 33,
51, 92, 94, 97. Ⓜ Louise, Porte de
Hal.

Known colloquially as "Les
Marolles", this quarter of
Brussels is traditionally working
class. Situated between the two
city walls, the area was home
to weavers and craftsmen.
Street names of the district,
such as Rue des Brodeurs
(Embroiderers' St) and Rue
des Charpentiers (Carpenters'
St), reflect its artisanal history.

Today the area is best known
for its fine daily flea market,
held in the **Place du Jeu de
Balle**. The flea market has
been held on this site since
1640. Between 7am and 2pm,
with the biggest and best markets on Thursday and Sunday,
almost anything from junk to
pre-war collector's items can
be found among the stalls.

Shopping of a different kind
is on offer on nearby Rue
Haute, an ancient Roman road.
A shopping district since the
19th century, it is still popular
with arty types with its specialist stores, interior and
antique shops. The street has
a long artistic history, too –
the elegant red-brick house at
No. 132 was home to Pieter
Brueghel the Elder and the
sculptor Auguste Rodin had a
studio at No. 224. No. 132
now houses the small **Maison
de Brueghel**, dedicated to the
16th-century painter.

At the southern end of Rue
Haute is Porte de Hal, the
stone gateway of the now-
demolished outer city walls.

Looming over the Marolles is
the imposing Palais de Justice
(see p69), which has hilltop
views of the area west of the
city, including the 1958 Atomium *(see p87)* and the Basilique
Sacré-Coeur *(see p84)*.

> 🏛 **Maison de Brueghel**
> Rue Haute 132, 1000 BRU.
> **Tel** (02) 513 8940. ◯ May–Sep:
> Wed & Sun pm (groups with written
> permission only). ● Oct–Apr. 🖼

Busy restaurants and cafés
outside Halles St-Géry

Halles St-Géry ❻

Place St-Géry 23, 1000 BRU. **Map** 1
C2. 🚌 46, 48, 86, 95. 🚊 3, 4, 31,
32, 33. Ⓜ Bourse.

In many ways, St-Géry can be
considered the birthplace of
the city. A chapel to Saint Géry
was built in the 6th century,
then in AD 977 a fortress took
over the site. A 16th-century
church followed and occu-
pied the location until the
18th century. In 1881 a

covered meat market was erected in Neo-Renaissance style. The glass and intricate ironwork was renovated in 1985, and the hall now serves as a cultural centre with an exhibition on local history.

La Bourse ❼

Palais de la Bourse, 1000 BRU. **Map** 1 C2. **Tel** (02) 509 1373. 🚌 46, 48, 86, 95. 🚊 3, 4, 31, 32, 33. Ⓜ Bourse. ⊘ to the public.

Brussels' Stock Exchange, La Bourse, is one of the city's most impressive buildings, dominating the square of the same name. Designed in Palladian style by architect Léon Suys, it was constructed from 1867 to 1873. Among the building's most notable features are the façade's ornate carvings. The great French sculptor, Auguste Rodin, is thought to have crafted the groups representing Africa and Asia, as well as four caryatids inside. Beneath the colonnade, two beautifully detailed winged figures representing Good and Evil were carved by sculptor Jacques de Haen. Once the scene of frantic trading, La Bourse now houses the offices of Euronext, owners of the Belgian Stock Exchange, and all trading is computerized. The building is no longer open to the public.

Bruxella 1238 ❽

Rue de la Bourse, 1000 BRU. **Map** 1 C3. **Tel** (02) 279 4350. 🚌 29, 38, 46, 47, 48, 63, 65, 66, 71, 86, 88, 95. 🚊 3, 31, 32, 33. Ⓜ Bourse, De Brouckère. ⊘ 1st Wed of month: 10:15am (English), 11:15am (French), 2pm (Dutch); by appt only at other times. 🎦 📷 obligatory, starts from Maison du Roi, Grand Place.

Once home to a church and 13th-century Franciscan convent, in the early 19th century this site became a Butter Market until the building of the Bourse started in 1867.

In 1988 municipal roadworks began alongside the Place de la Bourse. Medieval history must have been far from the minds of the city authorities but, in the course of working on the foundations, important relics were found, including 13th-century bones, pottery and the 1294 grave of Duke John I of Brabant. Visitors can see these and other pieces in a small museum built on the site.

Eglise St-Nicolas ❾

Rue au Beurre 1, 1000 BRU. **Map** 1 C2. **Tel** (02) 513 8022. 🚌 29, 38, 46, 47, 63, 65, 66, 71, 86, 88. 🚊 3, 4, 31, 32, 33. Ⓜ Bourse, De Brouckère. ⊘ 8am–6pm Mon–Fri, 9am–6pm Sat, 9am–7:30pm Sun & public hols.

At the end of the 12th century a market church was built on this site, but, like much of the Lower Town, it was damaged in the 1695 French Bombardment. A cannon ball lodged itself into an interior pillar and the belltower finally collapsed in 1714. Many restoration projects were planned but none came to fruition until 1956, when the west side of the building was given a new, Gothic-style façade. Named after St Nicolas, the patron saint of merchants, the church contains choir stalls dating from 1381 which display detailed medallions telling St Nicolas' story. Another interesting feature is the chapel, constructed at an angle, reputedly to avoid the flow of an old stream. Inside the church, works of art by Bernard van Orley and Peter Paul Rubens are well worth seeing.

The 19th-century domed glass roof of Galeries St-Hubert

Galeries St-Hubert ❿

Rue des Bouchers, 1000 BRU. **Map** 2 D2. 🚊 25, 94. Ⓜ Gare Centrale. ♿

Sixteen years after ascending the throne as the first king of Belgium, Léopold I inaugurated the opening of these grand arcades in 1847.

St-Hubert has the distinction of being the first shopping arcade in Europe, and one of the most elegant. Designed in Neo-Renaissance style by Jean-Pierre Cluysenaar, the vaulted glass roof covers its three sections, Galerie du Roi, Galerie de la Reine and Galerie des Princes, which house a range of luxury shops and cafés. The ornate interior and expensive goods on sale soon turned the galleries into a fashionable meeting place for 19th-century society, including resident literati – Victor Hugo and Alexandre Dumas attended lectures here. The arcades remain a popular venue, with shops, a cinema, theatre, cafés and restaurants.

Detail of a Rodin statue, La Bourse

Gothic-style façade of Eglise St-Nicolas

Pavement displays of restaurants along Rue des Bouchers

Rue des Bouchers ⓫

Map 2 D2. 🚌 27, 29, 38, 46, 47, 48, 63, 66, 71, 86, 88, 95. 🚊 3, 4, 31, 32, 33. Ⓜ De Brouckère, Gare Centrale, Bourse.

Like many streets in this area of the city, Rue des Bouchers retains its medieval name, reminiscent of the time when this meandering, cobblestoned street was home to the butchers' trade. Aware of its historic importance and heeding the concerns of the public, the city council declared this area the Ilot Sacré (sacred islet) in 1960, forbidding any of the architectural façades to be altered or destroyed, and commanding those surviving to be restored. Hence Rue des Bouchers abounds with 17th-century stepped gables and decorated doorways.

Today, this pedestrianized thoroughfare is best known as the "belly of Brussels", a reference to its plethora of cafés and restaurants offering many types of cuisine. But the most impressive sights during an evening stroll along the street are the lavish pavement displays of seafood, piled high on mounds of ice, all romantically lit by an amber glow from the streetlamps.

At the end of the street, at the Impasse de la Fidélité, is an acknowledgement of sexual equality. Erected in 1987, Jeanneke Pis is a coy, cheeky female version of her "brother", the more famous Manneken Pis *(see p45)*.

Théâtre Marionettes de Toone ⓬

Impasse Ste Pétronille, 66 Rue du Marché aux Herbes, 1000 BRU. **Map** 2 D2. **Tel** (02) 511 7137. 🚌 27, 29, 38, 46, 48, 63, 86, 95. 🚊 3, 4, 31, 32, 33. Ⓜ Bourse, Gare Centrale. ◯ bar: noon–midnight daily; theatre: performance times 4pm Sat, 8:30pm Thu–Sat. ● Mon, pub hols. 🎭 🎫 on request, for tour reservations **Tel** (02) 217 2753. **Museum** ◯ intervals. www.toone.be

Harlequin puppet

A popular pub by day, at night the top floor of this tavern is home to a puppet theatre. During the time of the Spanish Netherlands *(see p32)*, all theatres were closed because of the satirical performances by actors aimed at their Latin rulers. This began a fashion for puppet shows, the vicious dialogue more easily forgiveable from inanimate dolls. In 1830, Antoine Toone opened his own theatre and it has been run by the Toone family ever since; the owner is the eighth generation, Toone VIII. The classics are enacted by these wooden marionettes in the local Bruxellois dialect, and occasionally in French, English, German or Dutch.

Théâtre Royal de la Monnaie ⓭

Place de la Monnaie, 1000 BRU. **Map** 2 D2. **Tel** (02) 229 1200. 🚌 29, 38, 46, 47, 48, 63, 66, 71, 86, 88, 95. 🚊 4, 31, 32, 33. Ⓜ De Brouckère, Bourse. ◯ performance times, Tue–Sun; box office: noon–6pm Tue–Sat. ● Sun, public hols. 🎭 🎫 on written request. www.lamonnaie.be

This theatre was first built in 1817 on the site of a 15th-century mint but, following a fire in 1855, only the front and pediment of the original Neo-Classical building remain. After the fire, the theatre was redesigned by the architect, Joseph Poelaert, also responsible for the imposing Palais de Justice *(see p69)*.

The original theatre made its historical mark before its destruction, however, when on 25 August, 1830, a performance of *La Muette de Portici (The Mute Girl)* began a national rebellion. As the tenor began to sing the nationalist *Amour Sacré de la Patrie (Sacred love of the homeland)*, his words incited an already discontented city, fired by the libertarianism of the revolutions occurring in France, into revolt. The audience ran into the street in a rampage that developed into

The original Neo-Classical façade of Théâtre Royal de la Monnaie

The 19th-century glasshouse of Le Botanique in summer

the September Uprising *(see pp34–5)*. The theatre today remains the centre of Belgian performing arts; major renovations took place during the 1980s. The auditorium was raised 4 m (13 ft) to accommodate the elaborate stage designs, but the luxurious Louis XIV-style decor was carefully retained and blended with the new additions. The central dome is decorated with an allegory of Belgian arts.

Centre Belge de la Bande Dessinée ⑭

See pp50–51.

Le Botanique ⑮

Rue Royale 236, 1210 BRU. **Map** 2 E1. *Tel* (02) 218 3732. 🚌 61. 🚊 92, 94. Ⓜ *Botanique*. ⏱ *10am–6pm daily.* ♿ 🖥 **www**.botanique.be

In 1797, the city of Brussels created a botanical garden in the grounds of the Palais de Lorraine as a source of reference for botany students. The garden closed in 1826, and new gardens were relocated in Meise, 13 km (9 miles) from Brussels.

A grand glass-and-iron rotunda was designed at the centre of the gardens by the French architect Gineste. This

iron glasshouse still stands, as does much of the 19th-century statuary by Constantin Meunier *(see p15)*, including depictions of the Four Seasons. The glasshouse is now home to the French Community Cultural Centre and offers concerts and contemporary art exhibitions.

Rue Neuve ⑯

Map 2 D2. 🚌 29, 38, 46, 47, 48, 58, 61, 63, 66, 71, 86, 88, 95. 🚊 3, 4, 25, 31, 32, 33, 55. Ⓜ *Bourse, De Brouckère, Rogier.*

Brussels shoppers have been flocking to the busy Rue Neuve since the 19th century for its reasonably priced goods and

Rue Neuve, the longest pedestrian shopping street in the city

well-located stores. Similar to London's Oxford Street, but now pedestrianized, this is the heart of commercial shopping. It houses well-known international chainstores and shopping malls, such as **City 2**, which has shops, cafés and the media store Fnac all under one roof. Inno department store was designed by Horta *(see p78)*, but after a fire in 1967 was entirely rebuilt.

To the east of Rue Neuve is Place des Martyrs, a peaceful square where a monument pays tribute to the 450 citizens killed during the 1830 uprising.

🏬 **City 2**
Rue Neuve 123, 1000 BRU. *Tel* (02) 211 4060. ⏱ 10am–7pm Mon–Thu & Sat, 10am–8pm Fri. ⚫ Sun, public hols.

Hôtel Métropole ⑰

Place de Brouckère 31, 1000 BRU. **Map** 2 D2. *Tel* (02) 217 2300. 🚌 29, 38, 46, 47, 63, 66, 71, 86, 88. 🚊 3, 4, 31, 32, 33. Ⓜ *De Brouckère.* **www**.metropolehotel.be

The area lying between Place Rogier and Place de Brouckère is known as the hotel district of Brussels, and one of the oldest and grandest hotels in the area is the Métropole.

In 1891 the Wielemans Brewery bought the building and commissioned the architect Alban Chambon to redesign the interior, with money no object. The result was a fine Art Nouveau hotel which opened for business in 1895 and has since accommodated numerous acclaimed visitors, including actress Sarah Bernhardt. In 1911 the hotel was the location of the first science conference Conseil Physique Solvay, attended by the great scientists Marie Curie and Albert Einstein.

The Hôtel Métropole continues to welcome guests from all walks of life, at surprisingly reasonable cost given its beauty, history and location. It is particularly popular for drinks in its Café Métropole and heated pavement terrace, which are both open to non-residents to enjoy cocktails and coffees in elegant surroundings.

Centre Belge de la Bande Dessinée 🄫

Affectionately known as *cébébédé*, the Museum of Comic Strip Art pays tribute to the Belgian passion for comic strips or *bandes dessinées* and to many world-famous comic strip artists from Belgium and abroad.

Arranged over three levels, the collection is housed in a Horta-designed Art Nouveau building. One of the most popular permanent exhibitions is a tour of the great comic strip heroes, from *Tintin to The Smurfs*, both of whose creators were Belgian. Other displays detail the stages of putting together a comic strip, from examples of initial ideas and pencil sketches

The famous Tintin rocket

Three Comic Figures
Tintin, Professor Calculus and Captain Haddock greet visitors on the 1st floor.

through to final publication. The museum regularly holds major exhibitions featuring the work of famous cartoonists and studios, and also houses some 8,000 original plates, displayed in rotation, as well as a valuable archive of photographs and artifacts.

The Smurfs
These tiny blue characters first appeared in the Spirou journal in 1958. By the 1980s they had their own TV show and hit records.

A Suivre
Founded in 1978, A Suivre expanded the comic strip genre, and led to the new form of graphic novels: adult stories in cartoon form.

★ Life-size Cartoon Sets
A series of authentic comic scenes encourages children to enter the world of their favourite comic strip characters.

STAR SIGHTS

★ The Light Room

★ Life-size Cartoon Sets

★ The Light Room
*This airy space designed by
Victor Horta features stained
glass and wrought-ironwork.*

Comic Library
*The museum library
doubles as a study
centre for both art
students and enthu-
siasts of all ages. This
unique collection
includes a catalogue
of hundreds of old
comic strips, artists'
equipment, biogra-
phies, comic novels
and photographs.*

A HORTA-DESIGNED BUILDING

This beautiful building was constructed
between 1903 and 1906 to the design of
the Belgian Art-Nouveau architect Victor
Horta. Originally built as a fabric
warehouse, and known as the
Waucquez Building, it was one in a series of
department stores and warehouses in the city
designed by him. Saved from demolition by
the French Cultural Commission of Brussels,
in 1989 the building re-opened as a museum
dedicated to the comic strip, Belgium's so-
called Ninth Art *(see pp20–21)*. Carefully
restored, the building has many classic
features of Art Nouveau design, including
the use of curves on structural iron pillars.
In the impressive entrance hall is a display
of Horta's architectural drawings for the
building, and on the right the Brasserie
Horta serves traditional Belgian dishes in a
charming glass and marble Art Nouveau setting.

**Cast-iron
pillar**

THE CHANGING FACE OF HERGE'S TINTIN
Perhaps the best-known Belgian
comic character, *Tintin* made his
debut in a children's paper in 1929.
He began life as a simple black line
drawing, featuring the famous quiff,
but no mouth. By 1930 Hergé began
to produce *Tintin* in book-form and
gave him both a mouth and a more
complex character suggested by a
greater range of facial expressions.
By the 1940s *Tintin* was appearing
in colour, alongside such new
characters as Captain Haddock, the
Thompsons and Professor Calculus.

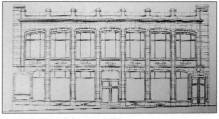

Horta's drawing of the CBBD building

Nineteenth-century building in Place de Brouckère

Place de Brouckère ⑱

Map 2 D2. ▦ 29, 38, 46, 47, 48, 63, 66, 71, 86, 88, 95. ▦ 3, 4, 31, 32, 33. Ⓜ De Brouckère, Bourse.

In 1872 a design competition was held to encourage the construction of buildings of architectural interest in de Brouckère. Twenty winning applicants were selected and commissioned to give prominence to this Brussels junction. The Parisian contractor Jean-Baptiste Mosnier was responsible for taking the original plans through to completion.

The French influence of Mosnier and his workers is still evident on the square. Many of the buildings were erected in stone, common in France at the end of the 19th century, whereas brickwork was more usual in Brussels. Several original façades survive today, including the 1874 Hôtel Continental by Eugene Carpentier.

One of the great hotels of Brussels, the Hôtel Métropole (see p49) is situated on the south side of the square. The 1900–10 interior is splendidly gilded and can be seen either through the doorway or by pretending to be a guest. Café Métropole next door is, however, open to the public; here the lavishly ornate surroundings date from around 1890.

In the 20th century, architectural style was still at a premium in the district. In 1933 a Neo-Classical cinema was erected with an impressive Art Deco interior. During the 1960s, two imposing glass buildings blended the contemporary with the classical. Today, the varied historic architecture of Place de Brouckère enhances one of the city's busiest squares, despite the addition of advertising hoardings.

Eglise St-Jean-Baptiste-au-Béguinage ⑲

Place du Béguinage, 1000 BRU. **Map** 1 C1. **Tel** (02) 217 8742. ▦ 47, 88. Ⓜ Ste-Catherine. ◐ 10am–5pm Tue–Sat, 10am–8pm Sun. ● Mon. &

This stone-clad church was consecrated in 1676 around the long-standing and largest béguine community in the country, established in 1250. Fields and orchards around the site contained cottages and houses for up to 1,200 béguine women, members of a lay religious order who took up charitable work and enclosed living after widowhood or failed marriages. In medieval times the béguines ran a laundry, hospital and windmill for the people of the city. Still a popular place of worship, the church is also notable for its Flemish Baroque details from the 17th century, especially the onion-shaped turrets and ornamental walls. The nave is also Baroque, decorated with ornate winged cherubs, angels and scrolls. The confessionals are carved with allegorical figures and saints. A more unusual feature are the aisles, which have been widened to allow more light in. In the apse is a statue of St John the Baptist. The 1757 pulpit is a fine example of Baroque woodcarving, showing St Dominic and a heretic.

Théâtre Royal Flamand ⑳

Quai au Pierre de Taille 9, 1000 BRU. **Map** 1 C1. **Tel** (02) 210 1112. ▦ 48, 58, 61, 88. ▦ 3, 4, 25, 31, 32, 33, 51, 55. Ⓜ Rogier, Yser. www.kvs.be

The former quay area of Brussels, on the banks of the old River Senne, still survives as a reminder that the city was once a thriving port. In 1882, architect Jean Baes was commissioned to enlarge one of the former waterfront warehouses and then turn it into a theatre but was asked to retain the original 1780 façade. Baes

The ornate façade of Eglise St-Jean-Baptiste-au-Béguinage

solved this problem by placing the façade directly behind the frontage of the new building. Other interesting design features are peculiar to the late 19th century. The four exterior metal terraces and a staircase leading to the ground were built for audience evacuation in the event of fire. Major renovations have restored the fabric of the original building and added a second building.

The 19th-century interior staircase of Théâtre Royal Flamand

Maison de la Bellone ㉑

Rue de Flandre 46, 1000 BRU. **Map** 1 C2. **Tel** (02) 513 3333. ▤ 47, 88. Ⓜ Ste-Catherine ◷ 10am–6pm Mon–Fri, ◐ Sat, Sun, Jul.

This 17th-century aristocratic residence, now shielded under a glass roof and no longer visible from the street, was once the headquarters of the Ommegang procession (see p25). The original façade is notable for its decoration. There is a statue of Bellona (goddess of war), after whom the house is named, above the central arch, and the window ledges have medallions of Roman emperors.

Today the house, its exhibition centre and once-private theatre are open for dance and cinema shows, and temporary exhibitions of art and furniture.

Stonework on the Maison de la Bellone

THE BÉGUINE MOVEMENT

The béguine lifestyle swept across Western Europe from the 12th century, and Brussels once had a community of over 1,200 béguine women. The religious order is believed to have begun among widows of the Crusaders, who resorted to a pious life of sisterhood on the death of their husbands. The women were lay nuns, who opted for a secluded existence devoted to charitable deeds, but not bound by strict religious vows. Most béguine convents disappeared during the Protestant Reformation in much

Béguine lay nun at prayer in a Brussels béguinage

of Europe during the 16th century, but begijnhofs (béguinages) continued to thrive in Flanders. The grounds generally consisted of a church, a courtyard, communal rooms, homes for the women and extra rooms for work. The movement dissolved as female emancipation spread during the early 1800s, although 20 convents remain, including those in Bruges (see p123) and Ghent.

Eglise Ste-Catherine ㉒

Place Ste-Catherine 50, 1000 BRU. **Map** 1 C2. **Tel** (02) 513 3481. ▤ 47, 88. Ⓜ Ste-Catherine, De Brouckère. ◷ 8am–5.30pm Mon–Sat, 10am–1.30pm Sun. ♿ on request.

Sadly, the only remnant of the first church here, built in the 15th century, is its Baroque tower, added in 1629. Inspired by the Eglise St-Eustache in Paris, the present church was redesigned in 1854–59 by Joseph Poelaert in a variety of styles. Notable features of the interior include a 14th-century statue of the Black Madonna and a portrait of St Catherine herself. A typically Flemish pulpit was installed at some stage; it may have come from the parish of Mechelen. Two impressive tombs were carved by Gilles-Lambert Godecharle. To the east of the church is the Tour Noire (Black Tower), a surviving remnant of the 12th-century stone city walls.

Although this area has been dedicated to the saint since the 13th century, the square of Place Ste-Catherine was only laid in front of this large church after the basin once here was filled in. Paved in 1870, the square contrasts the peacefulness of the religious building with today's vigorous trade in good fish restaurants.

The central square was once the city's main fish market, and this is still the best place to indulge in a dish or two of Brussels' famous seafood, but prices are generally high. Flanking the square, Quai aux Briques and Quai au Bois à Brûler (Brick Quay and Timber Quay, named after their industrial past), contain lively parades of fish restaurants.

Eglise Ste-Catherine showing the spacious Victorian interior

THE UPPER TOWN

Brussels' Upper Town is separated from the lower part of the city by an escarpment that runs roughly north-south from the far end of Rue Royale to the Palais de Justice. Modern developments are now scattered across the whole city, and the difference between the two areas is less distinct than in the past; traditionally the Lower Town was mainly Flemish-speaking and a bustling centre for trade,

Peter Pan statue in Palais d'Egmont

while the Upper Town was home to French-speaking aristocrats and royalty. Today the Upper Town is known for its beautiful Gothic churches, modern architecture and fine museums. The late 18th-century elegance of the Parc de Bruxelles and Place Royale is complemented by "King of the Belgians" Leopold II's sweeping 19th-century boulevards that connect the Parc du Cinquantenaire to the centre.

SIGHTS AT A GLANCE

Historic Streets and Buildings
Hôtel Ravenstein **6**
Palais de Charles
  de Lorraine **8**
Palais d'Egmont **14**
Palais de Justice **15**
Palais Royal pp58–9 **2**
Place du Grand Sablon **11**
Place du Petit Sablon **13**
Place Royale **4**
Square Ambiorix **19**

Parks and Gardens
*Parc du Cinquantenaire
  pp74–5* **25**
Parc Léopold **24**

Museums and Galleries
BELvue Museum and the
  Coudenberg **1**
Institut Royal des Sciences
  Naturelles **23**
Musée Charlier **9**
Musée des Instruments de
  Musique **7**
Musée Wiertz **21**
*Musées Royaux des Beaux-
  Arts de Belgique pp62–7* **10**

Churches and Cathedrals
*Cathédrale Sts Michel et Gudule
  pp70–71* **17**

Chapelle de la Madeleine **18**
Eglise St-Jacques-sur-
  Coudenberg **3**
Notre-Dame du Sablon **12**

Theatres and Concert Halls
Palais des Beaux-Arts **5**

Modern Architecture
Quartier Européen **20**
Parliament Quarter **22**

Shopping
Galérie Bortier **16**

0 metres 500
0 yards 500

KEY

■ Street-by-Street map
see pp56–57

🚆 Railway station

🚋 Tram stop

Ⓜ Metro station

🚌 Bus terminus

GETTING AROUND
The main metro stations for exploring the Upper Town are Parc and Porte de Namur in the west and Schuman and Maelbeek in the east. Most trams circle this area, so the best option is to take one of the many buses that run through the Upper Town.

◁ **Detail of a façade in a terrace of Art Nouveau houses in Square Ambiorix**

Street-by-Street: Quartier Royal

The Quartier Royal has traditionally been home to Brussels' nobility and rulers. Chosen because the air was purer on the hill than it was in the Lower Town, the area once known as Coudenberg Hill was occupied by the 15th-century Coudenberg Palace, home to the Dukes of Brabant and Renaissance rulers. In 1731, the palace was destroyed in just six hours by a fire. Slowly rebuilt during the 18th and 19th centuries, four new palaces and much of the park were designed in Neo-Classical style chosen by Charles de Lorraine (see p33). Today the Royal Quarter presents a peaceful elegance, with some of Europe's finest 18th-century buildings framing the tree-lined paths and fountains of Parc de Bruxelles.

Fountain in park

Rue Royale runs for 2 km (1 mile) from the Quartier Royal to Jardin Botanique. In contrast to the 18th-century Neo-Classicism of its beginnings, along its route many fine examples of Victorian and Art Nouveau architecture stand out.

Eglise St-Jacques-sur-Coudenberg
One of Brussels' prettiest churches, St-Jacques' 18th-century façade was modelled exactly on a classical temple. The barrel-vaulted nave and half-domed apse are sprinkled with floral plasterwork and contain several fine Neo-Classical paintings ❸

RUE ROYALE

★ **Place Royale**
In the centre of this attractive, symmetrical square is a statue of Godefroi of Bouillon, a Brabant soldier who fought the first Catholic Crusades and died in Palestine ❹

PLACE ROYALE

KEY

– – – Suggested route

STAR SIGHTS

★ Palais Royal

★ Parc de Bruxelles

★ Place Royale

Place des Palais divides Palais Royal and the park. In French, "Palais" refers to any large stately building, and does not have royal connotations.

0 metres 100
0 yards 100

★ **Parc de Bruxelles**
On the site of medieval hunting grounds once used by the dukes of Brabant, the park was redesigned in the 1770s with fountains, statues and tree-lined walks.

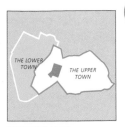

LOCATOR MAP
See Street Finder map 2

Palais de la Nation
Designed by French architect Barnabé Guimard, the Palais de la Nation was built in 1783 and restored in 1883 after a fire. Since 1831, it has been the home of both chambers of the Belgian Parliament.

★ **Palais Royal**
The largest of the palaces, the low rise Palais Royal is the official work place of the Belgian monarch and family. A flag flies to indicate when the king is in the country ❷

Palais des Académies
Built in 1823 as the residence of the Crown Prince, this has been the private premises of the Académie Royale de Belgique since 1876.

BELvue Museum and the Coudenberg ❶

Place des Palais 7, 1000 BRU. **Map** 2 E4. **Tel** *(070) 220 492.* 🚌 *21, 27, 29, 34, 38, 54, 63, 64, 65, 66, 71, 80, 95.* 🚊 *92, 94.* Ⓜ *Trone, Parc, Porte de Namur.* ⏲ *10am–5pm Tue–Fri, 10am–6pm Sat & Sun.* ⏺ *1 Jan, 25 Dec.* 📷 ♿ 🍴 🛍 **www**.belvue.be

The BELvue Museum houses a wide collection of paintings, documents and other royal memorabilia charting the history of the Belgian monarchy from independence in 1830 to the present day. Since 1992 it has been housed in the former Hôtel Bellevue, an 18th-century Neo-Classical building lying adjacent to the Palais Royal. A permanent exhibition across nine rooms presents the history of Belgium

The Neo-Classical façade of the BELvue Museum

through a collection of 1,500 unique historical documents, photographs, film extracts and objects. Complementary temporary exhibitions focus on a particular theme, era or perspective. The Coudenberg is a separate underground archeological site and museum that is within the grounds of the BELvue Museum.

Eglise St-Jacques-sur-Coudenberg ❸

Place Royale, 1000 BRU. **Map** 2 E4. **Tel** *(02) 511 7836.* 🚌 *21, 27, 29, 34, 38, 54, 63, 64, 65, 66, 71, 80, 95.* 🚊 *92, 94.* Ⓜ *Trone, Parc.* ⏲ *1–6pm Tue–Sat, 8:45am–5:45pm Sun.*

The prettiest building in the Place Royale, St-Jacques-sur-Coudenberg is the latest in a series of churches to have occupied this site. There has been a chapel here since the 12th century, when one was built to serve the dukes of Brabant. On construction of the Coudenberg Palace in the 12th century, it became the ducal chapel. The chapel suffered over the years: it was ransacked in 1579 during conflict between Catholics and Protestants, and was so badly damaged in the fire of 1731 that destroyed the

Palais Royal ❷

The Palais Royal is the most important of the palaces around the Parc de Bruxelles. An official residence of the Belgian monarchy, construction of the modern palace began in the 1820s on the site of the old Coudenberg Palace. Work continued under Léopold II (r.1865–1909), when much of the exterior was completed. Throughout the 20th century the palace underwent interior improvements and restoration of its older sections. It is open only from late July to early September, but this is a fine opportunity to tour Belgium's lavish state reception rooms.

The Pilasters Room contains an original Franz Winterhalter portrait of the first Belgian king, Léopold I, dating from 1846.

STAR SIGHTS

★ Throne Room

★ Small White Room

★ Throne Room
One of Brussels' original state-rooms, the huge throne room is decorated in grand style, with huge pilastered columns, 11 large candelabras and 28 wall-mounted chandeliers.

The 19th-century cupola of Eglise St-Jacques-sur-Coudenberg

Coudenberg Palace that it was demolished soon after. The present church was built in the Neo-Classical style and was consecrated in 1787, although it served several years as a Temple of Reason and Law during the French Revolution, returning to the

Catholic Church in 1802. The cupola was completed in 1849. The interior is simple and elegant, with two large paintings by Jan Portaels on either side of the transept.

Place Royale ●

Map 2 E4. ▦ 21, 27, 29, 34, 38, 54, 63, 64, 65, 66, 71, 80, 95. ▦ 92, 94. Ⓜ Trone, Parc, Porte de Namur.

The influence of Charles de Lorraine is still keenly felt in the Place Royale. As Governor of Brussels from 1741 to 1780 he redeveloped the site once occupied by the Coudenberg Palace along Neo-Classical lines reminiscent of Vienna, a city he greatly admired.

When the area was being worked on, the ruins of the burnt-down palace were demolished and the entire site

was rebuilt as two squares. However, in 1995, excavation work uncovered ruins of the 15th-century Aula Magna, the Great Hall of the former palace. This was part of the extension of the palace started under the dukes of Brabant in the early 13th century and then developed under the rule of the dukes of Burgundy, in particular Philip the Good. It was in this room that the Hapsburg emperor Charles V abdicated in favour of his son, Philip II. The ruins can now be seen as part of the BELvue Museum.

Although criss-crossed by tramlines and traffic, the Place Royale maintains a feeling of dignity with its tall, elegant, cream buildings symmetrically set around a cobbled square. Visitors can tour the area on foot, admiring the exceptional Neo-Classical buildings.

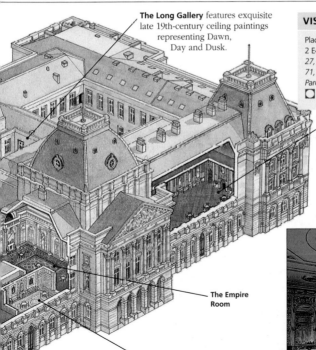

The Long Gallery features exquisite late 19th-century ceiling paintings representing Dawn, Day and Dusk.

Hall of Mirrors
This large room is famous for its grandiose effect similar to the mirrored chamber at Versailles. The ceiling is decorated in green beetle and wing designs by sculptor Jan Fabre.

The Empire Room

★ Small White Room
Rows of 19th-century royal portraits dominate this gilt chamber with its large candle-lit chandeliers and late 18th-century furnishings.

The Victor Horta-designed façade of the Palais des Beaux-Arts

Palais des Beaux-Arts ⑤

Rue Ravenstein 23, 1000 BRU.
Map 2 E3. *Tel* (02) 507 8200. 🚃 27, 29, 38, 63. Ⓜ Gare Centrale, Parc. ◯ 9am–6pm daily; for exhibitions 10am–6pm Tue–Sun. ● public hols. 🎫 🖥 ♿ www.bozar.be

The Palais des Beaux-Arts owes its existence to Henri Le Boeuf, a music-loving financier who gave his name to the main auditorium. In 1922 he commissioned the architect Victor Horta (see p78) to design a cultural centre which would house concert halls and exhibition areas open to all visitors and embracing the artistic fields of music, art, theatre, cinema, architecture and literature. The centre was the first of its kind in Europe.

The complex has a fine reputation and has played a key role in the cultural life of Brussels for more than 80 years. It is the focus for the city's music, hosting 250 classical music concerts each year, and is home to the Belgian National Orchestra. The programme also includes about 50 concerts of rock, pop, jazz and world music.

The complex also houses the **CINEMATEK**, set up in 1962, with its fine archive and exhibition of old cameras and lenses. It screens classic films.

🏛 **CINEMATEK**
Rue Baron Horta 9, 1000 BRU.
Tel (02) 551 1919. ◯ 4:30–10pm Mon, Tue, Fri, 2:30–10pm Wed, Thu, Sat, Sun. 🎫

Hôtel Ravenstein ⑥

Rue Ravenstein 3, 1000 BRU.
Map 2 E3. 🚃 27, 29, 38, 63, 65, 66. 🚋 92, 94. Ⓜ Gare Centrale, Parc. ◯ restaurant only.

Over the centuries the Hôtel Ravenstein has been the home of patrician families, soldiers and court officials, and, for the past 100 years, the Royal Society of Engineers. The building was designed at the end of the 15th century for Adolphe and Philip Cleves-Ravenstein; in 1515 it became the birthplace of Anne of Cleves. Consisting of two parts, joined by gardens and stables, it is the last remaining example of a Burgundian-style manor house. The Hôtel Ravenstein was acquired by the town in 1896 and used to store

The pretty open courtyard of the Hôtel Ravenstein

artworks. Sadly, it fell into disrepair and renovation took place in 1934. One half is now a Belgian restaurant, the other the Royal Society of Engineers' private HQ. However, the pretty, original inner courtyard can still be seen.

Musée des Instruments de Musique ⑦

Rue Montagne de la Cour 2, 1000 BRU. **Map** 2 E4. *Tel* (02) 545 0130. 🚃 27, 29, 38, 63, 65, 66. 🚋 92, 94. Ⓜ Gare Centrale, Parc. ◯ 9:30am–4:45pm Tue–Fri, 10am–4:45pm Sat & Sun. ● 1 Jan, 1 May, 1 & 11 Nov, 25 Dec. 🎫 🎫 🖥 🏧 ♿ www.mim.be

Once a department store, the building known as Old England is a striking showpiece of Art Nouveau architecture located by the Place Royale.

Architect Paul Saintenoy gave full rein to his imagination when he designed these shop premises for the Old England company in 1899. The façade is made entirely of glass and elaborate wrought iron. There is a domed gazebo on the roof, and a turret to one side. Surprisingly, it was only in the 1990s that a listed building policy was adopted in Brussels, which has secured treasures such as this. The building is now home to the Musée des Instruments de Musique, moved from the Sablon. Meanwhile, the Old England company is still flourishing, with its premises at No. 419 in the fashionable Avenue Louise.

The collection of the Musée des Instruments de Musique began in the 19th century when the state bought 80 ancient and exotic instruments. It was doubled in 1876 when King Léopold II donated a gift of 97 Indian musical instruments presented to him by a maharajah. A museum displaying all of these artifacts opened in 1877, and by 1924 the museum boasted 3,300

The façade of Old England

pieces and was recognized as a leader in its field. Today the collection contains more than 6,000 items and includes many fine examples of wind, string and keyboard instruments from medieval times to the present. Chief attractions include prototype instruments by Adolphe Sax, the Belgian inventor of the saxophone, mini violins favoured by street musicians and a violin maker's studio. In 2000 the museum moved to its specially designed home in the renovated Old England building, where there is much more room in which to display this world-class collection. Thanks to a clever infra-red headset system, visitors can discover the sound of each instrument at their own pace.

Antique violin

Palais de Charles de Lorraine ❽

Place du Musée 1, 1000 BRU. **Map** 2 D4. **Tel** (02) 519 5311. 27, 29, 38, 63, 65, 66. 92, 94. **M** Gare Centrale, Parc. ◯ 1–5pm Wed & Sat. ◯ Tue–Sun, Thu & Fri, last week in Aug, last week in Dec. for details **Tel** (02) 519 5786.

Hidden behind this Neo-Classical façade are the few rooms that remain of the

The state room with marble floor at the Palais de Charles de Lorraine

palace of Charles de Lorraine, Governor of Brussels during the mid-18th century. He was a keen patron of the arts, and the young Mozart is believed to have performed here. Few original features remain, as the palace was ransacked by marauding French troops in 1794. The bas-reliefs at the top of the stairway, representing air, earth, fire and water, reflect Charles de Lorraine's interest in alchemy. Most spectacular of all the original features is the 28-point star set in the floor of the circular drawing room. Each of the points is made of a different Belgian marble taken from Charles de Lorraine's personal mineral collection. The palace houses the Bibliothèque Royale (Royal Library) and the Musée du 18ème siècle.

Musée Charlier ❾

Avenue des Arts 16, 1210 BRU. **Map** 2 F2. **Tel** (02) 220 691. 22, 65, 66. 29, 63. **M** Madou, Arts-Loi. ◯ noon–5pm Mon–Thu, 10am–1pm Fri. ◯ public hols. French & Dutch only.

This quiet museum was once the home of Henri van Cutsem, a wealthy collector and patron of the arts. In 1890 he asked the young architect Victor Horta to re-design his house as an exhibition space for his extensive collections. When Van Cutsem died in 1904 his heir, the sculptor Charlier, took care of the house and the collections. On Charlier's death in 1925 the house and contents were left to the city as a museum.

The Musée Charlier opened in 1928. It contains paintings by a number of different artists, including portraits by Antoine Wiertz (see p72), landscapes by Hippolyte Boulenger and Guillaume Vogels, and impressionistic still lifes by James Ensor and Anna Boch. The collection also includes a large number of sculptures by Charlier and others by Rik Wouters, as well as glassware, porcelain, chinoiserie and silverware. Of special note are the tapestries, some from the Paris studios of Aubusson, on the staircases and the first floor, and the displays of Louis XV- and Louis XVI-style furniture on the first floor.

Musée Charlier, home to one of Belgium's finest individual collections of art and furnishings

Musées Royaux des Beaux-Arts: Musée d'Art Ancien ⑩

Officially known as the Musées Royaux des Beaux-Arts de Belgique, the Musée d'Art Ancien, Musée Fin de Siècle and Musée Magritte are Brussels' premier art museums. The museums' buildings are home to exhibits from two eras, *ancien* (15th–18th century) and *fin de sècle* (19th and 20th centuries). They house the world's largest collection of works by Belgian surrealist René Magritte (1898–1967). Housed in a Neo-Classical building, the Musée d'Art Ancien is the largest of the museum's sections and dates back to the 18th century when it consisted of the few valuable works left behind by the French Republican army. This small collection grew and the present gallery opened in 1887. The Musée d'Art Ancien is best known for the finest collection of Flemish art in the world, and many Old Masters, including van Dyck and Rubens, are also well represented.

Hercules Sculpture

Façade of Museum
Corinthian columns and busts of Flemish painters adorn the entrance.

Ground level

The Census at Bethlehem *(1610)*
Pieter Brueghel the Younger (c.1564–1638) produced a version of this subject some 40 years after the original by his father. Shown together, the two works illustrate the development of Flemish painting in its peak period.

Main Entrance

★ The Annunciation *(c.1406–7)*
The Master of Flémalle (c.1375–1444) sets the holy scene of the Archangel Gabriel announcing the impending birth of the Messiah in a homely, contemporary setting, with daily objects an apparent contrast to the momentous event.

Entrance to The Museum Shop

STAR PAINTINGS

★ The Assumption of the Virgin by Pieter Paul Rubens

★ The Annunciation by the Master of Flémalle

Upper level

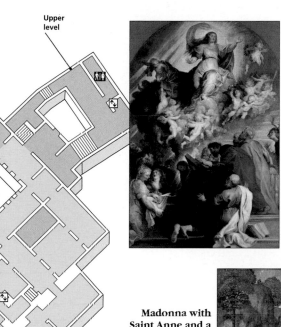

VISITORS' CHECKLIST

Rue de la Régence 3, 1000 BRU.
Map 2 D4. *Tel* (02) 508 3211.
📷 27, 29, 38, 63, 65, 66. 🚋
92, 94. Ⓜ Gare Centrale, Parc.
🕙 10am–5pm Tue–Sun. ●
Mon, public hols. ♿ 📷 📷 📷
🄷 www.fine-arts-museum.be

★ **The Assumption of the Virgin** *(c.1610)*
Pieter Paul Rubens (1577–1640) was the leading exponent of Baroque art in Europe, combining Flemish precision with Italian flair. Here, Rubens suppresses background colours to emphasize the Virgin's blue robes.

Madonna with Saint Anne and a Franciscan Donor
(1470)
Hugo van der Goes (c.1430–82) was commissioned to paint this symbolic work for the monk shown on the right for his personal devotional use.

To Musée Magrite →

Lower level

Interior of the Main Hall
Founded by Napoleon in 1801 to relieve the packed Louvre in Paris, these are the oldest museums in Belgium. More than 2,500 works are exhibited in the museums' buildings.

Auditorium

KEY

🟨	15th–16th century
🟨	17th–18th century
🟦	Temporary exhibitions
🟦	Non-exhibition space

GALLERY GUIDE
The gallery is divided up into two different eras of art, as shown in the key. Two large auditoriums on the ground floor and lower levels are used for occasional lectures as well as presentations. Visitors can enter the Musée Magritte and from there, the Musée Fin de Siècle, via the escalator behind the museum's restaurant.

Musées Royaux des Beaux-Arts: Musée Magritte and Musée Fin de Siècle

The modern section of the museum is situated in a unique setting: eight levels of the building are underground, but a lightwell allows many of the works to be seen by natural daylight filtering in from the Place du Musée. The collection of art is varied, and includes many well-known 20th-century artists from 1900 to the present day, though works by the Belgian Surrealists are the most popular. Since the opening of the Musée Magritte in 2009, the Musées Royaux des Beaux-Arts has seen many changes, and construction work is ongoing behind the scenes.

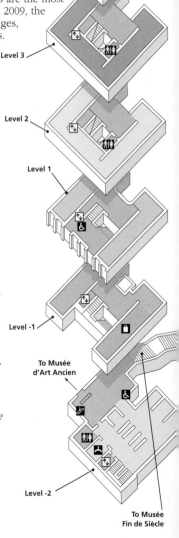

Level 4

Level 3

Level 2

Level 1

Level -1

To Musée d'Art Ancien

To Musée Fin de Siècle

Level -2

Le Joueur Secret *(1927)*
The museum owns this work, painted during Magritte's self-titled "Cavernous" period when he painted roughly a canvas each day.

★ The Domain of Arnheim *(1962)*
The museum contains the world's largest collection of work by surrealist René Magritte (see p17). Here, an eagle-mountain rears over a small bird's nest. The inexplicable nature of the eerie composition draws its elements into question, but answers are made deliberately difficult.

STAR EXHIBITS

- ★ La Seine à la Grande-Jatte by Georges Seurat

- ★ The Domain of Arnheim by René Magritte

GALLERY GUIDE

Access to the museums is available through the main ticket hall of the Musées Royaux des Beaux-Arts de Belgique. The Musée Magritte is arranged in chronological order over six floors. Level -2 is a multimedia area, showing Magritte's films. From here, stairs lead further underground to the Musée Fin de Siècle. The area shaded in green is this permanent collection, which displays work from the 19th and 20th centuries.

★ **La Seine à la Grande-Jatte** *(1888)*
It was in this painting that Georges Seurat first applied his pointilism technique on a large scale; colour dots are juxtaposed and optically fuse in the viewer's eye.

KEY

☐ Musée Fin de Siècle: 19th and 20th century

☐ Musée Magritte: 1898–1929

☐ Musée Magritte: 1930–1950

☐ Musée Magritte: 1951–1967

☐ Musée Magritte: multimedia area

☐ Temporary exhibitions

☐ Non-exhibition space

La Nature
(1899–1900)
Czech artist Alphonse Mucha was best known for his Art Nouveau poster designs, but he also created jewellery, stained glass and sculptures like this bronze, La Nature.

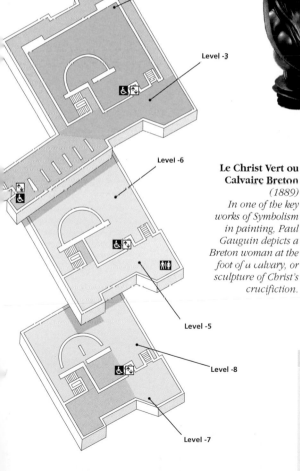

Level -4

Level -3

Level -6

Level -5

Level -8

Level -7

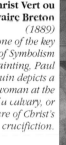

Le Christ Vert ou Calvaire Breton
(1889)
In one of the key works of Symbolism in painting, Paul Gauguin depicts a Breton woman at the foot of a calvary, or sculpture of Christ's crucifiction.

VISITORS' CHECKLIST

Place Royale 1, 1000 BRU. **Map** 2 D4. **Tel** *(02) 508 3211.* 🚌 *27, 29, 38, 63, 65, 66.* 🚋 *92, 94.* Ⓜ *Gare Centrale, Parc.* ⏰ *10am–5pm Tue–Sun (open till 8pm on Wed).* 🚫 *Mon, public hols.* ♿ 📷 🏪 www.fine-arts-museum.be *Musée Magritte* www.magrittemuseum.be

Exploring the Musées Royaux des Beaux-Arts de Belgique

Six centuries of art, both Belgian and international, are displayed in the museums that make up the Musées Royaux des Beaux-Arts. The combination of the museums contains works from many artistic styles, from the religious paintings of the 15th-century Flemish Primitives to the graphic art of the 1960s and 1970s. Regular temporary exhibitions are staged at the museums, which are very well set out, guiding the visitor easily through the full collection or, if time is short, directly to the art era of special interest. Each section is highly accessible, with both main museums divided into different sections which relate to the art of each century, taking the visitor through galleries representing the varied schools of art by period.

Flemish still life, *Vase of Flowers* (1704) by Rachel Ruysch

MUSÉE D'ART ANCIEN

The Musée d'Art Ancien exhibits works dating from the 15th to the 18th centuries. In the first few rooms are works by the renowned school of Flemish Primitives *(see p16)*. As is the case with most art from the Middle Ages, the paintings are chiefly religious in nature and depict biblical scenes and details from the lives of saints. Many of the works show deeds of horrific torture, martyrdom and violence, attended by the perplexing nonchalance of the elegantly attired bystanders. A typical example is the diptych *The Justice of Emperor Otto III* (c.1460) by Dirk Bouts, which includes a gory beheading (a famous miscarriage of justice in the 12th century) and an execution by burning at the stake. At the same time, the

detail is exquisite and provides a fascinating window on the textiles, architecture and faces of the 15th century. Also on display are works such as *Lamentation* (c.1441) by Rogier van der Weyden, the city painter to Brussels during the mid-15th century, and *The Martyrdom of Saint Sebastian* (c.1475) by Bruges artist, Hans Memling (c.1433–94).

Another unique aspect of the section is the extensive collection of paintings by the Brueghels, father and son. Both were renowned for their scenes of peasant life. On display are *The Fall of Icarus* (1558) by Brueghel the Elder and *The Struggle between Carnival and Lent* (c.1559) by his son, Pieter.

In the following rooms are works from the 17th and 18th centuries. A highlight of this section is the world-famous collection of paintings by Baroque artist, Pieter Paul

Rubens (1557–1640), which affords a fine overview of his art. As well as key examples of his religious works, there are some excellent portraits, such as *Hélène Fourment* (c.1614–73), of his young wife. Of special interest are the sketches made in preparation for Rubens's larger works, including *Four Negro Heads*, for his iconic *Adoration of the Magi* (1624).

Other works of note in this section are the paintings by Old Masters such as van Dyck's *Portrait of a Genoese Lady with her Daughter* from the 1620s and *Three Children with Goatcart* (c.1620) by Frans Hals. Representatives of the later Flemish schools include Jacob Jordaens and his depiction of myths such as *Pan and Syrinx* (c.1645) and *Satyr and Peasant*. Baroque and Flemish art are all well represented in the museum.

Also on display are some small sculptures that were studies of larger works by Laurent Delvaux, a leading sculptor of the 18th century. Most notably, *Hercules and Erymanthian Boar* is a study for the sculpture by the staircase in the Palais de Charles de Lorraine *(see p65)*. Works of the Italian, Spanish and French schools are also represented, notably the Classical landscape painter Claude Le Lorrain's poetic scene of *Aeneas Hunting the Stag on the Coast of Libya* (1672).

Other works on show include *Vase of Flowers* (1704) by Dutch artist Rachel Ruysch, who specialized in still-life paintings of flowers and fruits.

Lamentation (c.1441) by Rogier van der Weyden

MUSÉE FIN DE SIÈCLE

The Musée Fin de Siècle showcases European and international art from the end of the 19th century and the beginning of the 20th century. This part of the museum has become a flagship cultural institution in the world of art thanks to the exhibits from the 31 different European art academies who, in 1868, created the Société Libre des Beaux-Arts. The Société introduced modernism and the avant-garde to Belgium.

The rediscovery of the Primitives, Impressionism, Symbolism and Art Nouveau are all represented by such artists as Khnopff, Seurat, Spilliaert, Gauguin, van de Velde, Mucha, Horta, Ensor and de Vlaminick.

There is an excellent collection of Symbolist art, such as the poetic and disturbing classics *Des Caresses* by Fernand Khnopff (1858–1921), which shows an androgynous figure nuzzling a human head on a cheetah's body. Léon Spilliaert (1881–1946) is included via his 1909 symbolist landscape, *The Dike*.

Many of the artists, such as Nice-born Henri Evenepoel (1872–99), who brought his distinctive post-Impressionist style to *The Orange Market in Blidah* (1898), deserve a close inspection. There are characteristically bizarre paintings by proto-Expressionist James Ensor (1860–1949), including his 1892 work *Singular Masks*.

Pointillism is represented by *La Seine à la Grand-Jatte* (1888) by Georges Seurat (1859–91), who developed the technique *(see p65)*, followed by Henry van de

The Orange Market at Blidah (1898) by Henri Evenepoel

Velde's *Village Events VII. The Girl Mending* (1890). Belgian van de Velde (1863–1957) went on to become one of the main founders of Art Nouveau in Belgium.

A highlight of the museum is the extraordinarily rich Gillion Crowet Collection of Art Nouveau, which includes Alphonse Mucha's *La Nature (see p65)* and Fernand Khnopff's *Acrasia The Faerie Queen* (1892).

MUSÉE MAGRITTE

The works of the Belgian Surrealist movement have long proved a popular highlight of the Musées Royaux des Beaux-Art's collection. The art of René Magritte (1898–1967) in particular has created an extraordinary public fascination since the increase in his popularity in the 1960s. The museum's collection of Magritte's work began in 1953. To reflect public demand, and to afford the best possible display, his work is now housed in this separate section of the museum.

Born the son of a wealthy manufacturer in Lessines, Magritte entered the Brussels Academie des Beaux-Arts in 1916. A former poster and advertisement designer, he created visually striking work, frequently displaying a juxtaposition of familiar objects in unusual, sometimes unsettling, combinations and contexts. Many of the artist's best-known paintings are shown here in a striking collection of more than 200 works, including *L'Empire des Lumières* (1954), and *La Voleuse* (1927).

Of particular note are the paintings that date from Magritte's self-titled "Cavernous" period of 1927–30. At this time, while living in Paris, Magritte painted roughly a canvas a day. He then moved back to Brussels, where he lived for the rest of his life. Powerful, arresting paintings on display from this later period include the eerie *Domain of Arnheim (see p64)* and the melancholic *Saveur des Larmes* (1948). A cinema shows films dedicated to the artist and others who inspired his work.

Des Caresses (1896) by the symbolist artist, Fernand Khnopff.

Busy café scene at Place du Grand Sablon

Place du Grand Sablon ⑪

Map 2 D4. 🚌 *27, 29, 38, 63, 65, 66.* 🚋 *92, 94, 97.* Ⓜ *Gare Centrale, Louise, Parc.*

Situated on the slope of the escarpment that divides Brussels in two, the Place du Grand Sablon is like a stepping stone between the upper and lower halves of the city. The name "sablon" derives from the French "*sable*" (sand) and the square is so-called because this old route down to the city centre once passed through an area of sandy marshes.

Today the picture is very different. The square, more of a triangle in shape, stretches from a 1751 fountain by Jacques Berge at its base uphill to the Gothic church of Notre-Dame du Sablon. The fountain was a gift of the Englishman Lord Bruce, out of gratitude for the hospitality shown to him in Brussels. The square is surrounded by elegant town houses, some with Art Nouveau façades. This is a chic, wealthy and busy part of Brussels, an area of up-market antiques dealers, fashionable restaurants and trendy bars, which really come into their own in warm weather when people stay drinking outside until the early hours of the morning: a good place in which to soak up the

atmosphere. Wittamer, at No. 12, is a justifiably well-known *patisserie* and chocolate shop, which also has its own tea room on the first floor.

Every weekend the area near the church plays host to a lively and thriving, if rather expensive, antiques market.

Notre Dame du Sablon ⑫

Place du Grand Sablon, 1000 BRU. **Map** 2 D4. **Tel** *(02) 511 5741.* 🚌 *27, 29, 38, 63, 65, 66.* 🚋 *92, 94, 97.* Ⓜ *Gare Centrale, Louise, Parc.* ⬤ *8am–6pm daily.* ♿ 📷 *on request.*

Along with the Cathédrale Sts Michel et Gudule (*see p70–71*), this lovely church is one of the finest remaining examples of Brabant Gothic architecture in Belgium.

A church was first erected here when the guild of crossbowmen was granted permission to build a chapel to Our Lady on this sandy hill. Legend has it that a young girl in Antwerp had a vision of the Virgin Mary who instructed her to take her statue to Brussels. The girl carried the statue of the Virgin to Brussels down the Senne river by boat and gave it to the crossbowmen's chapel, which rapidly became a place of pilgrimage. Work to enlarge the church began around 1400 but, due to lack of funds, was not completed until 1550. All

Notre-Dame du Sablon window

that remains today are two carvings depicting the young girl in a boat, since the statue was destroyed in 1565.

The interior of the church is simple but beautifully proportioned, with inter-connecting side chapels and an impressive pulpit dating from 1697. Of particular interest, however, are the 11 magnificent stained-glass windows, 14 m (45 ft) high, which dominate the inside of the church. As the church is lit from the inside, they shine out at night like welcoming beacons. Also worth a visit is the chapel of the Tour et Taxis family, whose mansion once stood near the Place du Petit Sablon. In 1517 the family had tapestries commissioned to commemorate the legend that led to the chapel becoming a place of pilgrimage. Some now hang in the Musées Royaux d'art et d'histoire in Parc du Cinquantenaire (*see p75*), but others were stolen by the French Revolutionary army in the 1790s.

The magnificent interior of the church of Notre-Dame du Sablon

Place du Petit Sablon ⑬

Map 2 D4. 🚌 *27, 29, 38, 63, 65, 66.* 🚋 *92, 94, 97.* Ⓜ *Gare Centrale, Louise, Parc.*

These pretty, formal gardens were laid out in 1890 and are a charming spot to stop for a rest. On top of the railings that enclose the gardens are 48 bronze statuettes by Art Nouveau artist Paul Hankar, each one representing a

One of the lavish fountains in the gardens of Petit Sablon

different medieval guild of the city. At the back of the gardens is a fountain built to commemorate Counts Egmont and Hornes, the martyrs who led a Dutch uprising against the tyrannical rule of the Spanish under Philip II, and were beheaded in the Grand Place in 1568 (*see p31*). On either side of the fountain are 12 further statues of 15th- and 16th-century figures, including Bernard van Orley, whose stained-glass windows grace the city's cathedral, and the Flemish map-maker Gerhard Mercator, whose 16th-century projection of the world forms the basis of most modern maps.

Statue of Peter Pan in Palais d'Egmont gardens

has twice been rebuilt, in 1750 and again in 1891, following a fire. Today it belongs to the Belgian Foreign Ministry. It was here that Great Britain, Denmark and Ireland signed as members of the EEC in 1972.

Though the palace itself is closed to the public, the gardens, whose entrances are on the Rue du Grand Cerf and the Boulevard de Waterloo, are open. There is a statue of Peter Pan, a copy of one found in Kensington Gardens, in London. Many of the gardens' buildings are now run down, but the ancient orangery has been restored and houses a restaurant.

Palais d'Egmont 🄬

Rue aux Laines, 1000 BRU. **Map** 2 E4. 🚌 29, 63, 65, 66. 🚊 92, 94, 97. Ⓜ Louise, Parc. ♿

The Palais d'Egmont (also known as the Palais d'Arenberg) was originally built in the mid-16th century for Françoise of Luxembourg, mother of the 16th-century leader of the city's rebels, Count Egmont. This palace

Palais de Justice 🄯

Place Poelaert 1, 1000 BRU. **Map** 1 C5. *Tel* (02) 508 6578. 🚊 92, 94, 97. Ⓜ Louise. 🕐 8am–5pm Mon–Fri. ● Sat & Sun, public hols. ♿ 🎧 on request.

The Palais de Justice rules the Brussels skyline and can be seen from almost any vantage point in the city. Of all the ambitious projects of King Leopold II, this was perhaps the grandest. It occupies an area larger than St Peter's Basilica in Rome, and was one of the world's most impressive 19th-century buildings. It was built between 1866 and 1883 by architect Joseph Poelaert who looked for inspiration in classical temples, but sadly died mid-construction in 1879. The Palais de Justice is still home to the city's law courts.

Detail of a cornice at the Palais de Justice

Galérie Bortier

Rue de la Madeleine 55, 1000 BRU.
Map 2 D3. 27, 29, 38, 63. M
Gare Centrale.

Galérie Bortier is the only
shopping arcade in the city
dedicated solely to book and
map shops, and it has become
the haunt of students, enthus-
iasts and researchers looking
for secondhand French books
and antiquarian finds.

The land on which the
gallery stands was originally
owned by a Monsieur Bortier,
whose idea it was to have a
covered arcade lined with
shops on either side. He put
160,000 francs of his own

money into the project,
quite a considerable sum in
the 1840s. The 65-m (210-ft)
long Galérie Bortier was
built in 1848 and was
designed by Jean-Pierre
Cluysenaar, the architect of
the Galéries St-Hubert nearby
(see p47). The Galérie Bortier
opened along with the then-
adjacent Marché de la
Madeleine, but the latter was
unfortunately destroyed by
developers in 1958.

A complete restoration of
Galérie Bortier was ordered by
the Ville de Bruxelles in 1974.
The new architects kept strictly
to Cluysenaar's plans and
installed a replacement glass
and wrought-iron roof made

to the original 19th-century
Parisian style. The Rue de la
Madeleine itself also offers
plenty of browsing material
for bibliophiles and art lovers.

**Crammed interior of a bookshop
at the Galérie Bortier**

Cathédrale Sts Michel et Gudule ⑰

The Cathédrale Sts Michel et Gudule is the national
church of Belgium, although it was only granted
cathedral status in 1962. It is the finest surviving example
of Brabant Gothic architecture. There has been a church
on the site of the cathedral since at least the 11th
century. Work began on the Gothic cathedral in 1225
under Henry I, Duke of Brabant, and continued over a
period of 300 years. It was finally completed with the
construction of two front towers at the beginning of
the 16th century under Charles V. The cathedral is
made of a sandy limestone, brought from local
quarries. It was fully restored and cleaned in the 1990s
and now reveals its splendour.
Of particular interest inside
the cathedral are the Grenzig
organ and the Baroque pulpit
depicting Adam and Eve's
expulsion from Paradise.

The twin towers rise above
the city. Unusually, they were
designed as a pair in the
1400s; Brabant architecture
typically has only one.

★ **Last Judgement Window**
At the front of the cathedral,
facing the altar, is a magnificent
stained-glass window of 1528
depicting Christ awaiting saved
souls. Its vivid reds, blues and
yellows place it in the 16th-century
style. The Renaissance panes are
surrounded by later Baroque
garlands of flowers.

STAR SIGHTS

★ Last Judgement
   Window

★ Baroque Pulpit

Romanesque remains of
the first church here, dating
from 1047, were discovered
during renovation work.
They can be seen and
toured in the crypt.

Chapelle de la Madeleine ⑱

Rue de la Madeleine, 1000 BRU. **Map**
2 D3. **Tel** (02) 410 2957. ⊞ 27, 29,
38, 63. Ⓜ Gare Centrale. ✝ noon &
7pm Mon–Fri; 4:30pm & 7pm Sat;
7:30am, 9:30am, 10:30am & 7pm
Sun. ♿

This church once stood on the
site now occupied by the Gare
Centrale, but it was moved,
stone by stone, further down
the hill to make way for the
construction of the Art Deco-
style station in the early 1950s.
    The 17th-century façade of
the church has been restored.
The original 15th-century
interior has been replaced by

A view of the Chapelle de la Madeleine with restored brickwork

a plain, modest decor, with
simple stone pillars and modern stained-glass windows. Off
the regular tourist track, the

chapel is used by people as a
quiet place for worship. The
Baroque chapel which was
once attached has now gone.

The transept
windows repre-
sent the rulers
of Belgium in
1537/38. Jan Haeck
made the designs
after Bernard van
Orley's sketches.

The Lectern

Sainte Gudule
*This 7th-century saint is
very dear to the people of
Brussels. Her relics were
scattered to the winds
by ransacking
Protestants in 1579,
but this only served to
reinforce her cult.*

Sainte Gudule

VISITORS' CHECKLIST

Parvis Ste-Gudule, 1000 BRU.
Map 2 E2. **Tel** (02) 217 8345.
⊞ 27, 29, 38, 63, 65, 66. ⊞
92, 94. Ⓜ Gare Centrale, Parc.
◌ 7am 6pm Mon–Fri (8:30am
Sat & Sun). 🈺 to crypt. 🎦 ✝
♿ on request.

**The Statue of
St Michael** is the
cathedral's symbol
of its links with the
city. While the gilded
plaster statue is not
itself historically
exceptional, its long
heritage is; the patron
saint of Brussels, the
Archangel St Michael
is shown killing the
dragon, symbolic of his
protection of the city.

★ Baroque Pulpit
*The flamboyantly carved pulpit in the
central aisle is the work of an Antwerp-born
sculptor, Henri-François Verbruggen. Designed
in 1699, it was finally installed in 1776.*

The Art Nouveau façade of No. 11 Square Ambiorix

Square Ambiorix ⑲

Map 3 B2. 🚌 12, 21, 22, 36, 60, 79. Ⓜ Schuman.

Close to the EU district, but totally different in style and spirit, lies the beautiful Square Ambiorix. Together with the Avenue Palmerston and the Square Marie-Louise below that, this marshland was transformed in the 1870s into one of the loveliest residential parts of Brussels, with a large central area of gardens, ponds and fountains.

The elegant houses have made this one of the truly sought-after suburbs in the city. The most spectacular Art Nouveau example is at No. 11. Known as the Maison St Cyr after the painter

whose home it once was, this wonderfully ornate house, with its curved wrought-iron balustrades and balconies, is a fine architectural feat considering that the man who designed it, Gustave Strauven, was only 22 years old when it was built at the turn of the 20th century.

Quartier Européen ⑳

Map 3 B3. 🚌 12, 21, 22, 27, 36, 59, 60, 64, 79. Ⓜ Maelbeek, Schuman.

The area at the top of the Rue de la Loi and around the Schuman roundabout is where the main buildings of the European Union's administration are found.

The most recognizable of all the EU seats is the tricorn-shaped Berlaymont building, which has now reopened following the removal of large quantities of asbestos discovered in its structure. This is the headquarters of the European Commission, whose workers are, in effect, civil servants of the EU. The Council of Ministers, which comprises representatives of member-states' governments, now meets in the sprawling pink granite block across the road from the Berlaymont. This building is known as Justus Lipsius, after a Flemish philosopher.

Further down the road from the Justus Lipsius building is the Résidence Palace, a luxury 1920s housing complex that boasts a theatre, a pool and a roof garden as well as several floors of private flats. It now houses

the International Press Centre. Only the theatre is open to the public, but EU officials have access to the Art Deco pool.

This whole area is naturally full of life and bustle during the day, but much quieter in the evenings and can feel almost deserted at weekends. What is pleasant at any time, though, is the proximity of a number of the city's wonderful green spaces, which include Parc du Cinquantenaire (see pp74–5), Parc Léopold and the verdant Square Ambiorix.

Paintings and sculpture on show in the Musée Wiertz gallery

Musée Wiertz ㉑

Rue Vautier 62,1050 BRU. **Map** 3 A4. **Tel** (02) 648 1718. 🚌 12, 21, 22, 27, 34, 36, 38, 54, 59, 60, 64, 71, 79, 80, 95. Ⓜ Maelbeek, Schuman, Trone. ◻ 10am–noon, 1–5pm Tue–Fri. ● Mon, weekends, public hols. **www**.fine-arts-museum.be

Musée Wiertz houses some 160 works, including oil paintings, drawings and sculptures, that form the main body of Antoine Wiertz's (1806–65) artistic output. The collection fills the studio built for Wiertz by the Belgian state, where he lived and worked from 1850 until his death in 1865, when the studio became a museum.

The huge main room contains Wiertz's largest paintings, many depicting biblical and Homeric scenes, some in the style of Rubens. Also on display are sculptures and his death mask. The last of the six rooms contains his more gruesome efforts, one entitled *Madness, Hunger and Crime*.

The Justus Lipsius, the pink granite EU Council building

A tall European parliament building rising up behind the trees of Parc Léopold in the Parliament Quarter

Parliament Quarter ㉒

Map 3 A4. 🚌 12, 21, 22, 27, 36, 59, 60, 64, 79. Ⓜ *Maelbeek, Schuman.*

The vast, modern, steel-and glass complex, situated just behind Quartier Léopold train station, is one of three homes of the European Parliament, the elected body of the EU. Its permanent seat is in Strasbourg, France, where the plenary sessions are held once a month. The administrative centre is in Luxembourg and the committee meetings are held in Brussels.

This gleaming state-of-the-art building has many admirers, not least the parliamentary workers and MEPs themselves. But it also has its critics: the huge domed structure housing the hemicycle that seats the 700-plus MEPs has been dubbed the *"caprice des dieux"* ("whim of the gods"), which refers both to the shape of the building which is similar to a French cheese of the same name, and to its lofty aspirations. Many people also regret that, to make room for the new complex, a large part of Quartier Léopold has been lost. Though there are still plenty of restaurants and bars, a lot of the charm has gone. When the MEPs are absent, the building is often used for meetings of European Union committees.

Institut Royal des Sciences Naturelles ㉓

Rue Vautier 29, 1000 BRU. **Map** 3 A4. **Tel** (02) 627 4238. 🚌 12, 21, 22, 27, 34, 36, 38, 54, 59, 60, 64, 71, 79, 80, 95. Ⓜ *Maelbeek, Schuman, Trône.* ⏰ 9:30am–5pm Tue–Fri, 10am–6pm Sat & Sun 🚫 Mon, 1 Jan, 1 May, 25 & 31 Dec. 🎫 📷 ♿ 🍴 🏪 **www.**sciencesnaturelles.be

The Institut Royal des Sciences Naturelles is best known for its fine collection of iguanadon skeletons dating back 250 million years. The museum also contains interactive and educational displays covering all eras of natural history.

Parc Léopold ㉔

Rue Belliard. **Map** 3 B4. 🚌 12, 21, 22, 27, 36, 59, 60, 64, 79. Ⓜ *Maelbeek, Schuman.*

Parc Léopold occupies part of the grounds of an old estate and a walk around its lake follows the old path of the Maelbeek river.

At the end of the 19th century, scientist and industrialist Ernest Solvay put forward the idea of a science park development. Solvay was given the Parc Léopold, the site of a zoo since 1847, and set up five university centres here. Leading figures including Marie Curie and Albert Einstein met here to discuss new scientific issues. The park is still home to many scientific institutes, as well as a haven of peace in the heart of this busy political area.

Whale skeleton inside the Institut Royal des Sciences Naturelles

Parc du Cinquantenaire 25

The finest of Leopold II's grand projects, the Parc and Palais du Cinquantenaire were built for the Golden Jubilee celebrations of Belgian independence in 1880. The park was laid out on unused town marshes. The palace, at its entrance, was to comprise a triumphal arch and two large exhibition areas, but by the time of the 1880 Art and Industry Expo, only the two side exhibition areas had been completed. Further funds were eventually found, and work continued for 50 years. Before being converted into museums, the large halls on either side of the central archway were used to hold trade fairs, the last of which was in 1935. They have also been used for horse races and to store homing pigeons. During World War II, the grounds of the park were used to grow vegetables to feed the Brussels people.

Musée de l'Armée gun

★ Musée de l'Armée
Opened in 1923, the museum covers all aspects of Belgium's military history, and exhibits over 200 years of militaria. Historic aircraft are on display in the hall next door.

View of Park with Arch
Based on the Arc de Triomphe in Paris, the arch was not completed in time for the 50th Anniversary celebrations but was finished in 1905.

The Grand Mosque was built in Arabic style as a folly in 1880. It became a mosque in 1978.

Tree-lined Avenue
In part formal garden, part forested walks, many of the plantations of elms and plane trees date from 1880.

Pavillon Horta

STAR SIGHTS

★ Cinquantenaire Museum

★ Musée de l'Armée

Underpass

0 metres   100

0 yards   100

The Central Archway
Conceived as a gateway into the city, the arch is crowned by the symbolic bronze sculpture Brabant Raising the National Flag.

VISITORS' CHECKLIST

Ave de Tervuren, 1040 BRU. **Map** 3 C3. 🚌 *12, 21, 22, 27, 36, 60, 61, 79, 80, 81, 83.* Ⓜ *Schuman, Mérode.* ♿ 🏛 **Autoworld:** *(02) 736 4165.* ⏰ *10am–5pm (Sat, Sun & Apr–Sep: to 6pm).* ♿ 📷 🛍 **Grand Mosque:** *(02) 735 2173.* ⏰ *9am–4pm Mon–Thu. Please dress with respect.*

Autoworld
Housed in the south wing of the Cinquantenaire Palace, Autoworld is one of the best collections of automobiles in the world. There are some 300 cars, including an 1886 motor, and a 1924 Model-T Ford that still runs.

The park is popular with Brussels' Eurocrats and families at lunchtimes and weekends.

★ Cinquantenaire Museum
Belgian architect Bordiau's plans for the two exhibition halls, later permanent showcases, were partly modelled on London's Victorian museums. The use of iron and glass in their construction was inspired by the Crystal Palace.

Cinquantenaire Museum
Parc du Cinquantenaire 10. **Tel** *(02) 741 7211.* ⏰ *9:30am–5pm Tue–Fri (from 10am Sat, Sun and public hols).* ● *1 Jan, 1 May, 1 & 11 Nov, 25 Dec.* 📷 ♿
Part of the Musées Royaux d'Art et d'Histoire, the Cinquantenaire Museum has occupied its present site since the early 1900s. It houses four main collections: Antiquity, National Archaeology, European Decorative Arts and Non-European Civilizations, which includes sections on Byzantium and Islam, China, South-East Asia and the Indian Subcontinent, and the Pre-Columbian civilizations of the Americas. There are decorative arts from all ages, with glassware, silverware and porcelain as well as a fine collection of tapestries. Religious sculptures and stained glass are displayed around a courtyard in the style of church cloisters.

The aircraft display at the Musée Royal de l'Armée

Musée Royal de l'Armée et d'Histoire Militaire
Parc du Cinquantenaire 3. **Tel** *(02) 737 7833.* ⏰ *9am–noon, 1–4:45pm Tue–Sun.* ● *Mon, 1 Jan, 1 May, 1 Nov, 25 Dec.* ♿
Together with the section on aviation, displays cover the Belgian Army and its history from the late 1700s to today, including weapons, uniforms, decorations and paintings. There is a section covering the 1830 struggle for independence *(see p34–5)*. Two other sections show both World Wars, including the activities of the Resistance.

A 90-Minute Walk Around the Heart of Brussels

It is impossible to tire of the Grand Place, and there is no better place to start a walk that traces the history of the city. The route leads first to the island site where Brussels originated, and follows the watery landscape of the old, walled city before the river and canals disappeared. The walk then passes the opera house where Belgian independence was born *(see p48)*, leads to the cathedral, and then to the grand Galeries Royales de Saint-Hubert. Finally, it meanders through the Îlot Sacré, the web of medieval streets around the Grand Place.

No.23 Place St-Géry ⑦ some of the river can still be seen. Leave the square by the Rue Pont de la Carpe (carp bridge) and turn left at Rue Dansaert. ⑧

Place Ste-Catherine
The Rue du Vieux Marché aux Grains (old grain market) opens up into the Place Ste-Catherine ⑨, with the Eglise Ste-Catherine *(see p53)* ⑩ in its midst. Walk to the right of the church; at the far end, on the right, you

The Grand Place, Brussels' theatrical centrepiece

Grand Place and Place St Géry
You could start with a quick wander around the Grand Place, to savour its magnificent gilded architecture *(see pp42–3)*. The fact that this was once the medieval trading centre is recorded in the names of the streets all around it: Rue des Harengs (herrings), Rue Chair et Pain (meat and bread), and so on. At No. 4 Grande Place is La Maison des Maîtres Chocolatiers Belges, which showcases ten artisans who create Belgian chocolate by traditional methods. Leave the

square on the Rue au Beurre (butter), an appropriate address of the Biscuiterie Dandoy ① at No. 31, famous for its traditional, buttery biscuits. On the opposite side of the road is the atmospheric Église St-Nicholas *(see p47)* ②, while ahead lies the Neo-Classical façade of the Stock Exchange, La Bourse ③. Go left; facing the Bourse on Rue Henri Maus is Falstaff ④, one of the few genuine Art Nouveau cafés in Brussels, dating from 1903. Ahead lies the Boulevard Anspach ⑤; this was once the route of Brussels' river, the Senne, which was canalized and covered over in around 1870. The Halles St-Géry *(see p46)* – the old meat market on Place St-Géry ⑥ – is now the hub of a trendy area of the city; this square was an island until the mid-19th century, and the site of one of Brussels' earliest chapels. The River Senne still runs beneath here; in the courtyard of renovated apartments at

TIPS FOR WALKERS
Starting point: *Grand Place*
Length: *3.25 km (2 miles)*
Getting there: *The nearest Metro stop is Bourse; numerous buses also go to the Bourse, and to De Brouckère/Place de la Monnaie a short walk away.*
Stopping off points: *This area is packed with places to eat and drink. The area around Place Ste-Catherine is famous for its fish restaurants. Among the many attractive yet average establishments in the Îlot Sacré, Aux Armes de Bruxelles stands out.*

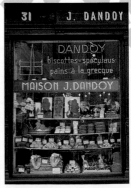

Traditional Belgian butter biscuits at Biscuiterie Dandoy ①

will see the Tour Noire (Black Tower) ⑪. This is a rare remnant of the first ring of city walls built to protect Brussels in the 13th century. Loop round the eastern end of the Eglise Ste-Catherine to the broad, open space lined by the Quai au Bois à Brûler (firewood quay) and Quai aux Briques (brick quay) ⑫. The area between them – filled with pools and fountains – was once a canal; it was covered over in 1870, and the fish market was relocated here. This tradition is maintained

by the numerous fish restaurants in these streets. The Rue du Peuplier leads to the Eglise St-Jean-Baptiste-au-Béguinage (see p52) ⑬; this beautiful Baroque church once stood at the heart of a béguinage (see p53) that occupied much of northwest Brussels in medieval times.

Place des Martyrs and La Monnaie

Via the Rue de Laeken, Rue des Hirondelles, and Boulevard Émile Jacquumain, you can reach the Place de Brouckère (see p52). On the opposite side is the Hôtel Métropole (see p49) ⑭, one of the city's grandest hotels. From the Boulevard Adolphe Max, turn right to walk through the Passage du Nord ⑮, a shopping arcade built in 1882. At the end lies Rue Neuve (see p49) ⑯, one of Brussels' main shopping streets. At one end you will find the Centre Anspach, at the other City 2 (see p169). From here the Rue St-Michel leads to the Place des Martyrs ⑰. In the middle is a marble statue of "Belga", under which is a mausoleum for the 450 "martyrs" killed in the 1830 Revolution that secured Belgium its independence. The building on the north of the square, decked with Flemish flags, is the seat of the Flemish government ⑱. Retrace your steps, then continue to the Place de la Monnaie ⑲, the site of the fine Neo-Classical opera house, the Théâtre Royal de la Monnaie (see p48) ⑳.

The Îlot Sacré

By walking some 200 m (220 yd) along the Rue de l'Écuyer, you come to the

The entrance to the Hôtel Métropole, one of Brussels' oldest Art Nouveau hotels ⑭

Marionettes de Toone puppet ⑳

northern entrance of the Galeries St-Hubert (see p47) ㉑, a magnificent shopping arcade built in 1847. Walk through the arcade to the point, halfway along, where it is intersected by the pedestrianized Rue des Bouchers ㉒, the "butchers street" lined with colourful restaurants. You are now in the Îlot Sacré, a term that dates back to 1960 when this area was decreed a "sacred island" to be protected from development. Take the second left, the Petite Rue des Bouchers ㉓; halfway down, on the left-hand side, is an alley called the Impasse

Galeries St-Hubert, continental Europe's oldest shopping arcade ㉑

Schuddeveld, at the end of which is the Théâtre Marionettes de Toone (see p48) ㉔, the famous and historic puppet theatre. By continuing along the Petite Rue des Bouchers and the Rue Chair et Pain, you will return to the Grand Place.

KEY

••• Walk Route

Ⓜ Metro station

0 metres 100
0 yards 100

A 90-Minute Walk in the Sablons and Coudenberg

Brussels was historically divided into an Upper and Lower Town. The Upper Town, on the Coudenberg ("Cold Hill"), was the royal quarter, the site of a palace destroyed by fire in 1731. This walk climbs gently from the Grand Place in the Lower Town, past remnants of the old city walls and the working-class Marolles district, before entering the chic area of Sablon. On the Coudenberg, the route passes the elegant 18th-century palace of Charles of Lorraine before descending to Brussels' cathedral and returning to the Grand Place.

Cafés and restaurants in the Grand Place, or Grote Markt

Manneken Pis and the Marolles

Leave the Grand Place via the Rue Charles Buls, named after a Burgomaster of the 1890s who did much to preserve the historic face of Brussels. At the first crossroad is the Hôtel Amigo ①, on the site of a prison named the Amigo by the 16th-century rulers of the Spanish Netherlands. Opposite, on the wall of Rue des Brasseurs 1, is a plaque ② marking the hotel where, in 1873, the French poet Paul Verlaine shot fellow poet Arthur Rimbaud at the end of their affair. The next street, the Rue de la Violette, contains the lace museum, the Musée

du Costume et de la Dentelle *(see p44)* ③. Continue along Rue de l'Étuve ④, the site of a public bathhouse in the Middle Ages. At the corner with the Rue du Chêne is the famous statue of the Manneken Pis *(see pp44–5)* ⑤. Take the Rue du Chêne, then the Rue de Villers to reach the Tour de Villers ⑥, the remains of a tower and section of the 12th-century city walls. Across Boulevard de l'Empereur is the church of Notre-Dame de la Chapelle *(see p46)* ⑦, with its black bell tower. Rue Blaes and Rue Haute lead off to the south into the Quartier Marolles *(see p46)*. If you

walk along Rue Haute to the north, you reach the Tour d'Angle (or Tour d'Anneessens) ⑧, another remnant of the old city walls.

The Sablon

Walk up the picturesque Rue de Rollebeek ⑨. At the top, take a look down Rue Joseph Stevens to where the Maison du Peuple ⑩ once stood on the Place E. Vandervelde. Built for the Société Coopérative, it was one of Victor Horta's great Art Nouveau masterpieces, but it was demolished in 1965. The sloping triangular space nearby is the Place du Grand Sablon *(see p68)* ⑪.

Musee du Costume et de la Dentelle ③

High-quality patisseries at renowned chocolatiers Wittamer ⑬

GRAND PLACE GROTE MARKT

RUE DU MIDI ZUIDSTRAAT

R DU MAR AUX HERB GRAS MARK

RUE DE

LOMBARD STRAAT

PLACE ST JEA ST JANSPLEIN

RUE DES ALEXIENS CELLEBROERS STR

PL DE LA CHAPELLE KAPELLE MARKT

RUE STEVENS S

The Musées Royaux de Beaux-Arts de Belgique

The fountain of Minerva ⑫, in the middle of the square, was erected in 1751 with funds from Thomas Bruce, an exiled friend of King James II of England. The Sablon still retains an upmarket air, and it is home to Wittamer ⑬, one of Brussels' most celebrated chocolate makers (shop and small café at No.12; café at No.6). At Rue des Sablons 11 is a branch of Le Pain Quotidien ⑭, famed for its bread and pastries. At the upper end of the Place du Grand Sablon is the beautiful Notre-Dame du Sablon (see p68) ⑮. On the Rue de la Régence, look right for a view of the Palais de Justice (see p69) ⑯. Directly opposite you is the Place du Petit Sablon (see pp68–9) ⑰, a pretty garden with statues of medieval guildsmen.

Place Royale and cathedral

Heading north along the Rue de la Régence, you reach the Musées Royaux des Beaux-Arts de Belgique (see pp62–7) ⑱, the city's most important art gallery, which houses the Musée Magritte. Beyond lies the Place Royale (see p59) on the top of the Coudenberg, the site of royal palaces since medieval times. The present royal palace is just around the corner (see pp57–9), and is

directly connected to the Eglise St-Jacques-sur-Coudenberg (see pp58–9) ⑲. On the opposite side of the square is the Musée des Instruments de Musique (see pp60–61) ⑳, which offers spectacular views from the terrace. Leave the Place Royale by the cobbled Rue du Musée, which leads to the Palais de Charles de Lorraine (see p61) ㉑. The Protestant Chapelle Royale ㉒, to the right, was where King Léopold I worshipped. At the top of Rue Ravenstein is the 15th-century Hôtel Ravenstein (see p60) ㉓, birthplace of Anne of Cleves. You can see the spire of the Hôtel de Ville (in the Grand Place) over the gardens on the Mont des Arts to the northeast. The modern building to the left of the gardens is the Bibliothèque Royale Albert I ㉔, the national library. Walk through the gardens to the equestrian statue of Albert I (reigned 1909–34) ㉕, the "Soldier King" revered for leading Belgian troops in World War I. The arch at the lower end of the street called Mont des Arts has a carillon clock ㉖ on the side facing up the hill that includes figures from Belgian history that move on the hour. From here, a walk of 400 m (437 yd) leads to the Cathédrale Sts Michel et Gudule (see pp70–1) ㉗. On the route back to the Grand Place, stop in the Place Agora to admire Burgomaster Charles Buls and his dog, portrayed in a charming bronze statue ㉘.

The modern carillion clock on the arch in the Mont des Arts ㉖

---

0 metres 100

0 yards 100

KEY

• • • Walk Route

Ⓜ Metro station

GREATER BRUSSELS

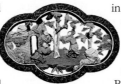

Detail from annexe of Chinese Pavilion, Laeken

Past the heart-shaped ring-road of Brussels city centre lie 19 suburbs *(communes)* which form the Bruxelles-Capitale region. While many are residential, a handful are definitely worth the short ride to sample outlying treasures of Brussels' fascinating history. For fans of early 20th-century architecture, the suburb of St-Gilles offers numerous original examples of striking Art Nouveau buildings including Musée Horta. In Koekelberg and visible from the Upper Town is the huge Sacré-Coeur basilica, started

in 1904. To the north, Heysel offers attractions whose modernity contrasts with the historical city centre. The 1958 Atomium, now restored, stands next to the Bruparck theme park. To the east, the Central Africa Museum reflects Belgium's colonial past in the Congo, and the tram museum takes a journey through Brussels' urban past. Peace and tranquillity can be found close to the metropolis, in the orderly landscape of Royal Laeken and the lush green spaces of the Bois de la Cambre and the Fôret de Soignes.

SIGHTS AT A GLANCE

Churches and Cathedrals
Basilique Nationale du Sacré-Coeur **8**

Historic Monuments, Buildings and Districts
Anderlecht **7**
Avenue Louise **2**
Ixelles **4**
St-Gilles **3**
Uccle **6**

Parks and Gardens
Bruparck **13**
Domaine de Laeken see pp86–7 **11**
Fôret de Soignes **5**

Museums and Exhibition Areas
The Atomium **12**
Musée Horta see p82 **1**
Musée du Tram **9**

Musée Royal de l'Afrique Centrale **10**

KEY

■	Central Brussels
□	Greater Brussels
✈	Airport
▬	Major Road
▬	Minor Road

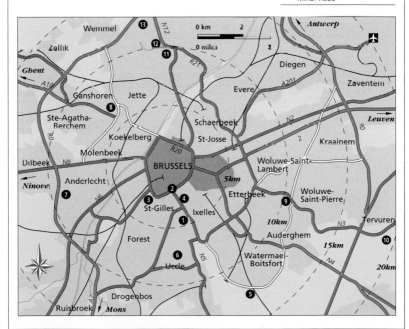

Musée Horta ❶

Art Nouveau candelabra

Architect Victor Horta (1861–1947) is considered by many to be the father of Art Nouveau, and his impact on Brussels architecture is unrivalled by any other designer of his time. A museum dedicated to his unique style is today housed in his restored family home, which he designed from 1898 to 1901. His skill lay not only in his grand, overall vision but in his equal talent as an interior designer, blending themes and materials into each detail. The airy interior of the building displays trademarks of the architect's style – iron, glass and curves – in every detail, while retaining a functional approach.

VISITORS' CHECKLIST

Rue Américaine 25, 1060 BRU. **Tel** *(02) 543 0490.* 48, 54. 3, 4, 33, 51, 92, 94, 97. Albert, Louise. 2–5:30pm Tue–Sun. Mon, public hols.

★ Central Staircase
Decorated with curved wrought iron, the stairs are enhanced further by mirrors and glass, bringing natural light into the house.

The bedroom
features Art Nouveau furniture, including a wardrobe inlaid with pale and dark wood.

★ Dining Room
White enamel tiles line the walls, rising to an ornate ceiling, decorated with the scrolled metalwork used in other rooms.

Madame Horta's sitting-room features blue-and-cream wool rugs woven to Horta's design, and a marble fireplace.

Front Entrance

STAR FEATURES

★ Central Staircase

★ Dining Room

Living Room
The detail of Horta's work can be best seen here, from sculpted bannister ends to finely wrought door handles that echo larger forms.

Exclusive boutique in the chic Avenue Louise

Avenue Louise ②

Map 2 D5. 🚊 *92, 94, 97.* Ⓜ *Louise.*

Most visitors to Brussels travelling by car will come across this busy thoroughfare, its various underpasses constructed in the 1950s and 1960s to link up the city centre with its suburbs. In fact, the avenue was constructed in 1864 to join the centre with the suburb of Ixelles. However, the north end of the avenue retains a chic atmosphere; by the Porte de Namur, fans of designer labels can indulge themselves in Gucci and Versace, as well as investigating the less expensive but no less chic boutiques.

The avenue also has its architectural treasures. The **Hôtel Solvay** at No. 224 was built by Victor Horta in 1894 for the industrialist Solvay family. Its ornate doorway, columns and balconies are a fine example of Art Nouveau style *(see pp18–19)*. The house is a private home, but visits can be arranged (www.hotel solvay.be). At No. 346, **Hôtel Max Hallet** is one of Horta's masterpieces, built in 1903. Continuing south leads to peaceful Ixelles.

St-Gilles ③

🚌 *27, 48.* 🚊 *3, 4, 33, 51.* Ⓜ *Porte de Hal, Parvis St-Gilles.*

Named after the patron saint of this district's main church, St-Gilles is traditionally one of Brussels' poorer areas. However, amid the low-quality functional housing are architectural survivors which make the suburb well worth a visit. Art Nouveau and *sgraffiti* gems *(see p19)* can be found in streets such as Avenue Jean Volders and Rue Vanderschrick. The **Hôtel Hannon** (1902), now a photography gallery, remains one of the city's most spectacular Art Nouveau structures. Restored in 1985, it has a stained-glass window and ornate statuary that take this architectural style to its peak *(see p18)*. Art Nouveau details can be seen in the nearby streets, particularly in Rue Félix Delhasse and in the nearby Rue Africaine.

One of the most striking features of St-Gilles is the **Porte de Hal**. Brussels' second set of town walls, built in the 14th century, originally included seven gateways, of which Porte de Hal is the only survivor *(see p14)*. Used as a prison from the 16th to 18th centuries, it was restored in 1870. Today it houses a small museum dedicated to medieval Brussels, and is part of the Musées Royaux d'Art et d'Histoire.

Art Nouveau detail on façade in Rue Africaine

Ixelles ④

🚌 *34, 54, 64, 71, 80.* 🚊 *24, 25, 81.* Ⓜ *Porte de Namur.*

Although one of Brussels' largest suburbs and a busy transport junction, the heart of Ixelles remains a peaceful oasis of lakes and woodland.

The idyllic **Abbaye de la Cambre** was founded in 1201, achieving fame and a degree of fortune in 1242, when Saint Boniface chose the site for his retirement. The abbey then endured a troubled history in the wars of religion during the 16th and 17th centuries. It finally closed as an operational abbey in 1796 and now houses a school of architecture. The abbey's pretty Gothic church can be toured and its grassy grounds and courtyards offer a peaceful walk.

South of the abbey, the Bois de la Cambre remains one of the city's most popular public parks. Created in 1860, it achieved popularity almost immediately when royalty promenaded its main route. Lakes, bridges and lush grass make it a favoured picnic site.

The **Musée Communal d'Ixelles** nearby has a fine collection of posters by 19th- and 20th-century greats, such as Toulouse Lautrec and Magritte, as well as sculptures by Rodin. The former home of one of Belgium's finest sculptors is now **Musée Constantin Meunier**, with 170 sculptures and 120 paintings by the artist, and his studio preserved in its turn-of-the-century style.

🏛 **Abbaye de la Cambre**
Ave de Général de Gaulle, BRU 1050.
🕐 *9am–noon, 3–6pm Mon–Fri.*
🔴 *public hols.*

🏛 **Musée Communal d'Ixelles**
Rue J Van Volsem 71, BRU 1050.
Tel *(02) 515 6421.* 🕐 *9:30am–5pm Tue–Sun.* 🔴 *public hols.* 📷

🏛 **Musée Constantin Meunier**
Rue de l'Abbaye 59, BRU 1050.
Tel *(02) 648 4449.* 🕐 *10am–noon, 1–5pm Tue–Fri.* 🔴 *public hols.*

🏛 **Hôtel Hannon**
Ave de la Jonction 1, BRU 1060.
Tel *(02) 538 4220.* Ⓜ *Albert.*

🏛 **Porte de Hal**
Blvds du Midi & de Waterloo, BRU 1000. **Tel** *(02) 534 1518.* 🚌 *27, 48, 134, 136, 137, 365.* 🚊 *3, 4, 33, 51.* Ⓜ *Porte de Hal.* 🕐 *9:30am–5pm Tue–Sun.* 📷 ♿

The Forêt de Soignes, once a royal hunting ground and now a park

Forêt de Soignes ❺

🚌 41, 42, 72. 🚋 94. Ⓜ Demey,
Hermann Debroux. 🚶 guided walks
10am Thu & Sun. **Tel** (02) 215 1740.

The large forested area to the
southeast of Brussels' city
centre has a long history:
thought to have had prehistoric
beginnings, it was also here
that the Gallic citizens suffered
their defeat by the Romans
(see p29). However, the forest
really gained renown in the
12th century when wild boar
roamed the landscape, and
local dukes enjoyed hunting
trips in the woodland.

The density of the landscape
has provided tranquillity over
the ages. In the 14th and 15th
centuries it became a favoured
location for monasteries and
abbeys. Few have survived,
but Abbaye de Rouge-Cloître
is a rare example from this era.

In a former 18th-century
priory is the **Groenendaal
Arboretum**, in which more
than 400 forest plants are
housed, many of which are
extinct elsewhere. The most
common sight, however, is
the locals enjoying a stroll.

🏛 **Groenendaal Arboretum**
Duboislaan 6, 1560 BRU.
Tel (02) 657 5925. ◑ 1–5pm
Wed–Sun. **www**.bosmuseum.be

Uccle ❻

🚌 43, 60. 🚋 51.

Uccle is a smart residential
district, nestling in its
tree-lined avenues. Not
immediately a tourist
destination, it is worthwhile

taking a trip to the **Musée
David et Alice van Buuren**.
The 1920s residence
of this Dutch couple
is now a small
museum, displaying
their eclectic
acquisitions. Amid
the Dutch Delftware
and French Lalique
lamps are great
finds, such as
original sketches by
Van Gogh. Visitors
will also enjoy the
modern landscaped gardens
at the rear.

🏛 **Musée David et Alice
van Buuren**
Ave Léo Errera 41, 1180 BRU. **Tel**
(02) 343 4851. ◑ 2–5:30pm Wed–
Mon. ● Tue, 1 Jan, 25 Dec. 📷

Anderlecht ❼

🚌 46, 49, 75. 🚋 31, 81. Ⓜ Bizet,
Clemenceau, St-Guidon.

Considered to be Brussels' first
genuine suburb (archaeological
digs have uncovered remnants
of Roman housing), Anderlecht

is now best known as an
industrial area, for its meat
market, and its successful
football club of the same
name. Despite this, the
Modernist Spanish painter
Joan Miró added a unique
artistic contribution inspiring
bright cartoon-like murals on
Rue Porcelaine.

Although only a few pockets
of the suburb are now residential, during the 15th century
this was a popular place
of abode and some houses
remain from that era. **Maison
d'Erasme**, built in 1468, is now
named after the great scholar
and religious reformer, Erasmus
(1466–1536), who
lived here for five
months in 1521. The
house was restored
in the 1930s. Now a
museum dedicated
to the most respect-
ed thinker of his
generation, it
displays a collection
of 16th-century
furniture and
portraits of the great
humanist by Holbein and van
der Weyden.

Nearby is the huge edifice of
Eglise Sts-Pierre-et-Guidon. This
14th-century Gothic church,
completed with the addition of
a tower in 1517, is notable for
its sheer size and exterior
gables, typical of Brabant architecture. The life of St Guidon,
patron saint of peasants, is de-
picted on interior wall murals.

Illustrating a more recent
history, the **Musée Gueuze** is
a family brewery that has
opened its doors to the public
to witness the production of
classic Belgian beers.

Mirò-style drawings,
Anderlecht

Maison Erasme in Anderlecht, with its courtyard and fountain

The Basilique Nationale du Sacré-Coeur rising over the city

🏛 **Maison d'Érasme**
Rue du Chapitre 31, 1070 BRU.
Tel (02) 521 1383. ⬜ 10am–6pm
Tue–Sun. ⬤ Mon, 1 Jan, 31 Dec. 🖼

⛪ **Eglise Sts-Pierre-et-Guidon**
Place de la Vaillance, 1070 BRU.
⬜ 2–5pm Mon–Fri. ⬤ Sat & Sun.

🏛 **Musée Gueuze**
Rue Gheude 56, 1070 BRU. *Tel* (02)
521 4928. ⬜ 8:30am–5pm Mon–
Fri, 9am–5pm Sat. ⬤ Sun, public
hols. 🖼 including 1 free beer.

Basilique Nationale du Sacré-Coeur ❽

Parvis de la Basilique 1, Koekelberg,
1083 BRU. *Tel* (02) 425 8822.
Ⓜ Simonis. 🚌 13, 14, 15, 20, 87.
🚋 19. ⬜ summer: 9am–5pm daily;
winter: 10am–4pm daily. 🖼 🎞 by
appointment.

Although a small and popular
suburb among Brussels'
residents, there is little for the
visitor to see in Koekelberg
other than the striking Basilique Nationale du Sacré-Coeur,
but this does make the
journey worthwhile for those
interested in Art Deco.
King Léopold II was keen
to build a church in the city
which could accommodate
vast congregations to reflect
the burgeoning population of
early 20th-century Brussels.
He commissioned the church

in 1904, although the building
was not finished until 1970.
Originally designed by
Pierre Langerock, the final
construction, which uses
sandstone and terracotta, was
the less expensive adaptation
by Albert van Huffel. Very
much a 20th-century church,
in contrast to the many
medieval religious buildings
in the city centre, it is
dedicated to those who died
for Belgium, in particular the
thousands of Belgian soldiers
who were never to return
from the two world wars,
killed in battles fought on
their own terrain.
The most dominating feature
of the church is the vast green
copper dome, rising 90 m
(295 ft) above ground. For
those who do not manage to
visit the church itself, it is this
central dome that is visible
from many points in the city,
including the Palais de Justice.

Musée du Tram ❾

Ave de Tervuren 364b, BRU 1150. *Tel*
(02) 515 3108. 🚋 39, 44. ⬜ Apr–
Sep: 1–7pm Sat & Sun, pub hols.
Group tours possible. Every Sun and
pub hol, the museum organizes a tour
to Heysel (9:45am). ⬤ Oct–Mar. 🖼

This museum traces the history
of public transport in Belgium,
with marvellous displays of
heritage machinery. Horse-
drawn trams are available to
transport visitors round the
site, which features fully-
working early versions of the
electric tram, buses and plenty
of interactive exhibits.

Musée Royal de l'Afrique Centrale ❿

Leuvensesteenweg 13, Tervuren
3080. *Tel* (02) 769 5211. 🚋 44.
⬜ 10am–5pm Tue–Fri, 10am–6pm
Sat & Sun. ⬤ Mon, public hols. 🖼
www.africamuseum.be

In the 19th century, the colony
of the Belgian Congo was
Belgium's only territorial
possession. It was handed
back to self-government in
1960 and eventually renamed
Zaire (now the Democratic
Republic of Congo). This
museum, opened in 1899,
is a collection gleaned from
over 100 years of colonial rule.
Galleries show ceremonial
African dress and masks,
and displays on colonial life.
Dugout canoes, pagan idols,
weapons and stuffed wildlife,
feature heavily. There is a
horrifying collection of con-
served giant African insects,
much beloved by children.
The museum hosts temporary
exhibitions year round.

The Musée Royal de l'Afrique Centrale façade in Tervuren

Domaine de Laeken ⑪

In the 11th century Laeken became popular among
pilgrims after reported sightings of the Virgin Mary.
Since the 19th century, however, it has been firmly
associated in the minds of all Belgians with the nation's
monarchy. A walk around the sedate and peaceful area
reveals impressive buildings constructed in honour of
the royal location, not least the sovereign's official
residence and its beautifully landscaped parkland. More
surprising is the sudden Oriental influence. The great
builder, King Léopold II, wanted to create an architectural world tour; the Chinese and Japanese towers are
the only two buildings that came to fruition, but
show the scope of one monarch's vision.

★ **Pavillon Chinois**
*Architect Alexandre Marcel
designed this elaborate building (built 1901–09) that
houses Oriental porcelain.*

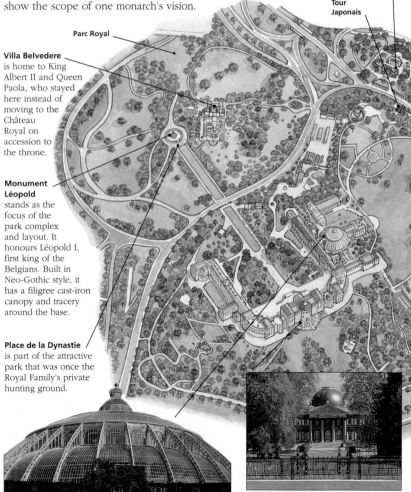

Tour
Japonais

Parc Royal

Villa Belvedere
is home to King
Albert II and Queen
Paola, who stayed
here instead of
moving to the
Château
Royal on
accession to
the throne.

**Monument
Léopold**
stands as the
focus of the
park complex
and layout. It
honours Léopold I,
first king of the
Belgians. Built in
Neo-Gothic style, it
has a filigree cast-iron
canopy and tracery
around the base.

Place de la Dynastie
is part of the attractive
park that was once the
Royal Family's private
hunting ground.

★ **Serres Royales**
*These late 19th-century glasshouses are home to
exotic trees, palms and camellias. Open to the public
annually in April, they are the King's private property.*

Château Royal
*The Belgian royal residence was
built in the late 18th century by
architect-contractor Louis Montoyer
following plans by renowned French
architect Charles de Wailly.*

VISITORS' CHECKLIST

Laeken, 1020 BRU. 🚌 *84, 88.*
🚋 *23, 51.* Ⓜ *Heysel.* **Château
Royal** *Ave du Parc Royal.* ● *to
public.* **Serres Royales** *Ave de
Prince Royal.* **Tel** *(02) 551 2020.*
○ *mid-Apr–mid-May (phone for
details).* 📷 *8–10pm Fri–Sun.*
Pavillon Chinois *Ave J van Praet
44.* **Tel** *(02) 268 1608.* ○
*9:30am–5pm Tue–Fri, 10am–5pm
Sat & Sun.* 📷 **Tour Japonais**
Avenue J van Praet 44. **Tel** *(02)
268 1608.* ○ *10am–5pm Tue–
Sun.* 📷 **Eglise Notre Dame de
Laeken** *Paris Notre Dame.* **Tel** *(02)
479 2362.* ○ *2–5pm Tue–Sun.*

**Domaine Royale de
Laeken** is the royal estate,
adjacent to the Parc de
Laeken in the city district
of Laeken; the woodland
features old magnolias
and blooming hawthorns.

0 metres 250

0 yards 250

STAR SIGHTS

★ Serres Royales

★ Pavillon Chinois

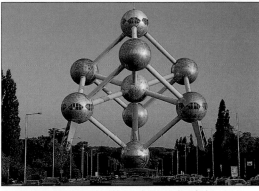

The Atomium rising 102 m (335 ft) over the Bruparck at dusk

The Atomium ⑫

Square de l'Atomium, 1020 BRU.
Tel *(02) 475 4775.* 🚌 *84, 88.* 🚋
23, 51. Ⓜ *Heysel.* ○ *10am–6pm
daily.* 📷 🚻 www.atomium.be

Built for the 1958 World
Fair *(see p37)*, the Atomium is
probably the most identifiable
symbol of Brussels. As the
world moved into a new age
of science and space travel at
the end of the 1950s, so the
design by André Waterkeyn
reflected this with a structure
of an iron crystal, magnified
165 billion times. Each of the
nine spheres that make up
the "atom" are 18 m (60 ft)
in diameter, and linked
by escalators and stairs.
They include exhibition
rooms and a smart
restaurant at the top of
the structure.

Bruparck ⑬

Boulevard du Centenaire, 1020 BRU.
Tel *(02) 474 8377.* 🚌 *84, 88.* 🚋
23, 51. Ⓜ *Heysel.* **Mini-Europe
& Océade Tel** *(02) 474 1313 (Mini-
Europe); (02) 478 4320 (Océade).*
○ *Apr–Sep: 9:30am–6pm daily
(Jul–Aug: to 8pm); Oct–mid-Jan:
10am–6pm daily.* ● *end Jan–Mar.*
📷 **Kinepolis Tel** *(02) 474 2600.*
○ *perfomances.* 📷 *for films.* 🚻
www.minieurope.be

Although nowhere near as
large or as grand as many of
the world's theme parks, Bruparck's sights and facilities are
a popular family destination.
 The first and favourite port
of call for most visitors is Mini-

Europe, where more than 300
miniature reconstructions take
you around the landscapes of
the European Union. Built at
a scale of 1:25, the collection
displays buildings of social or
cultural importance, such as
the Acropolis in Athens, the
Brandenburg Gate of Berlin
and the Houses of Parliament
from London. Even at this
scale the detail is such that it
can be second only to visiting
the sights themselves.
 For film fans, Kinepolis
cannot be beaten. Large
auditoriums show a range of
popular films from different
countries on 29 screens. The
IMAX cinema features surround
sound and a semi-circular 600
sq m (6,456 sq ft) widescreen.
 If warmth and relaxation
are what you are looking for,
Océade is a tropically heated
water park, complete with
giant slides, wave machines,
bars, cafés and even realistic
re-created sandy beaches.

London's Houses of Parliament in
small scale at Mini-Europe

Bruges Market ▷

BEYOND
BRUSSELS

BEYOND BRUSSELS

B russels is at the heart not only of Belgium, but also of Europe. The city marks the divide between the Flemish north and the French-speaking Walloon south. Its central position makes Brussels an ideal base for visitors: within easy reach are the ancient Flemish towns of Antwerp, Ghent and Bruges, each with their exquisite medieval architecture, superb museums and excellent restaurants.

Although Belgium is a small country, it has one of the highest population densities in Europe. An incredibly efficient road and rail network also means that large numbers of people move around the country every day, with around half the population employed in industry, particularly in textiles, metallurgy and chemicals. Despite this, parts of Belgium are still farmed. Stretching south from the defences of the North Sea is the plain of Flanders, a low-lying area which, like the Netherlands, has reclaimed land or *polders*, whose fertile soil is intensively cultivated with wheat and sugar beet. Bordering the Netherlands is the Kempenland, a sparsely populated area of peat moors, which in the 19th century was mined for coal.

There are small farms here today which cultivate mainly oats, rye and potatoes. Northeast Belgium also contains the large port of Antwerp, a major centre of European industry, with its ship-building yards and car factories. The towns of Leuven, Lier and Mechelen are noted for their medieval town centres. Ghent has an elegant grandeur and Bruges has superb medieval buildings and excellent museums.

Brussels itself is surrounded by both Flemish and Walloon Brabant, a fertile region famous for its wheat and beet farms and pasture for cows. Just a few kilometres south of the capital is Waterloo, the most visited battlefield in the world, where Napoleon was defeated by Wellington in 1815.

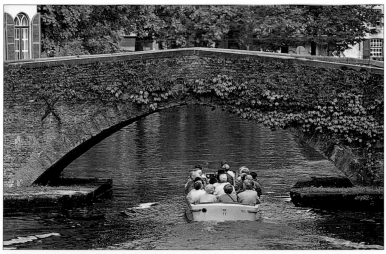

Visitors sail under the Blinde Ezelstraat Bridge on a tour of Bruges

◁ The Brabo Fountain in Antwerp's Grote Markt

Exploring Beyond Brussels

Belgium occupies one of the most densely populated parts of Europe, with a concentration of towns and villages across the flat landscapes of the Flemish plain. Along the North Sea coast there are fewer settlements, set among fertile farmland. To the north and west of Brussels are the three easy-to-reach towns of Antwerp, Ghent and Bruges which, with their ancient buildings and vibrant cultural life, are attractive destinations. East of Brussels is the charming university town of Leuven, and to the south of the city is the site of Napoleon's defeat at the hands of the British army at Waterloo.

Bronze statue of Silvius Brabo in Antwerp's Grote Markt

SEE ALSO

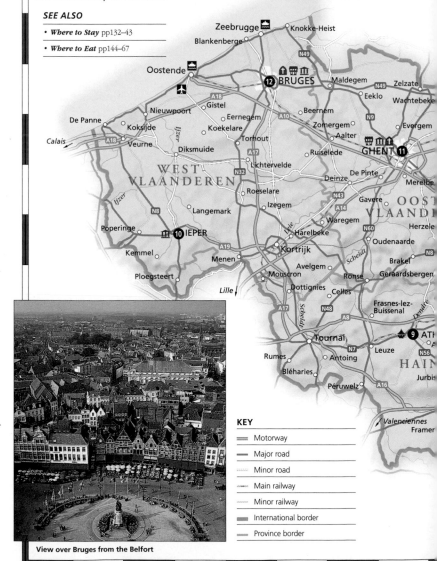

View over Bruges from the Belfort

KEY

▬▬	Motorway
▬	Major road
⋯⋯	Minor road
▬⋯	Main railway
▬	Minor railway
▬	International border
▬	Province border

For additional map symbols *see back flap*

GETTING AROUND

In Belgium distances are short, with a wide choice
of routes – even the tiniest village is easily reached.
Brussels sits at the hub of several major highways
such as the A10 and the A1 (which link the capital
to the country's principal towns). The fully integrated public transport system has frequent train
services and a comprehensive bus network.

The imposing walls of Ghent's Het Gravensteen

SIGHTS AT A GLANCE

Antwerp **1**	Ieper **10**
Ath **9**	Leuven **8**
Bruges **12**	Lier **2**
Dendermonde **4**	Mechelen **3**
Ghent **11**	Pajottenland **5**
Halle **6**	Waterloo **7**

Antwerp

Antwerp is Belgium's second city and the largest city in
Flanders, and it has one of Europe's busiest ports (its
docks situated well to the north of the centre). Beginning
as a settlement on the banks of the River Scheldt in the
2nd century, Antwerp became part of the Duchy of
Brabant in 1106, and its main port. Within 200 years it
was a thriving hub of the European cloth industry. But
its golden age came during the era of Spanish rule (see
p31), when it was illuminated by the artistic genius of
its most famous son, Pieter Paul Rubens (1577–1640).
Today, mirroring this vigorous mercantile and cultural
past, Antwerp is undergoing a spirited regeneration,
seen in its widespread programme of rebuilding and
renovation, and in its reputation as a key European
source of cutting-edge fashion design.

Carvings above the cathedral door depicting the Last Judgement

Visitors touring Antwerp on a horse-drawn bus in the summer

top of which is a statue of St
George and the dragon. The
central Brabo fountain is one
of Antwerp's noted landmarks.

KEY

Street-by-Street pp96–7

0 metres   400
0 yards   400

Key to Symbols see
back flap

Getting Around

The best way to get around
Antwerp is by using the public
transport system. The excellent
bus and tram network is
focused on Centraal Station,
where most visitors arrive.
Fast and frequent trams and
buses travel from here to the
centre. Most of the city's main
sights are within walking
distance of the Grote Markt.

Grote Markt

Grote Markt. **Tel** (03) 232 0103
(tourist office).
Antwerp's central square, or
Grote Markt, is flanked by the
ornately gabled Stadhuis (town
hall), which was completed in
1564 by the architect and
sculptor Cornelis Floris. The
square's north side has a series
of guildhouses, each of which
is decorated with gilded
figures. The tallest of these
is the House of the Crossbowmen at number seven, on

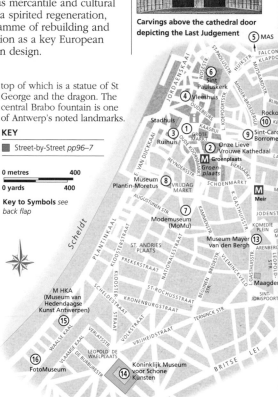

Fresco paintings of the dukes of Brabant in the Stadhuis, Grote Markt

🔒 Onze Lieve Vrouwe Kathedraal

Groenplaats 21 or Handschoenmarkt. **Tel** *(03) 213 9951.* ⬜ *10am–5pm Mon–Fri, 10am–3pm Sat, 1–4pm Sun.* 🚫 ♿ **www.dekathedraal.be**

The building of Antwerp's Onze Lieve Vrouwe Kathedraal (Cathedral of Our Lady) took almost two centuries, from 1352 to 1521. This magnificent structure has a graceful tiered spire that rises 123 m (404 ft) above the winding streets of the medieval city centre. Inside, the impression of light and space owes much to its seven-aisled nave and vaulted ceiling. The collection of paintings and sculpture includes three works by Rubens, of which two are trip-tychs – the *Raising of the Cross* (1610) and the *Descent from the Cross* (1612).

🏛 Antwerp Canals

Ruihuis, Suikerrui 21. **Tel** *(03) 232 01 03.* ⬜ *10am–5:30pm Thu–Mon.* 🔵 *Tue, Wed.* 🚫 🎫 *10am, 2pm, 3pm.* **www.**visitantwerpen.be

The Antwerp canals, or *ruien*, form the subterranean belly of the city and reveal a part of its history. It's possible to take a 15–20 minute walk along the canals without a guide, but there is also the "Long RUI" guided walk which takes three hours, (two hours underground and one hour above), during which you can ask the guide questions. Both walks include an exhibition on the history of the *ruien*, and you will be provided with a protective suit and boots (women are advised not to wear skirts).

🏯 Vleeshuis

Vleeshouwersstraat 38–40. **Tel** *(03) 292 6100.* ⬜ *10am–4:45pm Tue–Sun, Easter Mon.* 🔵 *Mon, 1 & 2 Jan, 1 May, Ascension, 1 & 2 Nov, 25 & 26 Dec.* 🚫

There has been a Vleeshuis (Meat Hall) on this site since 1250, but the existing hall was completed in 1504 to a design by architect Herman de Waghemakere. The structure features slender towers with five hexagonal turrets and rising gables, all built in alternate strips of stone and brick – giving the building a streaky bacon-like appearance.

The fine Gothic interior has been renovated to create a museum called "City Sounds", presenting 500 years of Antwerp's musical life.

🏛 Museum Aan De Stroom (MAS)

Hanzestedenplaats. **Tel** *(03) 338 4400.* **www.**mas.be

Located in the old docks area just north of the historical centre is Antwerp's most innovative project, the Museum Aan De Stroom (MAS), meaning Museum on the River, which opened in 2011. This museum combines the best of the collections from the former Maritime and

Folklore Museums along with some of the Vleeshuis's collection. A broad range of objects on display cover everything from paintings and silverware to wood carvings, archaeological finds, folk art, maritime artifacts and model ships. These pieces span the prehistoric era through to the present day. The museum also features a cultural events space, and it will display high-lights from the Koninklijk Museum voor Schone Kunsten while it is closed for refurbishment until 2017.

Imposing exterior of Antwerp's Sint Pauluskerk

🔒 Sint Pauluskerk

St-Paulusstraat 22 or Veemarkt 14. **Tel** *(03) 232 3267.* ⬜ *Apr–Oct: 2–5pm daily.* 🎫 *3pm Sun & pub hols.*

Completed in the early 17th century, this splendid church is distinguished by its combi-nation of both Gothic and Baroque features. The exterior dates from about 1517, and has an added elaborate Baroque gateway. The interior is noted for its intri-cately carved wooden choir stalls. St Paulus also possesses a series of paintings illustrating the Fifteen Mysteries of the Rosary, one of which, *The Scourging of the Pillar*, is an exquisite canvas by Rubens. There are also paintings by van Dyck and Jordaens.

[Map labels: VEKESTRAAT, R. P VAN HOBOKENSTR., Kerk, ST JACOBS MARKT, STRAAT, FRANKLIN ROOSEVELT PLAATS, GEMEENTESTR., Astrid, De Vlaamse Opera, Bus Station, CARNOTSTRAAT, MEIR, LEYSSTR., STATIESTR., KONINGIN ASTRIDPLEIN, ubenshuis, Opera, DE KEYSERLEI, Diamond Museum (17), Diamant, APPELMANSSTRAAT, QUELLINSTRAAT, Centraal Station, FRANKRIJKLEI, VESTINGSTRAAT, PELIKAANSTRAAT, Zoo, QUINTEN MATSIJSLEI, RUPENZLEI, LANGEVIEVITSTR., PLOEGSTRAAT, Stadspark, LIER, HELEN SSELS, VAN EYCKLEI, Antwerp Airport 6 km (3.5 miles)]

SIGHTS AT A GLANCE

Street-by-Street: Around Grote Markt

Fanning out from the east bank of the River Scheldt, Antwerp was and is one of the leading trading cities of northern Europe. Today, the city's industries lie away from its medieval core whose narrow streets and fine buildings cluster around the cathedral and the Grote Markt. Packed with evidence of Antwerp's rich history, this is a delightful area to wander in. Most sites of interest are within easy walking distance of the Grote Markt whose surrounding streets house museums, shops and exuberant cafés and bars.

Gilt statue on guildhouse

To Koninklijk Museum voor Schone kunsten

The Vleeshuis
Occupied by the Butcher's Guild for three centuries, this beautiful 1504 building has striking layers of brick and stone that look like alternating strips of fat and lean meat.

Stadhuis
Flanking Antwerp's spectacular central square is the elegant 16th-century Stadhuis (town hall), designed by Cornelis Floris (1514–75).

KEY

– – – Suggested route

STAR SIGHTS

★ Grote Markt

★ Kathedraal

The Brabo Fountain
This statue, in the centre of the Grote Markt, depicts the fearless soldier, Silvius Brabo. Said to be the nephew of Julius Caesar, Brabo is shown throwing the hand of the mythical giant, Antigonius, into the River Scheldt.

Sint-Pauluskerk

This imposing church was built in 1517, but has a magnificent Baroque gate and spire dating from the late 17th century. Inside, there is a noted collection of paintings, including one especially fine work by Rubens.

To Central Station

★ Grote Markt

Antwerp's golden age of trade in the 16th century is reflected in the square's cosmopolitan 1564 town hall, built by architects from all over Europe.

★ Onze-Lieve-Vrouwe Kathedraal

The largest Gothic cathedral in Belgium, this building occupies a 1-ha (2.5-acre) site in Antwerp's centre. Work began on this elegant church in 1352 and took almost two centuries to complete.

ZIRKSTRAAT

VERSMIDSTRAAT

To Rubenshuis

Groenplaats

The Groenplaats or Green Square is a pleasant open space with trees. Lined with cafés, bars and restaurants, the square is a popular spot with both locals and visitors for a peaceful stroll or meal.

| 0 metres | 50 |
| 0 yards | 50 |

Exploring Antwerp

Antwerp stretches out from its centre into its sprawling suburbs to a distance of some 7 km (4.3 miles). Badly damaged in both World Wars, the city has a broad mixture of architecture, ranging from the medieval to the ultra-modern. The old city centre is concentrated around the cathedral, Onze Lieve Vrouwe Kathedraal, and the Grote Markt *(see pp96–97)*. The area around the Centraal Station is the centre of the international diamond trade. The Zuid (South) district is an area of drained docks; now rejuvenated, this is a vibrant part of town, and the old dockland architecture of the Waalse Kaai and Vlaamse Kaai has become home to clubs, bars and museums. The area around the old, water-filled docks to the north of the city centre is now also undergoing rapid redevelopment. To the east of the cathedral – beyond Antwerp's pioneering 1930s skyscraper, the Boerentoren – lies the Meir, Antwerp's premier shopping street.

Printing press in the Museum Plantin-Moretus/Prentenkabinet

One of the changing exhibits at the Modemuseum

🏛 Modemuseum (MoMu)

Nationalestraat 28. *Tel (03) 470 27 70.* ◯ *10am–6pm Tue–Sun; 10am–9pm first Thu of every month.* ● *Mon.* 🌐 *www.momu.be*
Following the rise to celebrity of the influential fashion designers called the Antwerp

Six in the 1980s, the city has entered the stratosphere of international haute-couture, and maintains a glowing reputation for nurturing new talent. This fashion museum provides the historical context to Antwerp's rise. Fashion items and accessories are shown in innovative ways in changing exhibitions, to serve as both an instructive resource and a fount of inspiration.

🏛 Museum Plantin-Moretus/ Pretenkabinet

Vrijdagmarkt 22–23. *Tel (03) 221 1450.* ◯ *10am–5pm Tue–Sun, Easter Mon.* ● *Mon, 1 & 2 Jan, 1 May, Ascension, 1 & 2 Nov, 24, 25 & 31 Dec.* 🎫 *free last Wed of month.* **www.**museumplantinmoretus.be
This fascinating museum on the UNESCO World Heritage List occupies a large 16th-century house that belonged to the printer Christopher

Plantin, who moved here in 1576. The house's ancient rooms and narrow corridors resemble the types of interiors painted by Flemish and Dutch masters. The museum is devoted to the early years of printing, when Plantin and others began to produce books that bore no resemblance to earlier, illuminated manuscripts.

Antwerp was a centre for printing in the 15th and 16th centuries, and Plantin was its most successful printer. Today, his workshop displays several historic printing presses, as well as woodcuts and copper plates. Plantin's library is also on show. One of the gems here is an edition of the Gutenberg Bible – the first book to be printed using moveable type, a new technique invented by Johannes Gutenberg in 1455.

🔒 Sint-Carolus Borromeuskerk

Hendrik Conscienceplein. *Tel (03) 231 3751.* ◯ *10am–12:30pm and 2–5pm Mon–Sat.*
This Jesuit church is celebrated for its elegant Baroque façade, which forms one flank of a charming 17th-century square. Rubens played a part in the design of both the exterior and interior when the church was built in 1615–21, and supplied 39 ceiling paintings, but sadly these were lost in a fire in 1718. The surviving parts of the interior indicate how lavish it once was – a triumphant showpiece of the Counter-Reformation.

The Baroque interior of Sint-Carolus Borromeuskerk

Rockoxhuis

Keizerstraat 12. **Tel** (03) 201 9250.
◯ 10am–5pm Tue–Sun. ● Mon, 1
& 2 Jan, Ascension, 1 & 2 Nov, 25 &
26 Dec. 🖮 www.rockoxhuis.be
Nicholaas Rockox (1560–1640)
was mayor of Antwerp, a
humanist, philanthropist, and
a friend and patron of
Rubens. These attributes are
reflected in his beautifully
renovated home – a series of
rooms set around a formal
courtyard garden. They
contain a fine collection of
contemporary furniture and
miscellaneous artifacts, all
interesting and well-chosen.
The paintings and
drawings include
work by Rubens,
Jordaens and Van
Dyck, as well as
work by Frans
Snyders (1579–1657),
who lived next
door, was much
admired by Rubens,
and painted flowers
and fruit in
Rubens' work.

Detail from Fishmarket Antwerp, by Frans Snyders, at the Rockoxhuis

🔒 Sint Jacobskerk

Lange Nieuwstraat 73–75,
Eikenstraat. **Tel** (03) 225 0414.
◯ Apr–Oct: 2–5pm Wed–Mon;
Nov–Mar: 9am–noon, Mon–Sat. 🖮
Noted as Rubens' burial place
– his tomb is in his family's
chapel behind the high altar –
this sandstone church was
built from 1491 to 1656. Sint
Jacobskerk's rich interior
contains the tombs of several
other notable Antwerp
families, as well as a
collection of 17th-century art,
including sculptures by
Hendrik Verbruggen, and
paintings by van Dyck, Otto
Venius (Rubens' first master)
and Jacob Jordaens.

🏛 Rubenshuis

See pp102–3.

🏛 Museum Mayer van de Bergh

Lange Gasthuisstraat 19.
Tel (03) 232 4237. ◯
10am–5pm Tue–Sun, Easter
Mon. ● Mon, 1 & 2 Jan,
1 Nov, 24, 25 & 31 Dec. 🖮
www.museummayer
vandenbergh.be
Fritz Mayer van den
Bergh (1858–91) was
the scion of a wealthy
trading family, but instead of
following in his father's
footsteps, he chose to
devote himself to
collecting art and curios.
After his death aged just
33, his mother
created this museum
to display his
collections. Among
the many treasures
are tapestries,
furniture, ivories,
stained glass,
medieval and
Renaissance
sculpture and a
number of excellent paintings,
including *Dulle Griet* (Mad
Meg), a powerful image of a
chaotic world by Pieter
Brueghel the Elder.

🏛 Koninklijk Museum voor Schone Kunsten

See pp100–101.

🏛 Museum van Hedendaagse Kunst Antwerpen (M HKA)

Leuvenstraat 32. **Tel** (03) 260 9999.
◯ 11am–6pm Tue–Sun (to 9pm
Thu). ● Mon, 1 Jan, 1 May,
Ascension, 1 Nov, 25 & 31 Dec. 🚹
🖮 www.muhka.be
This museum is what you
might expect from a city famed

A room at the Museum Mayer van de Bergh

for its sense of style and
design. A huge, sculptural
building that was once a
1920s dockside grain silo
and warehouse has been
transformed into a series of
unusual spaces to display art
from the front line of
international contemporary art
(1970–present). This includes
work by many of the artists
who have helped to place
Belgium at the forefront of
the art scene, such as
Panamarenko, Luc Tuymans,
Jan Fabre and Wim Delvoye.

FotoMuseum

Waalse Kaai 47. **Tel** (03) 242 9300
◯ 10am–6pm Tue–Sun.
● Mon, 25 & 26 Dec, 1 & 2 Jan 🚹
www.fotomuseum.be
Antwerp's excellent museum
of photography, displaying a
wide range of historical
artifacts and images, has
undergone a complete
makeover, and has embraced
the moving image as well by
incorporating the Antwerp
Film Museum (which offers
scheduled film viewings). In
addition to its extensive,
thematically organized
permanent collection, the
museum mounts regular
exhibitions of photography.

🏛 Diamond Museum

Koningin Astridplein 19–23.
Tel (03) 202 4890. ● Closed for
relocation. Call the tourist office, (03)
232 0103, for the latest information.
This museum is dedicated to
the world of diamonds and
includes treasure chambers as
well as multimedia exhibits
highlighting the processes used
to extract and cut the precious
stone. The museum is
currently closed while a new
site is found. It is expected to
reopen during 2013.

A stained-glass window in Sint Jacobskerk

Koninklijk Museum voor Schone Kunsten

Antwerp's largest and most impressive fine art collection is exhibited in the Museum voor Schone Kunsten, which occupies a massive late 19th-century Neo-Classical building. The permanent collection contains both ancient and modern works. The earlier collection contains medieval Flemish painting and continues through the 19th century, with the "Antwerp Trio" of Rubens, van Dyck and Jordaens well represented. Modern exhibits include the work of Belgian artists Magritte, Ensor and Delvaux, as well as a major collection of work by Rik Wouters. Tissot and van Gogh are among the foreign artists on show. The museum is currently closed for renovations, however collection highlights can be found at the Cathedral of Our Lady and the Museum Aan De Stroom, MAS (see p95).

First Floor

Main Entrance

Façade of Gallery
Building began on this imposing structure in 1884. The Neo-Classical façade with its vast pillars has carved women charioteers atop each side. It was opened in 1890.

★ Woman Ironing *(1912)*
This peaceful domestic scene by Rik Wouters employs the muted colours of Impressionism. This was a productive period for Wouters who painted 60 canvases in 1912.

Madame Récamier *(1967)*
René Magritte's macabre version of the original painting by David is a classic Surrealist work.

Pink Bows *(1936)*
Paul Delvaux's dream-like style clearly shows the influence of Sigmund Freud's psychoanalytic theories on Surrealist painting.

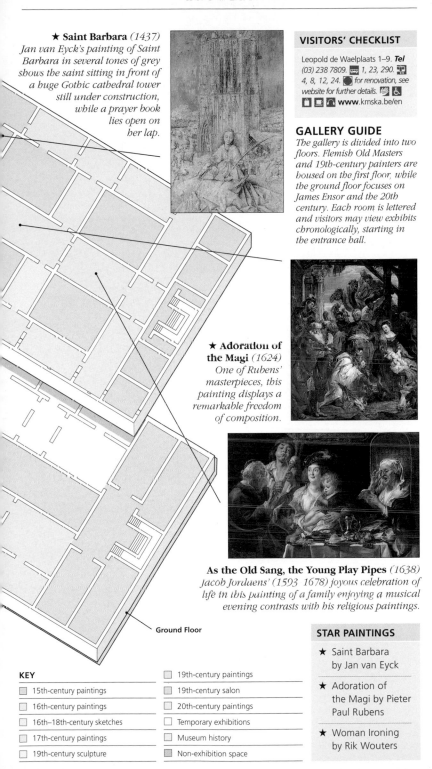

★ Saint Barbara *(1437)*
Jan van Eyck's painting of Saint Barbara in several tones of grey shows the saint sitting in front of a huge Gothic cathedral tower still under construction, while a prayer book lies open on her lap.

VISITORS' CHECKLIST

Leopold de Waelplaats 1–9. **Tel**
(03) 238 7809. 1, 23, 290.
4, 8, 12, 24. *for renovation, see
website for further details.*
www.kmska.be/en

GALLERY GUIDE
The gallery is divided into two floors. Flemish Old Masters and 19th-century painters are housed on the first floor, while the ground floor focuses on James Ensor and the 20th century. Each room is lettered and visitors may view exhibits chronologically, starting in the entrance hall.

★ Adoration of the Magi *(1624)*
One of Rubens' masterpieces, this painting displays a remarkable freedom of composition.

As the Old Sang, the Young Play Pipes *(1638)*
Jacob Jordaens' (1593–1678) joyous celebration of life in this painting of a family enjoying a musical evening contrasts with his religious paintings.

Ground Floor

STAR PAINTINGS

★ Saint Barbara
by Jan van Eyck

★ Adoration of
the Magi by Pieter
Paul Rubens

★ Woman Ironing
by Rik Wouters

KEY

☐ 15th-century paintings	☐ 19th-century paintings
☐ 16th-century paintings	☐ 19th-century salon
☐ 16th–18th-century sketches	☐ 20th-century paintings
☐ 17th-century paintings	☐ Temporary exhibitions
☐ 19th-century sculpture	☐ Museum history
	☐ Non-exhibition space

Rubenshuis

Rubenshuis, on Wapper Square, was Pieter Paul Rubens' home and studio for the last 29 years of his life, from 1611 to 1640. The city bought the premises just before World War II, but by then the house was little more than a ruin, and what can be seen today is the result of careful restoration. It is divided into two sections. To the left of the entrance are the narrow rooms of the artist's living quarters, equipped with period furniture. Behind this part of the house is the kunstkamer, or art gallery, where Rubens exhibited both his own and other artists' work, and entertained his friends and wealthy patrons, such as the Archduke Albert and the Infanta Isabella. To the right of the entrance lies the main studio, a spacious salon where Rubens worked on – and showed – his works. A signposted route guides visitors through the house.

Statue of Neptune

Façade of Rubenshuis
The older Flemish part of the house sits next to the later house, whose elegant early Baroque façade was designed by Rubens.

Formal Gardens
The small garden is laid out formally and its charming pavilion dates from Rubens' time. He was influenced by architects of the Italian Renaissance when he built the Italian Baroque addition to his house in the 1620s.

★ Rubens' Studio
It is estimated that Rubens produced some 2,500 paintings in this large, high-ceilinged room. In the Renaissance manner, Rubens designed the work which was usually completed by a team of other artists employed in his studio.

STAR SIGHTS

★ Kunstkamer

★ Rubens' Studio

Bedroom

The Rubens family lived in the Flemish section of the house, with its small rooms and narrow passages. The portrait by the bed is said to be of Rubens' second wife, Helena Fourment.

The Familiakamer, or family sitting room, is cosy and has a pretty tiled floor. It overlooks Wapper Square.

Dining Room

Intricately fashioned leather panels line the walls of this room, which also displays a noted work by Frans Snyders.

★ Kunstkamer

This art gallery contains a series of painted sketches by Rubens. At the far end is a semi-circular dome, modelled on Rome's Pantheon, displaying a number of marble busts.

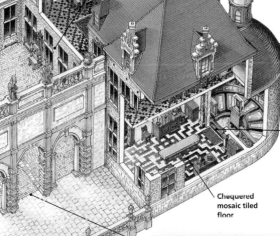

Chequered mosaic tiled floor

Baroque Portico

One of the few remaining original features, this portico was designed by Rubens, and links the older house with the Baroque section. It is adorned with a frieze showing scenes from Greek mythology.

A 90-Minute Walk Across Antwerp

Antwerp handles 80 per cent of the world's entire trade
in rough diamonds, yet this business is carried out in
a distinctly unglamorous quarter in the east of the city;
even the railway station is more elegant. This walk
starts in the diamond district and heads west to the Meir,
Antwerp's main shopping thoroughfare, before visiting
the haunts of Rubens and his contemporaries at the
Rubenshuis, Sint Jacobskerk and the Rockoxhuis. It
then passes through medieval Antwerp to reach
the broad sweep of the River Scheldt.

**The bar area in the impressive
Radisson Blu Astrid Hotel ②**

Diamond District and the Meir

Centraal Station ① is a palatial
Neo-Classical building
completed in 1905 that is
worth visiting in its own right.
It looks out over Koningin
Astridplein, named after the
hugely popular Queen Astrid
(wife of Leopold III and
mother of the present King
Albert II) who died tragically in
a car accident, aged 29,
in 1935. On the far side of
the square is the Radisson Blu
Astrid Hotel ②, a bold example
of post-modern architecture.
For a flavour of Antwerp's
connection with diamonds, go
to the diamond
district. Although
the Diamond
Museum
(see p99) ③ is
currently closed
for relocation, you
can still look at the
diamond shops
and get a flavour
of this distinctively
Jewish neighbour-
hood by walking
down Pelikaanstraat ④ and
Vestingstraat ⑤. By
continuing along De Keyserlei
and Leysstraat you enter the
Meir ⑥, a broad,
pedestrianized high street
packed with large shops.

**The Provincial Diamond
Museum ③**

Rubenshuis and Rockoxhuis

Turn left off the Meir into the
broad street called the
Wapper ⑦. On the left-hand
side of the street is
the Rubenshuis
(see pp102–03)
⑧, the
impressive
mansion
that
Rubens
bought as
his home and
studio in 1610.
At the end of
the Wapper, at
Hopland 2, is the
Grand Café Horta
⑨, a dynamic café-restaurant
built in 2000 around structural
remnants salvaged from
Victor Horta's classic Art
Nouveau building, the Maison
du Peuple, in Brussels (see
p78). Returning to the Meir,

look left – the
tallest building is the KBC
Tower ⑩. Complete with Art
Deco detailing, it was
Europe's highest skyscraper
when topped out in 1931. By
walking up Lange
Klarenstraat, you can reach
the Sint Jacobskerk (see p99)
⑪ on Lange Nieuwstraat. This
richly decorated church is
famous as the burial place of
Rubens. St-Jacobsstraat and
Keizerstraat lead to the
Rockoxhuis (see p99) ⑫,
which offers an insight into
how the homes of the rich
looked in the time of Rubens.
Wijngaardstraat will bring you
to the little square called
Hendrik Conscienceplein ⑬,
named after the Flemish
author who wrote the novel
The Lion of Flanders (1838),
a stirring tale about the
Battle of the Golden Spurs
of 1302; the book was a
landmark in the resurgence

One of the rooms inside the Rockoxhuis ⑫

of Flemish national pride. Overlooking the square is the fine Baroque façade of the Sint Carolus-Borromeuskerk (*see p98*) ⑭.

The Cathedral and the Scheldt

Continue along Wijngaardstraat to reach Lijnwaadmarkt (Linen Market) ⑮. The street names here recall the specialist markets that once clustered around the cathedral. Note how buildings have been constructed right up against the cathedral walls, such as the restaurant Het Vermoeide Model ("The Artist's Sleepy Model") ⑯. The bar on the corner on the other side of the street called Het Elfde Gebod ⑰, at Torfbrug 10, is packed with religious

The Grote Markt and its elegant 16th-century Stadhuis (town hall) ⑲

statuary and the walls adorned with paintings of saints – the name means "The Eleventh Commandment". Continue to the Handschoenmarkt (Glove Market) from where there is a magnificent view of Onze Lieve Vrouwe Kathedraal (*see p95*) ⑱. There is a well in the square decorated with metalwork foliage and a figure; this is said to have been forged by the painter Quentin Metsys in around 1495. The figure depicts the Roman soldier Silvius Brabo, throwing the hand of the evil giant Antigonius into the River Scheldt – the folkloric origin of the name Antwerp (*handwerpen* means "hand-throw"). Now go to the Grote Markt

(*see p94*) ⑲, Antwerp's spectacular main square, where you will see the more famous version of Brabo, by the noted Antwerp sculptor Jef Lambeaux, and the town hall. Head down the Oude Koornmarkt (Old Cornmarket) and Pelgrimsstraat. On the corner with Reyndersstraat is the pub called De Vagant ⑳, which specializes in jenever gin. De Groote Witte Arend (The Great White Eagle) ㉑, at Reyndersstraat 18, is an old and celebrated tavern with a courtyard. On Vrijdagmarkt (Friday Market) you will find the Museum Plantin-Moretus (*see p98*) ㉒, a museum of early printing, set in the 16th-century house of the printer who gave us the typeface called Plantin. From here walk down Steenhouwersvest to the square called St-Jansvliet, with the River Scheldt beyond. For the most part, Antwerp turns its back on its wide and windy river, but not the café-restaurant Zuiderterras ㉓ – an award-winning modern building with fine views across the water.

Boats moored on the busy dockside of the River Scheldt

KEY

••• Walk route

Ⓜ Metro station

TIPS FOR WALKERS

Starting point: *Centraal Station*
Length: *3.2 km (2 miles)*
Getting there: *Centraal Station is served by bus and tram routes from all over the city.*
Stopping-off points: *There are plenty of welcoming refreshment stops along the way. For a touch of class, try the Grand Café Horta (No. 9 on this walk). The walk also passes other noted watering holes, such as Het Vermoeide Model (No. 16), Het Elfde Gebod (No. 17), De Vagant (No. 20), and De Groote Witte Arend (No. 21). Or save yourself for the spectacular Zuiderterras (No. 23) overlooking the River Scheldt.*

0 metres   200

0 yards   200

The Centenary Clock on Lier's Zimmertoren or watchtower

Lier ❷

🏛 34,000. 🚉 🚌 ℹ️ *Grote Markt 57, (03) 800 0555.* www.toerismelier.be

Lier is an attractive small town, just 20 km (12 miles) southeast of Antwerp. The Grote Markt is a spacious cobbled square framed by handsome historic buildings. The Stadhuis (town hall) was built in 1740, and its elegant dimensions contrast strongly with the square, turreted 14th-century Belfort (belfry) adjoining. Nearby is the **Stedelijk Museum Wuyts**, with its collection of paintings by Flemish masters including Jan Steen, Brueghel and Rubens. East of here the church of St Gummaruserk, with its soaring stone pillars and vaulted roof, evokes medieval times, and the carved altarpiece is notable for its intricate biblical scenes. The stained-glass windows are among the finest in Belgium and were a gift from Emperor Maximillian I in 1516.

One of Lier's highlights is the **Zimmertoren**, a 14th-century watchtower that now houses the clocks of Lodewijk Zimmer (1888–1970). This Lier merchant wanted to share his knowledge of timepieces.

🏛 **Stedelijk Museum Wuyts**
Florent van Cauwenberg Straat 14. **Tel** (03) 800 0396. ☐ 10am–midday 1–5pm Tue–Sun. ● Mon, public hols. 🖼

🎏 **Zimmertoren**
Zimmerplein 18. **Tel** (03) 800 0395. ☐ Tue–Sun. 🖼

Mechelen ❸

🏛 77,000. 🚉 🚌 ℹ️ *Hallestraat 2, Grote Markt, (015) 29 7655.*

The seat of the Catholic Archbishop of Belgium, Mechelen was the administrative capital of the country under the Burgundian prince, Charles the Bold, in 1473. Today, it is an appealing town whose expansive main square is flanked by pleasant cafés and bars. To the west of the square is the main attraction, **St Romboutskathedraal**, a huge cathedral that took some 300 years to complete. The building might never have been finished but for a deal with the Vatican: the cathedral was allowed to sell special indulgences (which absolved the purchaser of their sins) to raise funds, on condition that the pope received a percentage. Completed in 1546, the cathedral's tower has Belgium's finest carillon, a set of 49 bells, whose peals ring out at weekends and on public holidays. The church also contains *The Crucifixion* by Antony van Dyck (1599–1641).

Less well-known in Mechelen are three 16th-century houses by the River Dilje. They are not open to visitors, but their exteriors are delightful. The "House of the Little Devils" is adorned with carved demons.

Mechelen is famous for its local beers, and visitors should try the Gouden Carolus, a dark brew, which is said to have been the favourite tipple of the Emperor Charles V.

🏛 **St Romboutskathedraal**
St Romboutskerkhof. **Tel** (015) 29 7655. 📷 obligatory for tower. ☐ Apr–Oct: 1:30–5:30pm daily; Nov–Mar: 1:30–4:30pm daily. Tours depart Tourist Office.

Mechelen's main square, the Grote Markt, on market day

Dendermonde ❹

🏛 40,000. 🚉 🚌 ℹ️ *Stadhuis, Grote Markt, (052) 21 3956.*

A quiet, industrial town, Dendermonde is about 20 km (12 miles) southeast of Ghent. Its strategic position, at the confluence of the Scheldt and Dender rivers, has attracted the attention of a string of invaders

Vleeshuis façade on the Grote Markt in Dendermonde

Wood panelled walls and paintings in the hall at Gaasbeek Castle

over the centuries, including the Germans who shelled Dendermonde in 1914. But the town is perhaps best-known as the site of the Steed Bayard, a carnival held every ten years at the end of August.

Today, the town's spacious main square is framed by the quaint turrets and towers of the the Vleeshuis or Meat Hall. The Town Hall is an elegant 14th-century building which was extensively restored in 1920. Dendermonde also possesses two exquisite early religious paintings by Anthony van Dyck which are on display in the Onze Lieve Vrouwekerk (Church of Our Lady).

Pajottenland ❺

🏛 113,000. 🄸 Toerisme Pajottenland en Zennevalaaei, (02) 356 4259.
www.visitflanders.com

The Pajottenland forms part of the Brabant province to the southwest of Brussels, and is bordered in the west by the Dender River. The gentle rolling hills of the landscape contain many farms, some of which date back to the 17th century. The village of Onze Lieve Vrouw Lombeek, just 12 km (7 miles) west of Brussels, is named after its church, an outstanding example of 14th-century Gothic architecture.

Just a short distance south of the village lies the area's main attraction, the castle and grounds of **Gaasbeek**. The

castle was remodelled in the 19th century, but actually dates from the 13th century, and boasts a moat and a thick curtain wall, strengthened by huge semi-circular towers. The castle's interior holds an excellent collection of fine and applied arts. Among the treasures are rich tapestries, 15th-century alabaster reliefs from England, silverware and a delightful ivory and copper hunting horn which belonged to the Protestant martyr Count Egmont in the 16th century. The Pajottenland is also known

for its beers, especially lambic and gueuze. Lambic is one of the most popular types of beer in Belgium *(see pp150–51)*.

⚓ **Gaasbeek**
Kasteelstraat 40. *Tel* (02) 531 0130.
🄾 Apr–Nov: 10am–6pm Tue–Sun.
⚫ Dec–Mar. (Park open all year.) 🄵

Halle ❻

🏛 36,800. 🄵 🚌 🄸 Stadhuis, Grote Markt, (02) 363 2211.
www.halle.be

Located on the outskirts of Brussels, in the province of Brabant, Halle is a peaceful little town. It has been a major religious centre since the 13th century because of the cult of the Black Virgin, an effigy in the Onze Lieve Vrouwebasiliek, the town's main church. The holy statue's blackness is due to its stained colour, which is said to have occurred through contact with gunpowder during the religious wars of the 17th century.

The virgin has long been one of Belgium's most venerated icons and each year, on Whit Sunday, the statue is paraded through the town.

THE STEED BAYARD

Dendermonde's famous carnival of the Steed Bayard occurs every ten years at the end of August. The focus of the festival is a horse, the Steed Bayard itself, represented in the carnival by a giant model. It takes 34 bearers to carry the horse which weighs 700 kg (1,540 lb) and is 5.8 m (19 ft) high. A procession of locals dressed in medieval costume re-enact the Steed Bayard legend – a complex tale of chivalry and treachery, family loyalty and betrayal. The four Aymon brothers (who were said to be the nephews of Emperor Charlemagne) ride the horse, and it is their behaviour towards the animal which serves to demonstrate their moral worth.

Waterloo ❼

The Battle of Waterloo was fought on 18 June, 1815. It pitted Napoleon and his French army against the Duke of Wellington, who was in command of troops mostly drawn from Britain, Germany and the Netherlands. The two armies met outside the hamlet of Waterloo, to the south of Brussels.

Death mask of Napoleon

The result was decisive. The battle began at 11:30am and just nine hours later the French were in full retreat. Napoleon abdicated and was subsequently exiled to the island of St Helena, where he died in mysterious circumstances six years later. Today, the battlefield is one of the biggest European historical and cultural sites, and one of the best preserved. The best place to start a visit is at the Musée Wellington, some 5 km (3 miles) from the battlefield, in the centre of Waterloo.

earthen mound built on the spot where the future King of the Netherlands, the Prince of Orange, was wounded during the battle. Steps lead to the top, which is guarded by a huge cast-iron lion, and from here there is a great view over the battlefield. The French army

The Butte du Lion viewed from the Waterloo battlefield

🏛 Musée Wellington

Chaussée de Bruxelles 147. *Tel (02) 357 2860.* ◯ *Apr–Sep: 9:30am–6pm daily; Oct–Mar: 10am–5pm daily.* ● *1 Jan, 25 Dec.* 🎟 📷 www.museewellington.be

The Waterloo inn where the Duke of Wellington spent the night before the battle has been turned into a museum, its rooms packed with curios alongside plans and models of the actual battle. One of the more quirky exhibits is the artificial leg of Lord Uxbridge, one of Wellington's commanders. His leg was blown off during the battle and buried in Waterloo. After his death, the leg was sent to join the rest of him in England and, as recompense, his relatives sent his artificial one back to Waterloo.

🏰 Eglise St-Joseph

Chaussée de Bruxelles. *Tel (02) 352 0910.*

Across the road from the Musée Wellington is the church of St-Joseph, which was originally built as a royal chapel at the end of the 17th century. Its dainty, elegant cupola predates the battle, after which it was extended, with the newer portions containing dozens of memorial plaques and flagstones dedicated to those British soldiers who died at Waterloo. Several of these plaques were paid for by voluntary contributions from ordinary soldiers in honour of their officers.

🏰 Butte du Lion

315 Route du Lion, Ring Ouest exit 25, 5 km (3 miles) S of Waterloo. *Tel (02) 385 1912.* ◯ *daily.* 🎟

Dating from 1826, the Butte du Lion is a 45-m (148-ft) high

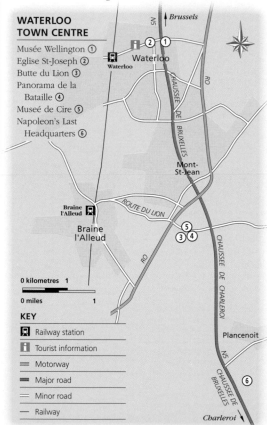

WATERLOO TOWN CENTRE

Musée Wellington ①
Eglise St-Joseph ②
Butte du Lion ③
Panorama de la Bataille ④
Musée de Cire ⑤
Napoleon's Last Headquarters ⑥

KEY

🚉 Railway station

ℹ Tourist information

━ Motorway

▬ Major road

═ Minor road

─ Railway

0 kilometres 1
0 miles 1

approached from the south and fought up the slope across farmland that became increasingly marshy as the day went on, while their opponents had the drier ridge at the foot of the mound. A plan of the battle is displayed at the top.

🏛 Panorama de la Bataille
252–254 Route du Lion, Braine-L'Alleud. N5, 5 km (3 miles) S of Waterloo. **Tel** (02) 385 1912. ☐ 10am–5pm daily. 🎨

This is perhaps the most fascinating of the several attractions beneath the Butte du Lion. This circular painting of the battle by artist Louis Demoulin was erected in 1912. It is 110 m (360 ft) long and stretches right round a circular, purpose-built gallery. This is one of the few late 19th-century panoramic, circular paintings that remain intact.

🏛 Musée de Cire
315 Route du Lion, N5, 5 km (3 miles) S of Waterloo. **Tel** (02) 384 6740. ☐ Apr–Oct: daily; Nov–Mar: pub hols, Sat & Sun. 🎨

The Musée de Cire is a wax museum where pride of place goes to the models of soldiers dressed in the military regalia of 1815. It seems strange today that the various armies dressed their men in such vivid colours, which made them easy targets. Indeed, many commanders paid for the uniforms of their men themselves.

🏛 Napoleon's Last Headquarters
66 Chaussée de Bruxelles, Vieux-Genappe, N5, 7 km (4.5 miles) S of Waterloo. **Tel** (02) 384 2424. ☐ daily. ● 1 Jan, 25 Dec. 🎨

Napoleon spent the eve of the battle in a farmhouse, Le Caillou. This is now a museum that is often referred to as the Caillou Museum, containing a number of artifacts from Napoleon's army, a bronze death mask of the Emperor, and his army-issue bed. A building in the garden contains the bones of some of the soldiers from the battle.

Leuven **❽**

See pp110–11.

The summer drawing room in the 18th-century Chateau d'Attre, near Ath

Ath **❾**

🏛 28,500. 🚉 🚌 🛈 Rue de Pintamont 18, (068) 26 5170.

This quiet town is known for its festival – the Ducasse – which occurs every year on the fourth weekend in August. It features the "Parade of the Giants", a procession of gaily decorated giant figures representing characters from local folklore and the Bible.

A few kilometres northeast is one of the most popular attractions in the region, the **Château d'Attre**. This handsome 18th-century palace was built in 1752 by the Count of Gomegnies, chamberlain to the Hapsburg Emperor Joseph II.

🏛 Château d'Attre
Attre. **Tel** (068) 45 4460. 🚌 to Attre. ☐ Jul–Aug: 1–5pm Sat & Sun, Apr–Jun & Sep–Oct: 2–5pm Sun. ● Nov–Mar.

Ieper **❿**

🏛 35,000. 🚉 🚌 🛈 34 Market Square, (057) 23 9220.

Ieper is the Flemish name of the town familiar to British soldiers as Ypres. During World War I, this town was used as a supply depot for the British army. The Germans shelled Ieper to pieces, but after the war the town was rebuilt to its earlier design, complete with a replica of its 13th-century Lakenhalle (cloth hall). Part of its interior has been turned into the "In Flander's Fields" Museum, a thoughtfully laid-out series of displays that attempt to conjure the full horrors of World War I.

There is also the Menin Gate memorial, inscribed with the names of over 50,000 British and Commonwealth troops who died in the area but have no known resting place.

THE YPRES SALIENT
The Ypres Salient was the name given to a bulge in the line of trenches that both the German and British armies felt was a good place to break through each others' lines. This led to large concentrations of men and four major battles including Passchendaele in July 1917, in which more than 500,000 men died. Today, visitors can choose to view the site with its vast cemeteries and monuments by car or guided tour.

View of the battlefield at Passchendaele Ridge in 1917

Leuven ⑧

Within easy striking distance of Brussels, the historic Flemish town of Leuven traces its origins to a fortified camp constructed here by Julius Caesar. In medieval times, the town became an important centre of the cloth trade, but it was as a seat of learning that it achieved international prominence. In 1425, Pope Martin V and Count John of Brabant founded Leuven's university, and by the mid-1500s it was one of Europe's most prestigious academic institutions, the home of such famous scholars as Erasmus and Mercator. Even today, the university exercises

Font Sapienza

a dominant influence over the town, and its students give Leuven a vibrant atmosphere. The bars and cafés flanking the Oude Markt, a large square in the centre of town, are especially popular. Adjoining the square is the medieval Grote Markt, and near the centre is the Stella Artois Brewery, part of the world's largest brewery group.

Lively café society in the Oude Markt

⌗ Oude Markt

This handsome, cobble-stoned square is flanked by a tasteful ensemble of high-gabled brick buildings. Some of these date from the 18th century; others are comparatively new. At ground level these buildings house the largest concentration of bars and cafés in town, and as such attract the town's university students in their droves.

⌗ Stadhuis

Grote Markt. *Tel (016) 20 3020.* ◻ daily. ▨ ▥ obligatory. At 3pm daily (Apr–Sep: also at 11am Mon–Fri). Built between 1439 and 1463 from the profits of the cloth trade, Leuven's town hall, the Stadhuis, was designed to demonstrate the wealth of the city's merchants. This distinctive, tall building is renowned for its lavishly carved and decorated façade. A line of narrow windows rise up over three floors beneath a steeply pitched roof adorned with dormer windows and

pencil-thin turrets. It is, however, in the fine quality of its stonework that the building excels, with delicately carved tracery and detailed medieval figures beneath 300 niche bases. There are grotesques of every description as well as representations of folktales and biblical stories, all carved in exuberant late-Gothic style. Within the niche alcoves is a series of 19th-century statues depicting local dignitaries and politicians. Guided tours of the interior are available, and include three lavishly decorated reception rooms.

Stone carvings of medieval figures decorate the Stadhuis façade

Huge buttresses supporting the tower of St Pieterskerk

⚑ St Pieterskerk and Museum Schatkamer van St Pieter

Grote Markt. *Tel (016) 29 5133.* ◻ Mar–Oct: daily, Nov–Feb: Tue–Sun. ▨ to museum. Across the square from the Stadhuis rises St Pieterskerk, a massive church built over a period of two hundred years from the 1420s.

Inside the church, the sweeping lines of the nave are intercepted by an impressive 1499 rood screen and a Baroque wooden pulpit.

The church also houses the Museum Schatkamer van St Pieter (Treasury) which has three paintings by Dirk Bouts (1415–75). Born in the Netherlands, Bouts spent most of his working life in Leuven, becoming its official artist.

🏛 Stella Artois Brewery

Vuurkruisenlaan. ◻ May–Oct: Sat & Sun. ▨ ▥ obligatory. Tour with beer tasting in Dutch at 2pm and in English at 3:30pm; tour without beer tasting at 11am Sat in Dutch and at 11am Sun in English. With brewing being an important part of Leuven's history since the 16th century, a visit to Belgium's beer capital would not be complete without a brewery tour. The Stella Artois Brewery offers a variety of tours on weekends from May to October. All tours take place in the brewing hall, covering local beer-making history and the secrets of the brewing process, with the option to finish with a beer in the bar.

⚏ Fochplein

Adjacent to the Grote Markt is the Fochplein, a narrow triangular square containing some of Leuven's most popular shops, selling everything from fashion to food. In the middle is the Fons Sapienza, a modern fountain that shows a student pouring water through his empty head – a pithy view of the town's student population.

🏛 M-Museum Leuven

Leopold Vanderkelenstraat 28.
Tel (016) 27 2929. ◯ 11am–6pm Fri–Tue (to 10pm Thu). 📷
www.mleuven.be

The former Museum Vander Kelen-Mertens has been revamped as "M" and provides a dynamic space for high profile art exhibitions. It also gives credance to Leuven's claim as a major city of the arts. The original collection still remains in the 17th–18th century mansion, which was owned by the Vander Kelen-Mertens family until it was donated to the city in 1918. The rooms were refurbished in a variety of styles, ranging from a Renaissance salon to a Rococo dining room, each with the appropriate antique furniture, silverware and ceramics.

Much of the art on permanent display is by the early Flemish Masters, including the work of Quentin Metsys (1446–1550), who was born in Leuven and introduced Italian style to northern European art.

🏛 St Michielskerk

Naamsestraat.
◯ Jun–Sep: Wed, Sat & Sun.
One of Leuven's most impressive churches, St Michielskerk was built for the Jesuits in the middle of the 17th century. The church was badly damaged during World War II, but has since been carefully restored. Its graceful façade with its flowing lines is an excellent illustration of the Baroque style. The interior is regularly open to visitors for three afternoons during the summer months. The stunning 1660 carved woodwork around the altar and choir are well worth seeing.

🏛 Groot Begijnhof

Schapenstraat. ◯ daily, for street access only.
Founded around 1230, the Groot Begijnhof was once one of the largest béguinages in Belgium, home to several hundred béguines (see p53).

VISITORS' CHECKLIST

🏠 97,300. 🚉 Bondgenoten-laan. 🚏 Grote Markt 9.
🛈 Naamsestraat 1, 3000 Leuven, (016) 20 3020.

The complex of 72 charming red-brick cottages (dating mostly from the 17th century) is set around the grassy squares and cobbled streets near the River Dijle. Leuven university bought the complex in 1961 and converted the cottages into student accommodation.

The red-brick houses of Leuven's Groot Begijnhof

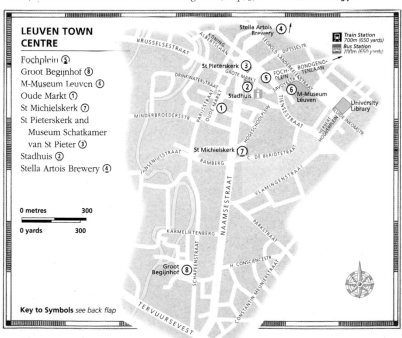

LEUVEN TOWN CENTRE

0 metres   300
0 yards   300

Key to Symbols see back flap

Street-by-Street: Ghent ⑪

As a tourist destination, the Flemish city of Ghent has long been over-shadowed by its neighbour, Bruges. In part this reflects their divergent histories. The success of the cloth trade during the Middle Ages was followed by a period of stagnation for Bruges, while Ghent became a major industrial centre in the 18th and 19th centuries.

Bell on display in the Belfort

The resulting pollution coated the city's antique buildings in layers of grime from its many factories. In the 1980s Ghent initiated a restoration programme. The city's medieval buildings were cleaned, industrial sites were tidied up and the canals were cleared. Today, it is the intricately carved stonework of its churches and antique buildings, as well as the city's excellent museums and stern, forbidding castle that give the centre its character.

★ Het Gravensteen
Ghent's centre is dominated by the thick stone walls and imposing gatehouse of its ancient Castle of the Counts.

★ Design Museum Ghent
This elegant 19th-century dining room is just one of many charming period rooms in the decorative arts museum. The collection is housed in an 18th-century mansion and covers art and design from the 1600s to the present.

Graslei
One of Ghent's most picturesque streets, the Graslei overlooks the River Leie on the site of the city's medieval harbour. It is lined with perfectly preserved guildhouses; some date from the 12th century.

To Ghent St-Pieters and Stadsmuseum

Korenmarkt
This busy square was once the corn market; the commercial centre of the city since the Middle Ages. Today, it is lined with popular cafés.

STAR SIGHTS

★ St Baafskathedraal

★ Het Gravensteen

★ Design Museum Ghent

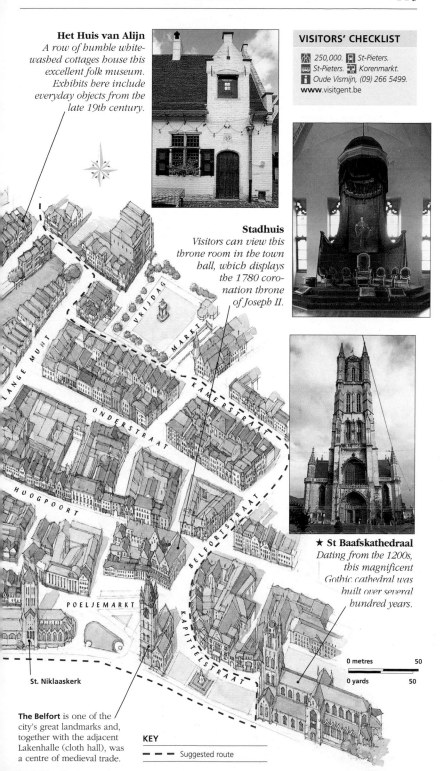

Het Huis van Alijn
A row of humble white-washed cottages house this excellent folk museum. Exhibits here include everyday objects from the late 19th century.

VISITORS' CHECKLIST

250,000. St-Pieters.
St-Pieters. Korenmarkt.
Oude Vismijn, (09) 266 5499.
www.visitgent.be

Stadhuis
Visitors can view this throne room in the town hall, which displays the 1780 coronation throne of Joseph II.

★ St Baafskathedraal
Dating from the 1200s, this magnificent Gothic cathedral was built over several hundred years.

LANGE MUNT

VRIJDAG MARKT

ONDERSTRAAT

KAMERSTRAAT

HOOGPOORT

BELFORTSTRAAT

POELJEMARKT

KAPITTELSTRAAT

St. Niklaaskerk

0 metres 50
0 yards 50

The Belfort is one of the city's great landmarks and, together with the adjacent Lakenhalle (cloth hall), was a centre of medieval trade.

KEY
- - - Suggested route

Exploring Ghent

Charles V's coat of arms

The heart of Ghent's historic centre was originally built during the 13th and 14th centuries when the city prospered as a result of the cloth trade. Ghent was founded in the 9th century when Baldwin Iron-Arm, the first Count of Flanders, built a castle to protect two abbeys from Viking raids. Despite many religious and dynastic conflicts, Ghent continued to flourish throughout the 16th and early 17th centuries. After 1648, the Dutch sealed the Scheldt estuary near Antwerp, closing vital canal links, which led to a decline in the fortunes of both cities. The 19th-century boom in cotton spinning reinvigorated Ghent and led to the building of wide boulevards in the south of the city. Today, textiles still feature in Ghent's industry, while its university lends a youthful vibrancy to city life.

Tiled flooring forms a maze in the Pacification Hall in Ghent's Stadhuis

Getting around
Ghent is a large city with an excellent bus and tram system. The main rail station, Ghent St-Pieters, adjoins the bus station from where several trams travel to the centre every few minutes. However, many of Ghent's main sights are within walking distance of each other. Canal boat trips are also available.

St Baafskathedraal
Sint Baafsplein. **Map** F2. **Tel** (09) 269 2045. ◯ daily. **Adoration of the Mystic Lamb** ◯ daily.
Built in several stages, St Baafskathedraal (St Bavo's Cathedral) has features representing every phase of Gothic style, from the early chancel through to the later cavernous nave, which is supported by slender columns and is the cathedral's architectural highlight. In a small side chapel is one of Europe's most remarkable paintings, Jan van Eyck's polyptych *Adoration of the Mystic Lamb* (1432). St Bavo (or Bavon) was Ghent's own 7th-century saint, who abandoned the life of a wealthy degenerate to become a missionary in France and Flanders and then a hermit. He was buried in about AD653.

Stadhuis
Botermarkt 1. **Map** F2. **Tel** (09) 266 5111. ◯ ◯ May–Oct: 3pm Mon–Thu. Tours depart 2:30pm from the Tourist Office.
The Stadhuis façade displays two different architectural styles. Overlooking Hoogstraat, the older half dates from the early 16th century, its tracery in the elaborate Flamboyant Gothic style. The plainer, newer part, which flanks the

THE ADORATION OF THE MYSTIC LAMB

The 12 panels of the painting, with the main image at the centre

In a side-chapel of Sint Baafskathedraal, in the centre of Ghent, is one of the greatest cultural treasures of Northern Europe. *The Adoration of the Mystic Lamb* is a monumental, multi-panelled painting by the first of the great early Flemish artists, Jan van Eyck, and his lesser-known brother, Hubrecht.

Completed in 1432, it is not only exquisitely painted; it is also an expression of the deepest beliefs of Christianity – that human salvation lies in the sacrifice of Christ, the Lamb of God. What you see today is almost entirely original; only the lower left panel is a modern copy, following its theft in 1934. This is a remarkable achievement, given the painting's history. It was rescued from Protestant church-wreckers in 1566 and from fire in 1822; parts of it were removed by French soldiers in 1794, and other parts were sold in 1816. Audioguides to the painting (included in the price of the entry ticket) explain the significance of the 12 panels.

Botermarkt, is a characteristic example of post-Reformation architecture. The statues in the niches on the façade were added in the 1890s. Among this group of figures it is possible to spot the original architect, Rombout Keldermans, who is shown studying his plans.

The building is still the city's administrative centre. Guided tours pass through a series of rooms, the most fascinating of which is the Pacification Hall. This was once the Court of Justice and the site of the signing of the Pacification of Ghent (a treaty between Catholics and Protestants against Hapsburg rule) in 1576.

🏯 Belfort
Sint Baafsplein. **Map** F2. *Tel (09) 233 3954.* ☐ *Open daily 10am–6pm 15 Mar–15 Nov.* 🔶 🔷 *May–Oct.*
Ghent's belfry, a prominent landmark rising 91 m (299 ft) to the gilded-copper dragon on the tip of its spire, is situated between the cathedral and the town hall. A lift to its parapet at 65 m (213 ft) offers magnificent views over the city. Originally built in 1380, the Belfort was restored in the 19th and 20th centuries. Its bells today include a 54-bell carillon, which plays tunes to accompany the clock chimes every 15 minutes, and for keyboard concerts every Friday and Sunday at noon. Below the Belfort is the *Lakenhalle* (Cloth Hall), a fine Flemish-Gothic building from 1425 where the city's cloth-trade was carried out (guided tours only, on request). The building also incorporates a small prison.

🏯 St Niklaaskerk
Cataloniëstraat. **Map** E2. ☐ *daily.*
This merchants' church, built in the 13th–15th centuries, was dedicated to their patron saint, St Nicholas, Bishop of Myra (and Santa Claus). The church is a fine example of the distinctive and austere style called Scheldt Gothic. The interior was once packed full of guild shrines and chapels, until Protestant church-wreckers destroyed them in 1566; today it is remarkable for its pure architectural forms, with

soaring columns brightly lit by high windows. The space is punctuated by a massive and extravagantly Baroque altar screen, a clarion call to the Counter-Reformation; unusually for such latter-day alterations, it harmonizes with the rest of the church to exhilarating effect.

🏯 Graslei and Korenlei
Map E2.
These are two embankments that face each other across the Tusschen Brugghen, once Ghent's main medieval harbour. The Graslei, on the eastern side, possesses a fine set of guildhouses. Among them, at No. 14, the sandstone façade of the Guildhouse of the Free Boatmen is decorated with finely detailed nautical scenes, while the Corn Measurers' guildhouse next door is adorned by bunches of fruit and cartouches. The earliest building here is the 12th-century *Spijker* (Staple House) at No. 10. This simple Romanesque structure stored the city's grain supply for hundreds of years until a fire destroyed its interior. The gabled buildings of the Korenlei, facing the Graslei across the water, date from later centuries, but gracefully complement the Graslei. The views from the St Michielsbrug, the bridge at the southern end, are among the most beautiful in Ghent.

Views of Graslei and 16th-century guildhouses along the River Leie

🏛 Design Museum Ghent
Jan Breydelstraat 5. **Map** E1. *Tel (09) 267 9999.* ☐ *10am–6pm Tue–Sun.* ● *1 Jan, 24, 25 & 31 Dec.* 🔶 **www.design.museum.gent.be**
This decorative arts museum has a large collection contained within an elegant 18th-century townhouse. The displays are arranged in two sections, beginning at the front with a series

Sofa at Design Museum

of lavishly furnished period rooms that feature textiles, furniture and artifacts from the 17th to the 19th centuries. At the back, an extension completed in 1992 focuses on modern design from Art Nouveau to contemporary works, and includes furniture by Victor Horta *(see p82)*, Marcel Breuer and Ludwig Mies van der Rohe.

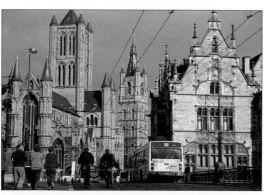
Gothic turrets of Sint-Niklaaskerk seen from St Michael's Bridge

🍴 Groot Vleeshuis

Groentenmarkt 7. **Map** E1. *Tel (09)*
223 23 24. ⬤ *10am–6pm Tue–Sun.*
⬤ *Mon.* 🔲 ⬤ 🔲 ⬤
www.grootvleeshuis.be

The "Great Meat Hall" was built
in 1407–19, and its long, low
interior space still reflects its
basic, original purpose as
a covered butchers' market,
complete with ancient beams
and wonky flooring. Into this
space a large, modern glass
box has been ingeniously
inserted to serves as a centre to
promote East Flemish food: on
the one side, a small restaurant
serves interesting and good-
value Flemish dishes; on the
other is a delicatessen.

**The original covered butchers'
market of the Groot Vleeshuis**

🍴 Dulle Griet. **Map** F1.

Groot Kanonplein (off Vrijdagmarkt).
This giant cannon, sitting on
the embankment
of the River Leie,
is famous in the
folklore of Ghent.
Cast in about 1450,
5 m (16 ft 5 in)
long and weighing
16 tonnes, it could
fire stone cannonballs the size
of a beachball; it was brought
to Ghent in 1578, during an era
of Calvinist government in
defiance of Spain. The name
Dulle Griet means "Mad Meg",
a legendary medieval character
who embodied mad, violent
frenzy and disorder. It was
recently repainted its original
red, reflecting its other
nickname "Groten Rooden
Duyvele" (Great Red Devil).

The Dulle Griet cannon

🏰 Het Gravensteen. **Map** E1.

Sint-Veerleplein. *Tel (09) 225 9306.*
⬤ *Apr–Sep: 9am–6pm daily; Oct–
Mar: 9am–5pm daily.* ⬤ *1 Jan,
24, 25 & 26 Dec.* 📷
Once the seat of the counts of
Flanders, the imposing stone

walls of Het
Gravensteen (or the
Castle of the Counts)
eloquently recall the
unsettled and violent
context of Ghent's
early medieval past.
Parts of the castle date
back to the late 1100s,
but most are later addi-
tions. Up to the 14th
century the castle was
Ghent's main military
stronghold, and from
then until the late
1700s it was used as
the city's jail. Later, it
became a cotton mill.

From the gatehouse,
a long and heavily
fortified tunnel leads
up to the courtyard,
which is overseen by
two large buildings, the
count's medieval residence
and the earlier keep. Arrows
guide visitors round the
interior of both buildings, and
in the upper rooms there is a
spine-chilling collection of
medieval torture instruments.

**Het Gravensteen, a classic medieval castle
complete with turrets and torture instruments**

🏛 Het Huis van Alijn. **Map** E1.

Kraanlei 65. *Tel (09) 269 23 50.*
⬤ *11am–5pm Tue–Sat, 10am–5pm
Sun.* ⬤ *Mon, 1 Jan, 25 Dec.* 📷 🔲
www.huisvanalijn.be (Dutch only)
This is one of Belgium's best
folk museums, graphically
evoking daily life in the
past through a
huge collection of
fascinating arte-
facts – dolls and
other toys,
games, clothes,
furniture, kitchen-
ware, funerary mementoes, as
well as complete shops and
craftsmen's workshops. There

is also a puppet theatre,
which presents plays (in
Dutch) throughout the year.
The museum is set out in a
sequence of rooms in a pretty
group of whitewashed
almshouses, "The House of
Alijn", surrounding a grassy
courtyard. Although mainly
16th-century, the almshouses
were originally founded in
1363 as a children's hospital –
not out of philanthropy, but
as an act of penance by the
Rijm family for the murder
of two members of the rival
Alijn family.

🍴 The Patershol. **Map** E1.

North of the Kraanlei are the
quaint little lanes and low
brick houses of the Patershol,
a district that developed in the
17th century to house the city's
weavers. This once down-at-
heel area underwent extensive
refurbishment in the 1980s and

The Patershol's 17th-century buildings which now house shops and cafés

is now one of the trendiest parts of town, with upmarket restaurants, cafés and shops.

🎭 Vlaamse Opera. Map E3.

Schouwburgstraat 3. *Tel (09) 268 1011.* ◯ *for performances; guided tours third Saturday of the month.* 🖳 www.vlaamseopera.be

This classic opera house was built in 1837–40; it has been restored to reclaim its reputation as one of the most spectacular theatres in Europe, with an auditorium and adjoining salons encrusted with gilding, chandeliers and sculptural decorations. The resident company is the much-respected Vlaamse Opera (Flemish Opera), which formed when the opera companies of Ghent and Antwerp merged.

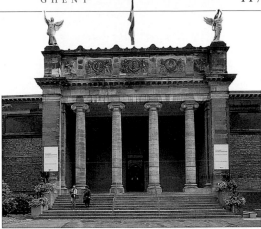

The grand, Neo-Classical façade of the Museum voor Schone Kunsten

The stunning interior of the Vlaamse Opera building

🎭 Klein Begijnhof

Lange Violettestraat 205. ◯ *6:30am–10pm daily.*

The Klein Begijnhof (Small Béguinage) is the prettiest of Ghent's three béguinages *(see p53)*. Rows of step-gabled, whitewashed houses – most

dating from the 17th century – enclose a small park and Baroque church, creating a tranquil refuge. This Begijnhof was founded as a community of single women in about 1235. It has been occupied ever since, but the residents today are no longer béguines.

🏛 STAM. Map E4. Bijlokesite,

Godshuizenlaan 2. *Tel (09) 267 1400.* ◯ *10am–6pm Tue–Sun.* ● *Mon, 1 Jan, 24, 25 & 31 Dec.* ♿ 🖳 🔢 www.stamgent.be

Located on a site that brings together a 14th-century Gothic abbey, a 17th-century monastery and the latest in 21st-century architecture, STAM is Ghent's excellent city museum. It provides an introduction to the city's history and cultural heritage, tracing its evolution to the present day. Visitors staying in Ghent for three days will find the Museum Pass an economical way of seeing the city's main museums.

🏛 Stedelijk Museum voor Actuele Kunst (SMAK). Map E5.

Citadelpark. *Tel (09) 240 7601.* ◯ *10am–6pm, Tue–Sun.* ● *Mon.* 🖳 🚻 🔢 www.smak.be

SMAK is one of Europe's most dynamic modern art galleries, a force in the art world that has helped to bring the spotlight to the Belgian art scene. Its extensive and challenging permanent collection includes work by artists such as Bacon, Beuys, Broodthaers, Long, Muñoz, Nauman, Panamarenko, Tuymans and Warhol, while temporary exhibitions feature international artists at the cutting edge of contemporary art. The airy and attractive building dates from 1949 but was remodelled in the 1990s.

🏛 Museum voor Schone Kunsten. Map F5.

Ferdinand Scribedreef, Citadelpark. *Tel (09) 240 0700.* ◯ *10am–6pm Tue–Sun.* 🖳 www.mskgent.be

Ghent's largest collection of fine art is displayed in this Neo-Classical building. Inside, a rotunda divides the works, with the older exhibits in a series of rooms on the right and 19th- and 20th-century art to the left. Medieval paintings include the *Bearing of the Cross* by Hieronymus Bosch (1450–1516). There are also works by Rubens *(see pp14–15)*, Anthony van Dyck (1599–1641) and Jacob Jordaens (1593–1678).

Visitors planning to also visit the Royal Museum of Fine Arts in Antwerp and the Groeninge Museum in Bruges should invest in the Flemish Art Collection combiticket.

A small garden surrounded by step-gabled houses in the Klein Begijnhof

Street-by-Street: Bruges ⑫

With good reason, Bruges is one of the most popular tourist destinations in Belgium. An unspoilt medieval town, Bruges' winding streets pass by picturesque canals lined with fine buildings. The centre of Bruges is amazingly well preserved. The town's trade was badly affected when the River Zwin silted up at the end of the 15th century. It was never heavily industrialized and has retained most of its medieval buildings. As a further bonus Bruges also escaped major damage in both world wars.

Today, the streets are well maintained: there are no billboards or high rises, and traffic is heavily regulated. All the major attractions are located within the circle of boulevards that marks the line of the old medieval walls.

Traditional organ grinder

View of the Rozenhoedkaai
A charming introduction to Bruges is provided by the boat trips along the city's canal network.

Onze Lieve Vrouwekerk
The Church of Our Lady employs many architectural styles. It took around 200 years to build, and its spire is Belgium's tallest in brick.

Memling in Sint-Jan Hospitaalmuseum
Six of the artist's works are shown in the small chapel of the 12th-century St Janshospitaal, a city hospital that was still operating until 1976.

0 metres		100
0 yards		100

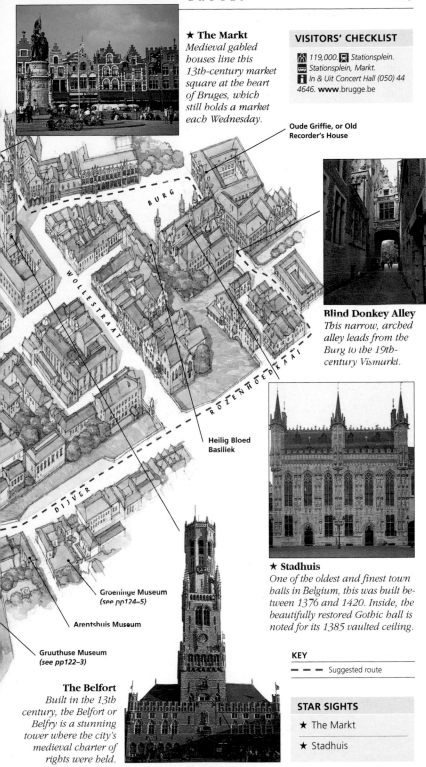

★ The Markt
Medieval gabled houses line this 13th-century market square at the heart of Bruges, which still holds a market each Wednesday.

VISITORS' CHECKLIST

119,000. Stationsplein. Stationsplein, Markt. In & Uit Concert Hall (050) 44 4646. www.brugge.be

Oude Griffie, or Old Recorder's House

Blind Donkey Alley
This narrow, arched alley leads from the Burg to the 19th-century Vismarkt.

Heilig Bloed Basiliek

★ Stadhuis
One of the oldest and finest town halls in Belgium, this was built between 1376 and 1420. Inside, the beautifully restored Gothic hall is noted for its 1385 vaulted ceiling.

Groeninge Museum (see pp124–5)

Arentshuis Museum

Gruuthuse Museum (see pp122–3)

The Belfort
Built in the 13th century, the Belfort or Belfry is a stunning tower where the city's medieval charter of rights were held.

KEY

– – – Suggested route

STAR SIGHTS

★ The Markt

★ Stadhuis

Exploring Central Bruges

Bruges developed around a 9th-century fortress, built to defend the coast against the Vikings. Despite the vagaries of successive invasions by the French, between the 14th and 16th centuries Bruges became one of northern Europe's most sophisticated cities. Today, it owes its pre-eminent position to the beauty of its historic centre, whose narrow cobbled lanes and meandering canals are lined by an ensemble of medieval buildings. These are mostly the legacy of the town's heyday as a centre of the international cloth trade, which flourished for 200 years from the 13th century. During this golden age, Bruges' merchants lavished their fortunes on fine mansions, churches and a set of civic buildings of such extravagance that they were the wonder of northern Europe.

Bell maker in market

Bruges' medieval buildings reflected in the River Dijver

Getting Around
The centre of Bruges is compact, and it is easiest to walk around. However, the bus service is useful for getting from the railway station to the centre. Half-hour boat trips along the canals leave from several jetties. From March to November, boats depart twice every hour.

The Vismarkt
Braambergstraat. **Map** B3.
◯ *8am–1pm Tue–Sat.*
From the Burg an attractive arched path called the Alley of the Blind Donkey (Blinde Ezelstraat) leads to the open-air fish market with its elegant 18th-century colonnades. Fish is still sold here early each morning and business is brisk.

♛ The Burg
Map B3.
This pleasant cobbled square a few metres from the Markt, was once the political and religious focus of Bruges. It is also the site of the original fort around which the city grew. Some of the most imposing civic buildings are located here. The beautiful sandstone Stadhuis or town hall has a

façade dating from 1375, and is adorned with turrets and statues. In contrast, the Proostdij or Provost's House was built of grey stone in 1662 in the Baroque style and boasts an ornate entrance.

♛ Stadhuis
Burg 12. **Map** B3. *Tel (050) 44 8711.* ◯ *9:30am–5pm daily.* ● *1 Jan, 25 Dec.* 🖼
The intricately carved façade of the Stadhuis was completed in 1375, but the niche statues are modern effigies of the counts and countesses of Flanders. These were added in the 1960s to replace those destroyed by the French army over a century before. The building is still used as a town hall. It is also a popular venue for weddings. Inside, a staircase leads up from the spacious foyer to the beautiful Gothic Hall, which is open to visitors year round. This magnificent parliamentary chamber was built around 1400. The ceiling boasts some lavish woodcarvings including 16 beautiful corbels (brackets) bearing representations of the seasons and the elements. A series of paintings around the hall was completed in 1895, each portraying a key event in the city's history.

In an adjacent building is the Renaissance Hall, which houses a massive wood, marble and alabaster chimney designed by Lanceloot Blondeel. The chimney is one of the best sculptural works of 16th-century Flanders.

♙ Heilig Bloed Basiliek
Burg 15. **Map** B3. *Tel (050) 33 6792, 33 3767.* ◯ *10am–noon, 2–5pm daily (opens at 9:30am in summer).*
The Basilica of the Holy Blood holds one of the most sacred reliquaries in Europe. The basilica divides into two distinct sections, the lower part being the evocative St Basil's chapel with its plain stone-pillared entrance and arches. The upper chapel was rebuilt in the 19th century after the French destroyed it in the 1790s. Here, brightly coloured decorations surround a silver tabernacle of 1611 which houses a sacred phial, supposed to contain a few

drops of blood and water washed from the body of Christ by Joseph of Arimathea. The phial was brought here from Jerusalem in 1150, and is still the object of great veneration. The church also has a museum of paintings, vestments and other artifacts.

⛪ The Markt
Map A3.

A market has been held on Bruges' main square since the 10th century. It is an impressive open space lined with 17th-century houses and overlooked by the Belfort on one side. The oldest façade on the square (dating from the 15th century) belongs to the Huis Bouchotte, which was the home of Charles II of England during part of his exile from 1656–7.

In the middle is a statue of Pieter de Coninck and Jan Breidel, two 14th-century guildsmen who led a rebellion against the French in 1302. Known as the *Bruges Matin*, they led Flemish soldiers to attack the French at dawn on May 18, 1302, killing almost all of them. This bloody uprising paved the way for a form of independence for the Low Countries' major towns. Rights such as the freedom to trade were subsequently enshrined in the towns' charters until the 15th century.

⛪ The Belfort
Markt. **Map** B3. ⏲ *daily.* 📷

The Markt is dominated by the belfry, whose octagonal belltower rises 83 m (272 ft) above the square. Built between the 13th and 15th centuries, the belfry is Bruges' most celebrated landmark as it was used to store the town's charter, and is therefore a constant reminder of the city's past as a centre of trade. Inside the tower a winding staircase leads up, past the chamber where the town's rights and privileges were stored, to the roof, where the views across Bruges are delightful.

Bruges' Belfort or belltower overlooking the Markt

Gruuthuse Museum
Map B4. *See pp122–3.*

🏛 Arentshuis Museum
Dijver 16. **Map** B4. *Tel (050) 44 8763.* ⏲ *9:30am–5pm daily.* ● *Mon (except Easter Mon and Whit Mon).* 📷

The Arentshuis Museum is housed in an 18th-century mansion overlooking the Dijver Canal. The interior is divided into two sections, with the ground floor devoted to a delightful selection of antique lace. Bruges was a centre of Belgian lace making and, although there were a few local factories, most of the work was done by women at home. The collection focuses on needlepoint

Statue of Breidel and Pieter de Coninck

and bobbin lace, with several fine examples of Bruges floral or Duchesse lace as well. Upstairs is the work of Frank Brangwyn (1867–1956), a painter and sculptor who was born in Bruges of Welsh parents. Most of Brangwyn's life was spent in Britain, but he bequeathed this collection to Bruges, as well as his drawings, furniture and carpets. The dark and powerful canvases depicting industrial scenes are perhaps the most diverting.

🎵 Concertgebouw
't Zand. **Map** A4. *Tel (070) 22 3302.* Built as part of the celebrations for Bruges' European City of Culture, this terracotta concert hall features a 28-m (92-ft) tower that offers great views.

Groeninge Museum
See pp124–5.

🔒 Onze Lieve Vrouwekerk
Mariastraat. **Map** A4. *Tel (050) 34 5314.* ⏲ *9:30am–5pm Mon–Sat, 1:30–5pm Sun & holy days.* ● *during services.* 📷 *mausoleum only.*

The Church of Our Lady took over 200 years to build, starting in 1220, and incorporates a variety of styles. The interior, with its white walls, stark columns and black-and-white tiled floor has a medieval simplicity, while the side chapels and pulpit are lavishly decorated.

One of the church's artistic highlights is Michelangelo's sculpture *Madonna and Child* (1504–5), at the end of the southern aisle. This marble statue was imported by a Flemish merchant, and was the only one of the artist's works to leave Italy during his lifetime. In the choir there are fine paintings by Pieter Pourbus including a *Last Supper* (1562), and the carved mausoleums of the Burgundian prince Charles the Bold and his daughter Mary.

The soaring spire of the Vrouwekerk

Gruuthuse Museum

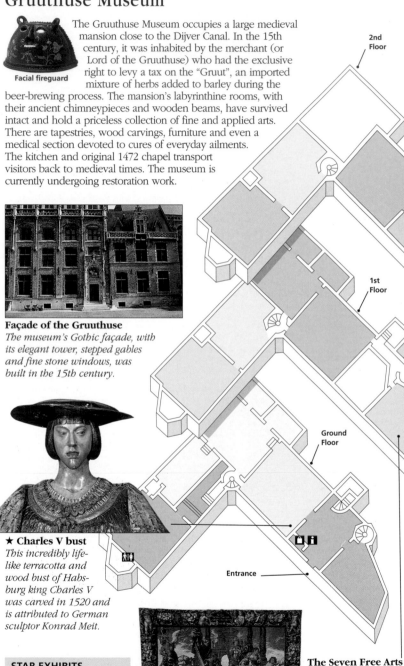

Facial fireguard

The Gruuthuse Museum occupies a large medieval mansion close to the Dijver Canal. In the 15th century, it was inhabited by the merchant (or Lord of the Gruuthuse) who had the exclusive right to levy a tax on the "Gruut", an imported mixture of herbs added to barley during the beer-brewing process. The mansion's labyrinthine rooms, with their ancient chimneypieces and wooden beams, have survived intact and hold a priceless collection of fine and applied arts. There are tapestries, wood carvings, furniture and even a medical section devoted to cures of everyday ailments. The kitchen and original 1472 chapel transport visitors back to medieval times. The museum is currently undergoing restoration work.

2nd Floor

1st Floor

Façade of the Gruuthuse
The museum's Gothic façade, with its elegant tower, stepped gables and fine stone windows, was built in the 15th century.

Ground Floor

★ Charles V bust
This incredibly life-like terracotta and wood bust of Habsburg king Charles V was carved in 1520 and is attributed to German sculptor Konrad Meit.

Entrance

STAR EXHIBITS

- ★ Charles V bust
- ★ Chapel

The Seven Free Arts
Dating from around 1675, this exquisite tapestry depicts the "free arts", which includes music.

GALLERY GUIDE
*Laid out over three floors, the
collection is organized into
types of object from glassware,
porcelain and ceramics to
medical instruments in a
series of 22 numbered rooms.
Visitors may view the rooms
in sequence from 1–22 and
get a good sense of the
original uses and layout of
the house in doing so.*

★ **Chapel**
*Built in 1472, this oak-
panelled chapel on the
museum's second floor
overlooks the high altar
of the church next door.*

KEY
- 🟨 Glassware, porcelain and ceramics
- 🟦 Kitchen
- ⬜ Chapel
- 🟦 Musical instruments
- ⬜ Coins
- ⬜ Tapestries
- ⬜ Tools, weights and measures
- 🟦 Entrance hall
- ⬜ Textiles and lace
- 🟦 Household implements
- ⬜ Renaissance works
- 🟦 Baroque works
- ⬜ Reliquary and furniture
- 🟦 Medical instruments
- ⬜ Great Hall
- 🟦 Weaponry

House on the Southern Bridge at Minnewater

🏛 Memling in Sint-Jan Hospitaalmuseum
Mariastraat 38, 8000 Bruges. **Map** A4.
⬜ Tue–Sun. 🌑 1 Jan, 25 Nov. 📷
This museum contains the
works of Hans Memling
(1430–94), one of the most
talented painters of his era.
Among them, *The Mystical
Marriage of St. Catherine*
(1479), the central panel of a
triptych, is superb. The former
wards also house a collection
of paintings and furniture
related to the hospital's history.

🔒 St Salvators-Kathedraal
Steenstraat 1, 8000 Bruges. **Map** A4.
Tel (050) 33 61 88. ⬜ Apr–Sep:
daily. 🌑 1 Jan, 25 Dec. 📷
Built as a parish church from
the 12th and 15th centuries,
this large, yellow-brick building became Bruges' cathedral
in 1834 when the French army
destroyed the existing one. The
interior is enormous and quite
plain except for a handsome
set of Brussels' tapestries hanging in the choir, and a 1682
organ adorned with angels.

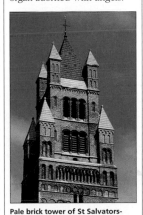
**Pale brick tower of St Salvators-
Kathedraal in Bruges**

🌼 Minnewater
Map A5–B5.
Just south of the Begijnhof,
Minnewater is a peaceful
park with a canalized lake.
There were already swans
here in 1448 when Maximilian
of Austria ordered they be
kept in memory of his
councillor, Pieter Lanchals,
who was beheaded by the
Bruges citizens.
Once this was a bustling
harbour which connected to
the canal network and the sea.
It is now a popular spot for
walkers and picnickers who
may view the pretty
15th-century lock gate and
house and the 1398 tower
(Poedertoren). There is an
adjoining park which holds
music concerts in summer.

🏚 Begijnhof
Wijngaardplein 1, 8000 Bruges. **Map**
A4–A5. **Tel** (050) 33 00 11. ⬜ daily.
Beguines were members of
a lay sisterhood founded in
1245. They lived and dressed
as nuns but did not take vows
and were therefore able to
return to the secular world
at will. The begijnhof or
beguinage is the walled complex in a town that housed
the beguines. In Bruges, this
is an area of quiet tree-lined
canals faced by white, gabled
houses, with a pleasant green
at its centre. Visitors and locals
enjoy strolling here and may
visit the small, simple church
which was built in 1602. The
nuns who live in the houses
are no longer beguines, but
Benedictine sisters who moved
here in the 1930s. One of the
houses is open to visitors and
displays simple rustic furniture
and artifacts that illustrate the
women's contemplative lives.

Groeninge Museum

Bruges' premier fine arts museum, the Groeninge, holds a fabulous collection of early Flemish and Dutch masters, featuring artists such as Jan van Eyck (d.1441) and Hieronymous Bosch (1450–94), famous for the strange freakish creatures of his moral allegories. Hugo van der Goes is well represented too, as is Gerard David (d.1523). These early works are displayed on the ground floor of the museum, as well as a collection of later Belgian painters, most notably Paul Delvaux (1897–1994) and René Magritte (1898–1967). Originally built between 1929 and 1930 on land belonging to the former Eeckhout Abbey, the museum is small and displays its collection in rotation, along with various temporary exhibitions.

★ Virgin and Child with Canon *(1436)*
Jan van Eyck's richly detailed painting is noted for its realism. It shows van Eyck's patron, the canon, being presented to St Donatian by St George.

★ The Moreel Triptych *(1484)*
This panel of the triptych, by German-born artist Hans Memling, was designed to adorn the altar in a Bruges church. It depicts the prominent Bruges family Moreel, and is said to be the first ever group portrait.

Last Judgement
Painted on three oak panels in the early 16th century, this detail from Hieronymous Bosch's famous tryptich depicts scenes of cruelty and torture. The strong moral tone of the work suggests that man's sinful nature has created a hell on earth.

STAR PAINTINGS

★ Virgin and Child with Canon by Jan van Eyck

★ The Moreel Tryptich by Hans Memling

Portrait of Bruges Family *(1645)*
Jacob van Oost the Elder's focus on the affluence of this family surveying their beloved city shows why he was Bruges' most popular artist of the Baroque period.

Judgement of Cambyses *(1498)*
Originally commissioned by the city of Bruges for the town hall, this left panel of a diptych by Gerard David depicts a judge sentenced to be flayed alive.

VISITORS' CHECKLIST

Dijver 12, 8000 Bruges. **Map** B4.
Tel (050) 44 8743. ⬜ Markt. ⬜
9:30am–5pm Tue–Sun (tickets till
4:30pm). ⬤ 1 Jan, 25 Dec. ♿ ⬜
www.museabrugge.be

Household Cares *(1913)*
Rik Wouters used his wife Nel as the model for this statue, cast in bronze. The work's Fauvist style (see p17), is reflected in the bold planes that enhance the figure's anxious stance

1st Floor

Entrance

Serenity *(1970)*
This unusually representative work by Paul Delvaux was commissioned by the museum, and retains elements of the artist's surrealist style.

GALLERY GUIDE
The Groeninge Museum is divided between two buildings. The main portion of the museum is on one level with a series of rooms displaying the early Flemish masters as well as works from the 17th to 20th centuries. Nearby the Arentshuis (see p121), displays temporary exhibitions and houses a permanent collection of work by the artist Frank Brangwyn on its first floor.

Museum Façade
Originally built in 1930, the gallery was extended in 1994 to a design by architect Joseph Viérin. The old entrance is based on that of a Romanesque convent.

KEY

- ⬜ 15th and 16th centuries
- ⬜ 17th to 19th centuries
- ⬜ 20th century
- ⬜ Cabinet displays
- ⬜ Non-exhibition space

Exploring Northeast Bruges

In the height of the summer and on holiday weekends, tourists pour into Bruges, and parts of the city centre often get too crowded for comfort. Fortunately, the narrow cobbled streets and picturesque canals to the north-east of the Markt never suffer from this, and this fascinating area remains one of the most delightful parts of Bruges. Streets of charming, medieval terraced houses are dotted with grand, yet elegant 18th-century mansions. The best approach is via Jan van Eyckplein, in medieval times the city's busiest harbour, from where it is a short stroll along Spinolarei and Potterierei streets to the many museums and churches that are found in this historic district.

Statue of Jan van Eyck

The historic buildings and lovely canals of northeast Bruges

Lace-making skills on show at the Kantcentrum lace centre

🏛 Kantcentrum
Peperstraat 3a. **Map** C2. *Tel (050) 33 0072.* ◯ *Mon–Sat.* 📷

The area from the white-washed cottages to the east of Potterierei Street is one of several old neighbourhoods where the city's lace workers plied their craft. Mostly, the women worked at home, receiving their raw materials from a supplier who also bought the finished product.

Lace-making skills are kept alive at the Kantcentrum, the Lace Centre at the foot of Balstraat, where local women (and a few men) fashion lace in a variety of styles, both modern and traditional. It is a busy place, and visitors can see the lace-making demonstrations held every afternoon during the summer. Some of the finished pieces are sold in the Kantcentrum shop at very reasonable prices.

🏛 Muur der Doodgeschotenen
Map C3.

Bruges was occupied by the German Army during both world wars. The bullet-marked "Wall of those who were shot dead", as its name roughly translates, is located just south of the Kruispoort and commemorates a dozen men executed by German firing squad in 1916. Eleven of them were Belgian, shot for resisting German rule. The twelfth was Captain Fryatt, a British merchant navy officer. His arrest and execution here caused almost as much outrage around Europe as the death of Edith Cavell in Brussels a year earlier.

🏛 Jeruzalemkerk
Peperstraat. **Map** B3. ◯ *Mon–Sat.* 📷

Next door to the Kantcentrum, the Jeruzalemkerk is Bruges' most unusual church. The present building dates from the 15th century, and was built on the site of a 13th-century chapel commissioned by a family of wealthy Italian merchants, the Adornes family, whose black marble tomb can be seen inside. Based on the design of the church of the Holy Sepulchre in Jerusalem, the structure possesses a striking tower with two tiers of wooden, polygon-shaped lanterns topped by a tin orb. Inside, the lower level contains a macabre altarpiece, carved with skulls and assorted demons. Behind the altar is a smaller vaulted chapel; leading from this is a narrow tunnel guarded by an iron grate. Along the tunnel, a lifelike model of Christ in the Tomb can be seen at close quarters.

🏛 The Kruispoort and the windmills
Map C2.

Medieval Bruges was heavily fortified. It was encircled by a city wall which was itself protected by a moat and strengthened by a series of massive gates. Most of the wall was knocked down in

The Jeruzalemkerk, built in 1497

the 19th century, but the moat has survived and so has one of the gates, the Kruispoort, a monumental structure dating from 1402 that guards the eastern approach to the city. The earthen bank stretching north of the Kruispoort marks the line of the old city wall, which was once dotted with some 20 windmills. Today, only three remain overlooking the canal. The first, the Bonne Chieremolen, was brought here from a Flanders village in 1911, but the second – St Janshuismolen – is original to the city, a restored structure erected in 1770. The northernmost mill of the three is De Nieuwe Papegai, an old oil mill that was relocated here in 1970.

The massive Kruispoort, all that remains of Bruges' old city walls

🔒 English Convent

Carmersstraat 85. **Map** C2. **Tel** (050) 33 2424. ◯ Mon & Tue; Mass 8:30am Sun. 🟤 *Obligatory.*

The English Convent was where dozens of English Catholics sought asylum following the execution of Charles I in 1642, and during Oliver Cromwell's subsequent rule as Lord Protector. The conventual buildings are not open to the public, but the nuns provide a well-informed tour of their beautiful church, which was built in the Baroque style in the 1620s. The interior has a delightful sense of space, its elegant proportions enhanced by its cupola, but the highlight is the altar, a grand affair made of around 20 types of marble.

🏛 Museum voor Volkskunde

Balstraat 43. **Map** B2–C2. **Tel** (050) 44 8764. ◯ 9:30am–5pm Tue–Sun, Easter & Whit Mon. 🖼

The Museum voor Volkskunde is one of the best folk museums in Flanders. It occupies

17th-century almshouses comprising the Museum voor Volkskunde

an attractive terrace of low, brick almshouses located behind an old neighbourhood café called the "Zwarte Kat" (Black Cat), which serves as the entrance. Each of the almshouses is dedicated to a different aspect of traditional Flemish life, with workshops displaying old tools. Several different crafts are represented here, such as a cobbler's and a blacksmith's, through to a series of typical historical domestic interiors.

🏯 Schuttersgilde St Sebastiaan

Carmersstraat 174. **Map** C2. **Tel** (050) 33 1626. ◯ May–Sep: 10am–noon Tue–Thu, 2–5pm Sat; Oct–Apr: 2–5pm Tue–Thu & Sat. 🖼

The Archers' guild (the Schuttersgilde) was one of the most powerful of the militia guilds, and their 16th- and 17th-century red-brick guildhouse now houses a museum.

The commercial life of medieval Bruges was dominated by the guilds, each of

which represented the interests of a particular group of skilled workmen. The guilds guarded their privileges jealously and, among many rules and customs, marriage between children whose fathers were in different guilds was greatly frowned upon. The guild claimed the name St Sebastian after an early Christian martyr, whom the Roman Emperor Diocletian had executed by his archers. The bowmen followed orders – medieval painters often show Sebastian looking like a pincushion – but miraculously Sebastian's wounds healed before he was finished off by club-wielding assassins. The guildhouse is notable for its collection of paintings of the guild's leading lights, gold and silver trinkets and guild emblems.

🏛 Museum Onze Lieve Vrouw ter Potterie

Potterierei 79. **Map** B1. **Tel** (050) 44 8711. ◯ 9:30am–noon, 1:30–5pm Tue–Sun, Easter & Whit Mon. 🖼

Located by the canal in one of the quietest parts of Bruges, the Museum Onze Lieve Vrouw ter Potterie (Our Lady of Pottery) occupies part of an old hospital that was founded in 1276 to care for elderly women. There is a 14th- and 15th-century cloister, and several of the sick rooms house a modest collection of paintings, the best of which are some 17th- and 18th-century portraits of leading aristocrats. The hospital church is in excellent condition, too; it is a warm, intimate place with fine stained-glass windows and a set of impressive Baroque altarpieces.

The St Sebastiaan guildhouse, now a museum

A 90-Minute Walk Around Bruges

Almost all the most famous sights of Bruges are in the centre and to the southwest of the centre. But the commercial and residential heart in Bruges' medieval golden age was to the north of the Markt. This is where a cosmopolitan collection of European merchants had their grand national "lodges", which oversaw the trade that passed into the city along a network of canals. Only small traces of this former glory remain, hidden among a collection of waterways, bridges, and residential streets of exceptional tranquillity and charm.

The Provinciaal Hof housing the local government offices ②

Markt and Vlamingstraat

Like most of the old trading cities of Flanders, Bruges clusters around its old market square, the Markt (see p121). The 19th-century statue in the centre celebrates Pieter de Coninck and Jan Breydel ①, the guildsmen who led a revolt against their French overlords in Bruges in 1302. It culminated in victory at the Battle of the Golden Spurs (see p30), a key date in Flemish nationalism. Goods came into the square on a canal, and were unloaded under the roof of the Waterhalle. The canal was filled in during the 1780s and now the site of the Waterhalle has been taken by the Provinciaal Hof ②, which is now used for

exhibitions and receptions. This Neo-Medieval building was designed by Louis Delacenserie (1838-1909), the architect responsible for much of the restoration of medieval Bruges. On the other side of the Markt, on the corner of St-Amandstraat, is the Huis Bouchoute ③; the compass on the façade, attached to a weathervane, was used by merchants to check the winds for the ships bringing goods to Bruges. Opposite it is the Craenenburg ④ (now a café), where Archduke Maximilian of Austria was imprisoned by the Bruges' authorities in 1488. A walk up Vlamingstraat leads past the Stadsschouwburg ⑤ (Municipal Theatre), a handsome Neo-Classical building from 1868. At No. 33 is the former Genuese Loge ⑥, the lodge of the Genoese traders, dating from 1399, which now houses the Friet Musuem. No. 35 was the Huis Ter Beurze ⑦, where merchants and bankers exchanged credit notes as early as the 13th century, making this perhaps the world's first stock exchange, and the origin of the French term for a stock-exchange, "Bourse".

Statue of Pieter de Coninck and Jan Breidel ①

Spiegelrei

On the right-hand side of the Academiestraat stands the Poortersloge ⑧ (Burghers' Lodge), a clubhouse for leading citizens in medieval Bruges. Almost all the city's grand buildings of that era had a tower; this is a rare example where the tower (rebuilt in 1775) has survived. On the other side of the street is the Oud Tolhuis ⑨, the Old Customs House. It overlooked a weighbridge where customs charges were assessed; that area has been replaced by the square, Jan van Eyckplein, named after the city's great artist who is represented by a statue ⑩. The canal that once led to the city centre now stops between Spiegelrei and

KEY

••• Walk Route

Spinolarei. On the corner of Spiegelrei and Genthof is Roode Steen ⑪; this was the home of Georges Rodenbach, the author of the controversial novel Bruges-la-Morte (Bruges the Dead, 1892). Koningstraat, off Spinolarei, leads to the St

Walburgakerk ⑫, Bruges' finest Baroque church, built for the Jesuits in 1612–42.

Jeruzalemkerk

Back on Spinolarei, cross the canal on Strooibrug. Straight ahead is Blekersstraat, with Café Vlissinghe ⑬ on the right. This is reputedly Bruges' oldest tavern, dating from 1515. Heading south down St-Annarei, the first left leads to the St Annakerk ⑭, a pretty parish church from 1497. The

A room at Bruges' folk museum, the Museum voor Volkskunde ⑯

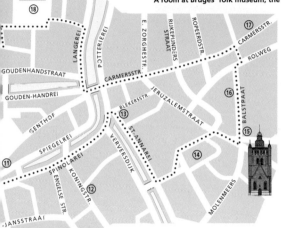

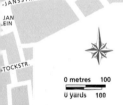

The Spinolarei canal, one of Bruges' principal waterways

Jeruzalemkerk *(see p126)* ⑬ on Peperstraat is very different, built in the 15th century and themed on pilgrimage sites in the Holy Land. Adjoining it is the Kantcentrum, the Lace Centre *(see p126)*. A row of almshouses in Balstraat is now the Museum voor Volkskunde *(see p127)* ⑯, a folk museum that paints a vivid picture of life in old Bruges. The only domed church in Bruges is in the English Convent (Engelsklooster) *(see p127)* ⑰, on Carmersstraat. Head back west along Carmerstraat, cross the canal on the Carmersbrug, and turn right to reach St Gilliskerk ⑱, an attractive church dating from the 13th–15th century. A series of cobbled streets leads to a picturesque section of canal at the Augustijnenbrug. The street on the opposite side called Spaanse Loskaai ⑲ recalls that this was once the Spanish quarter. Cross the

canal on the Vlamingbrug ⑳. At Naaldenstraat 19 is Hof Bladelin ㉑, a mansion built in about 1450 by Pieter Bladelin; after 1469, it was owned by the Medici Bank of Florence. Hotel Lucca ㉒, at Naaldenstraat 30, is on the site of the trading house of the merchants of the Italian city of Lucca. The alley off Naaldenstraat called Boterhuis ㉓ passes beneath the arch of the old Butter House and dairy market, and leads to St Jakobskerk ㉔. This fine Gothic church – with Baroque remodelling – contains art, ornate chapels, and tombs. The route along Moerstraat and Ontvangersstraat marks the bounds of the Prinsenhof, the former palace of the Dukes of Burgundy, which is now the first and only five star hotel in Bruges ㉕. Geldmuntstraat is named after the old mint that stood on the little square called Muntplein; it leads back to the Eiermarkt (Egg Market) ㉖ and the Markt.

TIPS FOR WALKERS

Starting point: *The Markt*
Length: *3.7 km (2.3 miles)*
Getting there: *The Markt is within walking distance of almost all hotels in Bruges; bus routes from all directions also go to this hub.*
Stopping off points: *There are a multitude of cafés and restaurants around the Markt, but very few beyond Vlamingstraat. A famous exception is the venerable old tavern called Cafe Vlissinghe in Blekersstraat (No. 13 on this walk).*

0 metres   100
0 yards   100

AIR
CONDITIONNING
Fruits de Mer
nos FRUITS
PLATEAU VIEUX BRUXELLES
PLATEAU ROYAL
6 Zélandes

TRAVELLERS' NEEDS

WHERE TO STAY

For most of the year, Brussels is primarily a business or political destination, and accommodation is often priced accordingly. The wide range of top hotels has one fine advantage for the visitor; weekend and summer deals make it possible even on a modest budget to stay in some of Europe's most luxurious establishments. The mid-range of hotels is also well represented

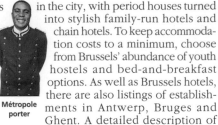

Métropole porter

in the city, with period houses turned into stylish family-run hotels and chain hotels. To keep accommodation costs to a minimum, choose from Brussels' abundance of youth hostels and bed-and-breakfast options. As well as Brussels hotels, there are also listings of establishments in Antwerp, Bruges and Ghent. A detailed description of each hotel is listed on pp136–43.

Hallway in the Hotel Métropole on Place de Brouckère (see p138)

BRUSSELS HOTELS

While Brussels does not have a specific hotel area, there are clusters of hotels in various parts of the city. Centrally, the most fertile ground is between Place Rogier and Place de Brouckère, which is within walking distance of both the Upper and Lower Town and a short bus ride from most major sights. The streets to the west of the Grand Place are also well supplied for those who want to be in the historic centre of town, but road noise can be a problem at night. To the north, Place Ste-Catherine or the streets behind Avenue de la Toison d'Or also have plenty of options. Following the pattern of cities worldwide, hotels generally reduce in price the further they are from the centre. Bed-and-breakfast rooms are dispersed across the capital and can often be found in residential

districts at very good rates. When arriving in the city from abroad by train or plane, it is worth knowing that the Gare du Midi and the airport both have nearby hotel colonies, although the station surroundings are run down in places. The airport has principally attracted chain hotels, which often offer good value package deals with the national airlines, although sightseeing from here is inconvenient.

ROOM RATES

Hotels at the top end of the market offer exceptional standards of comfort and convenience to their largely corporate clients, and their prices reflect this. In general, prices are higher than in the rest of Belgium, but on a par with other European capitals. For a night in a luxury hotel, expect to pay €250 to €300 for a double room; the price for a room in the city averages in the €150 to €175 bracket.

Façade of the Crowne Plaza Hotel, one of the hotel chain (see p137)

However, there are numerous discounts available (see Special Rates, p134).

Single travellers can often find reasonable discounts on accommodation, although few places will offer rooms at half the price of a double. It is usual to be charged extra if you place additional guests in a double room. Travelling with children is not the financial burden it might be in this child-friendly society (see p127). Youth hostels cater very well to the budget student traveller and some also have family rooms.

TAXES AND CHARGES

Room taxes and sales taxes should be included in the cost of your room, so the price quoted should be what appears as the total. The price of car parking may be added. Some hotels offer free parking, others charge up to €20 a night. In hotels with no private car park, it is worth checking discounts for public parking facilities if these are located nearby. While many hotels are happy to allow pets, many will add a small nightly charge to the bill.

Breakfast is not always included in the price of a room, even in very expensive establishments. However, many hotels do offer excellent free breakfasts, so ask when you book. The fare usually consists of continental breakfasts, including good coffee, warm croissants and brioche rolls, preserves and fruit juice. Bear in mind that if the expensive place where you are staying is charging €20 for breakfast, there will be plenty of places nearby offering equal quality for much less money. The usual price for a hotel breakfast ranges upwards from €2.50, but coffee and rolls are usually priced at around €6.20. Unusually, youth hostels also offer lunches and dinners at around €9.90 each.

Phone calls from hotel rooms can be extremely expensive, with unit charges of €.60 for even a local call not uncommon. To make a long-distance call, buying a phonecard and using the efficient public pay-phone service is several times less expensive. Hotel faxes or modem charges, when available, can also mount up.

Minibar charges are usually very high, although no more so than in any other western European city. Watching satellite or pay-TV stations can also be expensive. However, Belgium's advanced cable network and proximity to other countries means that there are usually more than 20 free channels to choose from including the BBC as well as French and German television.

HOTEL GRADINGS AND FACILITIES

Approved hotels are issued with a shield by the Belgian Tourist Board which must be displayed in a prominent position. Hotels carrying this sign conform to official standards set by Belgian law which guarantee certain standards of quality. Some hotels are also graded according to the Benelux

Unique frescoes decorate each room at the Hotel Bloom *(see p139)*

system, ranging from one to five stars, with one as the minimum. It is worth remembering, however, that membership of this scheme is voluntary and as a result, there may be high-quality hotels which are not graded in this way.

In a city with so many luxury hotels, fierce competition has led to ever more sophisticated gadgets and services for business-people. Several private phone lines, screened calls, free wireless internet access, automatic check-out services, 24-hour news via Reuters, secretarial services, free mobile phones and even executive suites designed expressly for women are all on offer. Most of the top hotels also house extensive fitness facilities, including saunas and full gymnasiums, although there are few large swimming pools.

Brussels' reputation as a centre for fine dining is significantly enhanced by the hotel trade, with major hotels

often offering several options, from expert gastronomy to excellent brasserie dining. For snacks and drinks, Brussels' hotels are known for their old-style, entertaining bars with piano music for those

19th-century courtyard of the Conrad International *(see p142)*

guests who prefer not to venture into the city at night. A handful have nightclub facilities where lively crowds meet in the evening for cocktails and dancing.

As one of Europe's major centres for the convention trade, Brussels is not short of meeting and function rooms, with the big hotels offering dozens of spaces for anything from conferences to society weddings and even relatively modest hotels offering good-sized rooms for business seminars and the like. Many expensive hotels have serviced apartments on offer; these can be useful for the greater freedom and increased space they provide.

The Hotel Ter Brughe, next to one of Bruges' many canals *(see p143)*

View of the Grand Place from a room at Auberge Saint-Michel *(see p136)*

HOW TO BOOK

Rooms are available in Brussels at most times of the year, but you should book several days in advance to ensure that you get the place you want. In mid- and top-range hotels, a credit card is the usual way to book, giving card details as a deposit; in smaller hotels, bookings can often be made simply by giving your name and details of the day and time of arrival.

The **Tourist Office** offers a free, same-day reservation service on-site. It also publishes a practical guide to Brussels hotels, updated annually, which is available on request. For booking by telephone, **Resotel** provides a free service for visitors and is very helpful.

If you are familar with the technology, internet bookings can be quick and efficient and the information available on hotel websites is often more regularly updated than the hotel brochure.

SPECIAL RATES

Brussels is an exceptional destination, in that relatively few people come for the weekend or in July and August, meaning that often remarkable deals can be acquired at these times.

The cost of staying in one of the top hotels over the weekend or at off-peak times can plummet by as much as 65 per cent (for example, from €300 to €100 for a double room), so checking before booking about any special deals may save a large sum of money. A few hotels also offer discounts for guests who eat in their restaurants.

Some reservation services charge a small fee, but they can usually find competitively priced accommodation. Any

deposit given is deducted from the final hotel bill.

Many travel agents also offer packages for visiting Brussels or Belgium, with accommodation working out less expensively than a custom-booked break.

It is worth checking with your airline about possible discounts through its reservation services, and to find out about frequent-flyer bargains for affiliated hotels.

DISABLED TRAVELLERS

Hotels in Brussels and the rest of Belgium take the needs of disabled travellers seriously. Many have one or more rooms designed with wheelchair-bound guests in mind. It is worth remembering that many hotel buildings in Brussels are historic and therefore may not be suitable. Most staff, however, will be helpful. It is wise to ask in

The Hilton Brussels, formerly the Albert Premier Rogier *(see p137)*

DIRECTORY

RESERVATION AGENCIES

Brussels Info Place (BIP)
Rue Royale 2–4, Brussels 1000. **Map** 2 E4.
Tel (02) 513 8940.
www.biponline.be

Resotel
Avenue E Van Nieuwenhuyse 6,
Brussels 1160.
Tel (02) 779 3939.
www.resotel.be

AUBERGES DE JEUNESSE/YOUTH HOSTELS

Generation Europe
Rue de l'Eléphant 4,
Brussels 1080. **Map** 1 A1.
Tel (02) 410 3858. www.lesaubergesdejeunesse.be

Jacques Brel
Rue de la Sablonnière 30,
Brussels 1000. **Map** 2 F1.
Tel (02) 218 0187

New Sleep Well
Rue du Damier 23,
Brussels 1000. **Map** 2 D1.

Tel (02) 218 50 50.
www.sleepwell.be

BED AND BREAKFAST

Bed and Breakfast Taxi Stop
Rue du Fossé-aux-Loups 28, Brussels 1000. **Map** 2 D2. *Tel (07) 22 2292.*
www.taxistop.be

Bed & Brussels
Rue Kindermans 9, Brussels 1050. *Tel (02) 646 0737.*
www.bnb-brussels.be

GAY AND LESBIAN ACCOMMODATION

The Rainbow House
Rue du Marché au Charbon 42, Brussels 1000.
Map 1 C3
Tel (02) 503 5990.
www.rainbowhouse.be

Tels Quels
Rue du Marché au Charbon 81, Brussels 1000.
Map 1 C3.
Tel (02) 512 4587.
www.telsquels.be

advance whether the hotel can cater to travellers with special needs. Most hotels will allow the visually handicapped to bring a guide dog onto the premises, although again it is best to make sure that this is the case before you arrive.

YOUTH ACCOMMODATION

Brussels has several central, excellent youth hostels, with modern facilities, reasonably priced food and more privacy than is usually associated with hostel stays. Perhaps the best are the **Jacques Brel**, close to Place Madou, and the **New Sleep Well**, which has disabled access. A bed in a four-person room should cost in the region of €19, rising to around €30 for a single room. Breakfast is sometimes included or costs from €2.50, with lunch and dinner for a charge of around €9.90. If you are not a member of Hostelling International, rates rise by up to €5 extra per night; membership cards, priced €9–15, are available at most hostels. Joining is worthwhile if you are travelling around Belgium, as there are over 30 hostels across the country and there are discounts at some attractions.

GAY AND LESBIAN ACCOMMODATION

Same-sex couples should have few problems finding welcoming accommodation. Maison

The lobby at the Meridien Hotel in Brussels' Lower Town *(see p139)*

Noble *(see p137)*, Brussels' first luxury gay guesthouse, opened in 2009. The **Tels Quels** association, located on the Rue de Marché au Charbon, is the best source of information about good places to choose. It has a documentation centre covering most aspects of gay life in the city and publishes a monthly magazine. **The Rainbow House**, across the road, is a good place to find details of events taking place in and around the centre of the city.

TRAVELLING WITH CHILDREN

Children are welcome at all hotels in Brussels, with many making a concerted effort to cater for the needs of those travelling with children. Most allow one or two under-12s to stay in their parents' room without extra charge and some hotels will extend this

principle to under-16s and under-18s. When travelling with children, it is worth reserving in advance as the hotel will find the room that best suits your needs. Families planning a long stay in Brussels should consider renting a suite or a self-catering apartment, which are more economical.

SELF-CATERING APARTMENTS

There is no shortage of self-catering accommodation in Brussels, with many places available for a short stay as well as by the week or month. A few places are attached to hotels as suites, with the rest run by private companies. Prices start at around €600 per week, for a fairly basic but furnished one- or two-bedroom apartment, to €1,000 or more for more luxurious lodgings. Contact Resotel or visit the Tourist Office for a detailed list of suggestions.

BED-AND-BREAKFAST

Bed-and-breakfast, also called *chambre d'hôte*, accommodation can be a very pleasant alternative to staying in a cheap hotel, and rooms can often be found even in the centre of town. You may come across a bargain by wandering the streets, but the easiest way to find bed-and-breakfast lodgings is through the Tourist Office or one of the capital's specialist agencies, either in person or online.

Brasserie at the Hotel Marivaux *(see p136)*

Choosing a Hotel

The hotels on the following pages have been selected across a wide price range for the excellence of their facilities, location or character. The chart below first lists hotels in Brussels by area, followed by a selection in Antwerp, Bruges, and Ghent. Hotels within the same price category are listed alphabetically. Map references refer to the Brussels Street Finders on pp190–93.

PRICE CATEGORIES
The following price ranges are for a standard double room and taxes per night during the high season. Breakfast is not included, unless specified.

€ under €80
€€ €80–€130
€€€ €130–€180
€€€€ €180–€260
€€€€€ over €260

LOWER TOWN

Astrid Centre
Place du Samedi 11, 1000 Brussels **Tel** *(02) 219 3119* **Fax** *(02) 219 3170* **Rooms** *100*   **Map** *1 C1*   €

A comfortable and efficient hotel in the centre of the city, the Astrid Centre Hotel can be found near the picturesque fish market and the popular restaurants of Place Ste Catherine. The rooms are large with modern furnishings and facilities. Conference facilities. Private parking at extra cost. Complimentary breakfast. **www.astridhotel.be**

Grande Cloche
Place Rouppe 10, 1000 Brussels **Tel** *(02) 512 6140* **Fax** *(02) 512 6591* **Rooms** *36*   **Map** *1 C4*   €

A welcoming hotel halfway between the Grand Place and Brussels' Gare du Midi, Grande Cloche occupies a renovated 19th-century townhouse. Rooms are comfortable with modern facilities, ideal for budget travellers. Breakfast is included in the price. Free parking on the square in front of the hotel. **www.hotelgrandecloche.com**

Queen Anne
Boulevard Emile Jacqmain 110, 1000 Brussels **Tel** *(02) 217 1600* **Fax** *(02) 217 1838* **Rooms** *60*   **Map** *2 D1*   €

Close to the De Brouckère metro station, the welcoming Hotel Queen Anne is small, but friendly, with clean, comfortable rooms and a generous buffet breakfast. All rooms have ensuite facilities. Eleven apartments are available for longer stays. The peaceful location and relaxed atmosphere is perfect for families. **www.queen-anne.be**

Manhattan
Boulevard Adolphe Max 132–140, 1000 Brussels **Tel** *(02) 219 1619* **Fax** *(02) 223 2599* **Rooms** *62*   **Map** *2 D1*   €

Situated between the Grand Place and the Botanical Gardens, Hotel Manhattan is very well priced but pretty basic. Rooms have an old-fashioned feel, but are clean and comfortable and the main sights are within walking distance. The price includes breakfast. Plenty of nearby restaurants, which staff can recommend. **www.hotelmanhattan.be**

Marivaux
Boulevard Adolphe Max 98, 1000 Brussels **Tel** *(02) 227 0300* **Fax** *(03) 218 0683* **Rooms** *100*   **Map** *2 D1*   €

The rooms of this comfortable, modern and business-friendly hotel, just north of Place de Brouckère, are large and pleasantly decorated with ensuite facilities. Breakfast is included in the price. Stylish bar and brasserie serving international cuisine. Convention facilities. Business club rooms (with Internet connections). **www.hotelmarivaux.be**

Aris Grand Place
Marché aux Herbes 78–80, 1000 Brussels **Tel** *(02) 514 4300* **Fax** *(02) 543 0119* **Rooms** *55*   **Map** *2 D3*   €€

This reasonably-priced hotel in the historical centre is just a minute from the Grand Place. Housed in a late 19th-century building, the rooms are modern and comfortable with double-glazing to keep out exterior city noise. Discounts for weekend bookings. Breakfast included. One room has wheelchair access. **www.arishotel.be**

Atlas
Rue du Vieux Marché aux Grains 30, 1000 Brussels **Tel** *(02) 502 6006* **Fax** *(02) 502 6935* **Rooms** *88*   **Map** *1 C2*   €€

Modern, three-star hotel just to the north of Grand Place. Offers basic, but comfortable rooms with free Wi-Fi Internet connection and breakfast included in the price. Families can rent duplex rooms, sleeping four (daily supplement applies). These rooms have a mini-kitchenette. **www.atlashotel.be**

Auberge Saint-Michel
Grand Place 15, 1000 Brussels **Tel** *(02) 511 0956* **Fax** *(02) 511 4600* **Rooms** *14*   **Map** *2 D3*   €€

A former mansion overlooking the Grand Place, the two-star Auberge Saint-Michel is well-placed. Be sure to ask for a room with a view over the square (as only seven have them). Rooms are basic, but clean, with ensuite facilities. Staff are friendly and helpful. Breakfast is served for a supplement and can be taken in the rooms.

Carrefour de l'Europe
Rue du Marché aux Herbes 110, 1000 Brussels **Tel** *(02) 504 9400* **Fax** *(02) 504 9500* **Rooms** *65*   **Map** *2 D3*   €€

An elegant, four-star hotel in the heart of Brussels, targeted at the business traveller. Eight conference rooms and 10 executive traveller rooms. Lobby bar. Large public parking next to the hotel. All rooms have Wi-Fi Internet connection and breakfast is included in the price. **www.carrefoureurope.net**

Key to Symbols *see back cover flap*

Centrale Hotel   🔲🅿️▤   €€
Rue des Colonies 10, 1000 Brussels **Tel** *(02) 504 9910* **Fax** *(02) 503 1451* **Rooms** *47*   **Map** *2 E3*

This historic four-star hotel near the Royal Palace offers comfortable and reasonably-priced accommodation in the centre of Brussels. Efficient staff provide sightseeing advice and restaurant recommendations. Complimentary buffet breakfast. Private parking is available at extra cost. **www.centrale-hotel.com**

Congres   🔲   €€
Rue du Congres 42, 1000 Brussels **Tel** *(02) 217 1890* **Fax** *(02) 217 1897* **Rooms** *70*   **Map** *2 F2*

This peaceful three-star hotel occupies four renovated 19th-century townhouses and is within walking distance of all the main sights. Rooms are modern but elegant, with business-friendly facilities. Complimentary buffet breakfast. Polite and friendly staff. **www.hotelducongres.be**

Crowne Plaza Hotel   🔲🈁🈶▤   €€
Rue Gineste 3, 1210 Brussels **Tel** *(02) 203 6200* **Fax** *(02) 203 5555* **Rooms** *354*   **Map** *2 E1*

An Art Nouveau hotel dating back to 1908, combining turn-of-the-century style with modern facilities. Rooms are clean and comfortable, and some have been refurbished. Generous buffet breakfast at extra cost. Helpful and friendly staff. Book in advance in the busy summer season. **www.crowneplazabrussels.be**

George V Hotel   🔲🅿️   €€
Rue T'Kint 23, 1000 Brussels **Tel** *(02) 513 5093* **Fax** *(02) 513 4493* **Rooms** *20*   **Map** *1 B3*

This friendly, very reasonably priced three-star hotel within walking distance of the Grand Place occupies an old English-inspired 19th-century townhouse. Rooms are large and opulently decorated with period furnishings and plenty of old-world charm. Hotel bar. Complimentary breakfast included in price. **www.hotelgeorge5.be**

Hilton Brussels City   🔲🅿️🈁🈶   €€
Place Rogier 20, 1210 Brussels **Tel** *(02) 203 3125* **Fax** *(02) 203 4331* **Rooms** *283*   **Map** *2 E2*

Situated in the heart of Brussels, near the Rue Neuve shopping district, the Grand Place and the Royal Palace, this sophisticated city hotel offers comfortable rooms and multiple facilities for both tourists and business travellers alike. The bar and brasserie serve Belgian beers and traditional specialities at reasonable prices. **www.hilton.com**

Hotel Floris Arlequin Grand'Place   🔲🈶   €€
Rue de la Fourche 17–19, Greepstraat, 1000 Brussels **Tel** *(02) 514 1615* **Fax** *(02) 514 2202* **Rooms** *92* **Map** *2 D2*

A modern, three-star hotel in the heart of the historical centre. Although not the most historically interesting of Brussels' hotels, it does have a great location. Some of the guest rooms boast great views over the city. Breakfast is included. There are plenty of restaurants and bars in the vicinity. Conference facilities available. **www.florishotels.com**

La Legende   🔲   €€
Rue du Lombard 35, 1000 Brussels **Tel** *(02) 512 8290* **Fax** *(02) 512 3493* **Rooms** *26*   **Map** *1 C3*

La Legende isn't the most modern of Brussels' two-star hotels but, given its central location, it is reasonably-priced and welcoming. Rooms are clean and functional, with four-bed family rooms on offer. A good choice for budget travellers. Guests can use a private car park for €20 per day. **www.hotellalegende.com**

La Vieille Lanterne   €€
Rue des Grands Carmes 29, 1000 Brussels **Tel** *(02) 512 7494* **Fax** *(02) 512 1397* **Rooms** *6*   **Map** *1 C3*

Centrally-located, La Vieille Lanterne is a good value hostel with six rooms. All are brightly decorated, with ensuite, and benefit from great views onto Manneken Pis. Breakfast is included in the price and is served in the rooms. No check-in after 10pm, when the doors are closed for the night. Book in advance in summer seasons. **www.lavieillelanterne.com**

Madeleine   🔲▤   €€
Rue de la Montagne 20–22, 1000 Brussels **Tel** *(02) 513 2973* **Fax** *(02) 502 1350* **Rooms** *56*   **Map** *2 D3*

Behind its slightly shabby exterior, Hotel La Madeleine is quite charming and offers rooms to meet all budgets – from small and cosy to executive suites. Double-glazing keeps out the exterior noise. Not all rooms have ensuite facilities. Complimentary buffet breakfast. All rooms have Wi-Fi access. **www.hotel-la-madeleine.be**

Maison Noble   🈶   €€
Rue Marcq 10, 1000 Brussels **Tel** *(02) 219 2339* **Fax** *(02) 219 3039* **Rooms** *4*   **Map** *1 C1*

This stylish gay-friendly hotel is located in a 19th-century townhouse close to Place St Catherine. There are painted wooden ceilings and sumptuous Art Deco stained glass windows alongside more modern conveniences such as free Wi-Fi and a steam room. Room rates are reduced for stays of two nights or more. **www.maison-noble.eu**

Matignon   🔲🈁   €€
Rue de la Bourse 8–12, 1000 Brussels **Tel** *(02) 511 0888* **Fax** *(02) 513 6927* **Rooms** *37*   **Map** *1 C2*

A small, reasonably-priced, three-star hotel in a good location with simple, but thoughtfully-decorated rooms. The price includes breakfast and a minibar. The Matignon also has a welcoming brasserie. Friendly staff are on hand to offer sightseeing advice. **www.hotelmatignon.be**

NH Grand Place Arenberg   🔲🅿️▤   €€
Rue d'Assaut 15, 1000 Brussels **Tel** *(02) 501 1616* **Fax** *(02) 501 1818* **Rooms** *155*   **Map** *2 D2*

A modern hotel within sight of Brussels' cathedral and a short stroll away from Place du Grand Sablon, with its famous chocolatiers. All rooms have modern facilities and have been renovated to their current spotless state. Breakfast not included in the price. Business-friendly amenities. **www.nh-hotels.com**

Noga
🖥️ 🅿️   €€
Rue du Béguinage 38, 1000 Brussels **Tel** *(02) 218 6763* **Fax** *(02) 218 1603* **Rooms** *19*   **Map** 1 C1

A friendly hotel near the church of St-Jean-Baptiste, Noga feels like a home away from home with its comfy lounge, popular games room with billiard table, library and music room with piano, not to mention the eclectic furnishing in its bedrooms. Internet access and laundry facilities. **www.nogahotel.com**

Novotel Tour Noire
🖥️ 🅿️ 🔢 ♨️ 📺 🍽️   €€
Rue de la Vierge Noire 32, 1000 Brussels **Tel** *(02) 505 5050* **Fax** *(02) 505 5000* **Rooms** *217*   **Map** 1 C2

A welcoming hotel with plenty of family-friendly facilities – including gym and pool – the Novotel Tour Noire offers an efficient and well-priced base in the heart of the city. Paid parking. Friendly staff. Generous buffet breakfast. Rooms have triple-glazing to keep out the noise. **www.novotel.com**

Opera
🖥️   €€
Rue Grétry 53, 1000 Brussels **Tel** *(02) 219 4343* **Fax** *(02) 219 1720* **Rooms** *49*   **Map** 2 D2

Situated just off the Grand Place, the two-star Hotel Opera is clean, quiet, friendly and well-located. Rooms are modern, comfortable and simply decorated. Reasonably priced for the location with discounts available if rooms are booked online. Complimentary buffet breakfast. **www.hotel-opera.be**

Scandic Grand Place
🖥️ 🅿️ 🔢 📺 🍽️   €€
Rue d'Arenberg 18, 1000 Brussels **Tel** *(02) 548 1811* **Fax** *(02) 548 1820* **Rooms** *100*   **Map** 2 D2

This luxury hotel in the Scandic chain is situated behind the façades of two listed townhouses and boasts a popular bar and restaurant, sauna, fitness room, "recreation area" and conference facilities. Close to Gare Centrale train station, it is well placed for exploring the city. **www.scandichotels.com**

Welcome Hotel
🖥️ 🅿️ 🍽️   €€
Quai au Bois à Brûler 23, 1000 Brussels **Tel** *(02) 219 9546* **Fax** *(02) 217 1887* **Rooms** *16*   **Map** 1 C1

Situated in a peaceful location to the north of Place Ste Catherine (the city's old fish market), Hotel Welcome sits in the midst of some fabulous fish restaurants. Complimentary breakfast is served in the Art Deco breakfast room. Metro stop just in front of the hotel. Shuttle bus from the airport. **www.hotelwelcome.com**

Bedford
🖥️ 🅿️ 🔢 📺 🍽️   €€€
Rue du Midi 135–137, 1000 Brussels **Tel** *(02) 507 0000* **Fax** *(02) 507 0010* **Rooms** *326*   **Map** 1 C3

The rooms in this four-star hotel are spacious and comfortable with plenty of lounge space. Within walking distance of the Grand Place and the area's busy restaurants. The hotel also has 18 sumptuously-decorated executive rooms and 12 suites suitable for families. Breakfast is included. **www.hotelbedford.be**

Citadines St Catherine
🅿️   €€€
Quai Au Bois A Bruler 51, 1000 Brussels **Tel** *(02) 221 1411* **Fax** *(02) 221 1599* **Rooms** *169*   **Map** 1 C1

This apartment hotel just north of the Grand Place (near the church of Ste-Catherine) offers studio apartments with a peaceful communal garden on a self-catering or half-board basis. A good choice for visitors coming for a week or more, the apartments come with all modern facilities. Wi-Fi connections available. **www.citadines.com**

Hôtel Cascade Midi
🅿️ 🍽️   €€€
Avenue Fosny 5–7, 1060 Brussels **Tel** *(02) 533 1099* **Fax** *(02) 533 1099* **Rooms** *99*   **Map** 1 B5

Located close to the central station, this modern hotel offers a range of comfortable, well-equipped rooms, making it a good choice for both leisure and business travellers. Guests can enjoy a buffet breakfast looking out onto the rear garden. In the evening, light snacks and drinks are available. Useful concierge desk. **www.cascadehotel.be**

Hotel Métropole
🖥️ 🔢 📺 🍽️   €€€
Place de Brouckère 31, 1000 Brussels **Tel** *(02) 217 2300* **Fax** *(02) 218 0220* **Rooms** *300*   **Map** 1 D2

Built in 1895, this plush hotel boasts striking architecture and a mix of French Renaissance, Empire and Art Deco styles. High ceilings, stained-glass restaurant and crystal chandeliers in the lobby, bar and gourmet restaurant. Not all rooms are period decorated. Complimentary breakfast. **www.metropolehotel.be**

Le Plaza
🖥️ 🅿️ 🔢 📺 🍽️   €€€
Boulevard Adolphe Max 118–126, 1000 Brussels **Tel** *(02) 278 0100* **Fax** *(02) 278 0101* **Rooms** *190*   **Map** 2 D1

An opulent five-star hotel which regularly provides accommodation to visiting stars and gentry, Le Plaza even has its own theatre. The building itself dates back to 1930 when it was built to model Paris' famous George V hotel. Rooms were renovated in 1996 to provide modern facilities. Business- and tourist-friendly. **www.leplaza-brussels.be**

Marriott Brussels
🅿️ 🔢 🍽️   €€€
Rue Auguste Orts 3–7, 1000 Brussels **Tel** *(02) 516 9090* **Fax** *(02) 516 9000* **Rooms** *221*   **Map** 1 C2

Five-star Marriott in the centre of Brussels, this hotel is perfectly placed for a shopping break. It lies near the top designer stores on Antoine Dansaert, the antique district is just a short walk away and if you arrive in the winter months, it is also in the midst of Brussels' famed Christmas market. Price includes breakfast. **www.marriott.com**

Amigo
🖥️ 🅿️ 🔢 📺 🍽️   €€€€
Rue de l'Amigo 1–3, 1000 Brussels **Tel** *(02) 547 4747* **Fax** *(02) 513 5277* **Rooms** *173*   **Map** 1 C3

This five-star hotel in the Rocco Forte Hotel chain provides an elegant setting and great location just near the Grand Place. Rooms have king-size beds and marble bathrooms. Family suites. Award-winning restaurant. Meeting room and fitness facilities. **www.hotelamigo.com**

Key to Price Guide *see p136* **Key to Symbols** *see back cover flap*

Hotel Café Pacific

⬚ €€€€

Rue Antoine Dansaert 57, 1000 Brussels **Tel** *(02) 213 0080* **Fax** *(02) 213 0083* **Rooms** *12*   **Map** *1 B2*

This boutique hotel is located in one of the trendiest areas of Brussels. Just five minutes' walk from Grand Place and the main shopping streets, guests can retreat to this little oasis complete with restaurant after taking in the nearby sights. It is ideal for both couples and families alike. Breakfast is included. **www.hotelcafepacific.com**

Meridien

⬚ 🍽 📺 ▤ €€€€

Carrefour de l'Europe 3, 1000 Brussels **Tel** *(02) 548 4211* **Fax** *(02) 548 4080* **Rooms** *224*   **Map** *2 D3*

A modern luxury hotel just south of the Grand Place, the Meridien offers a classy place to stay in the heart of old Brussels if you don't mind its proximity to the more seedy area around the Gare Centrale train station. Rooms are designed in Victorian/English style. The hotel organizes golf, canoeing and sightseeing trips. **www.lemeridienbrussels.com**

Radisson Blu Royal Hotel

⬚ P 🍽 📺 ▤ €€€€

Rue du Fosse-aux-Loups 47, 1000 Brussels **Tel** *(02) 219 2828* **Fax** *(02) 219 6262* **Rooms** *281*   **Map** *2 D2*

A fabulous five-star hotel behind a glorious Art Deco façade (designed by famed Belgian designer, Michel Haspers), Radisson is one of the best places to stay in the city. Stunning garden and two restaurants, along with Bar Dessiné filled with Tintin illustrations. The hotel will organize city tours. **www.radissonblu.com**

Royal Windsor

⬚ 🍽 📺 ▤ €€€€

5 Rue Duquesnoy, 1000 Brussels **Tel** *(02) 505 5555* **Fax** *(02) 505 5781* **Rooms** *166*   **Map** *2 D3*

A characterful hotel near the Grand Place, the Royal Windsor is as luxurious as its name would suggest. Despite their rather smallish size, the rooms are sumptuously decorated (including four-poster beds and French antiques), with marble bathrooms. The restaurant has a stunning stained-glass ceiling. **www.royalwindsorbrussels.com**

Van Belle

P 🍽 €€€€

Chaussée de Mons 39, 1070 Brussels **Tel** *(02) 521 3516* **Fax** *(02) 527 0002* **Rooms** *105*   **Map** *1 A3*

The Van Belle is a three-star hotel situated just off Brussels' busy Boulevard du Midi. Welcoming and efficient, it has rooms that are comfortable and well furnished, and the communal lounge area has a large open fire. Breakfast is included in the price. Underground garage. Free transportation to the Grand Place and the Gare du Midi. **www.hotelvanbelle.be**

Hotel Bloom

⬚ P 🍽 📺 ▤ €€€€€

Rue Royal 250 Koninsstraat, 1210 Brussels **Tel** *(02) 220 6611* **Fax** *(02) 217 8444* **Rooms** *305*   **Map** *2 E2*

This boutique hotel features comfortable, contemporary rooms, each decorated with a unique fresco by a different artist. Situated next to the Botanical Gardens, within a 20-minute walk of the historic centre, and with tram, bus and metro stops just outside, Hotel Bloom makes a stylish base from which to explore the city. **www.hotelbloom.com**

Le Châtelain All Suite Hotel

⬚ P 🍽 📺 ▤ €€€€€

Rue de Châtelain 17, 1000 Brussels **Tel** *(02) 646 0055* **Fax** *(02) 646 0088* **Rooms** *107*

Located just off the stylish Avenue Louise, this five star hotel prides itself on its traditional ideas of hospitality and attention to detail while at the same time having all the mod cons and gadgets you could wish to find. All the large rooms are soundproof and have large, luxuriously appointed bathrooms. **www.le-chatelain.com**

UPPER TOWN

Les Bluets

€

Rue Berckmans 124, 1060 Brussels **Tel** *(02) 534 3983* **Fax** *(02) 543 0970* **Rooms** *8*

Charming, family-run, non-smoking hotel in a 19th-century bourgeois townhouse. The eight rooms are decorated with a laidback mix of antique furnishings, objets d'art and modern facilities, making it an interesting place to stay. The hotel has been refurbished and some rooms now have kitchenettes. Small plant-covered annex. **www.bluets.be**

Best Western Hotel Royal Centre

⬚ P ▤ €€

Rue Royale 160, 1000 Brussels **Tel** *(02) 219 0065* **Fax** *(02) 218 0910* **Rooms** *73*   **Map** *2 F1*

A four-star hotel within walking distance of the Royal Palace, the President Centre has elegant rooms, luxurious hotel bar, business centre with meeting room and private garage (at a fee). Continental breakfast included in the price. Good last-minute rates available online. **www.royalcentre.be**

Chambord

⬚ 🍽 ▤ €€

Rue De Namur 82, 1000 Brussels **Tel** *(02) 548 9910* **Fax** *(02) 514 0847* **Rooms** *64*   **Map** *2 E4*

The Penthouse Suite of this hotel has a stunning view from its terrace and even some of the standard rooms have their own balconies. There is also a terrace bar. Good promotional rates for off-peak tourists and breakfast is included. The hotel does not have parking facilities but can find a place for your car nearby. **www.hotel-chambord.be**

Chambres en Ville

€€

Rue de Londres 19, 1050 Brussels **Tel** *(02) 512 9290* **Rooms** *3*   **Map** *2 F2*

This wonderfully chic guesthouse, designed by the artist-owner Philippe Guilmin, is itself a work of art. It's filled with original paintings and sculptures and the beautiful bedrooms are themed around Guilmin's love of travel. The breakfasts are equally sumptuous – Phillipe even makes his own jam. **www.chambresenville.be**

Dixseptième
🔲 €€

Rue de la Madeleine 25, 1000 Brussels **Tel** *(02) 517 1717* **Fax** *(02) 502 6424* **Rooms** *24*   **Map** *2 D3*

The former home of a 17th-century Spanish ambassador, this small, friendly hotel is a great choice for art aficionados. All rooms are named after famous Belgian artists and the lounge has its own art library! Communal rooms have opulent decorations, including crystal chandeliers and a Louis XVI staircase. Breakfast is included. **www.ledixseptieme.be**

NH Hotel du Grand Sablon
🔲 P 🍴 €€

Rue Bodenbroek 2–4, 1000 Brussels **Tel** *(02) 518 1100* **Fax** *(02) 512 6766* **Rooms** *196*   **Map** *2 D4*

Flagship Brussels establishment of the Italian Jolly chain, the Hotel du Grand Sablon boasts a fantastic location on the Place du Grand Sablon. Rooms are large and carefully decorated, with great amenities and free Internet connection. Mini Baroque art gallery in the lobby. **www.nh-hotels.com**

Sabina
🔲 €€

Rue du Nord 78, 1000 Brussels **Tel** *(02) 218 2637* **Fax** *(02) 219 3239* **Rooms** *24*   **Map** *2 F2*

The Sabina is a no frills hotel tucked away in a quiet corner of the city not far from the Parc de Bruxelles and the Botanical Gardens. While it's true that some of the rooms are on the small side, the hotel is exceptionally good value for somewhere so central. There are good deals available for online booking. **www.hotelsabina.eu**

The White Hotel
€€

Avenue Louise 212, 1000 Brussels **Tel** *(02) 644 2929* **Fax** *(02) 644 1878* **Rooms** *60*

Located on Brussels' luxury shopping street Avenue Louise, this four-star hotel is now part of the Design hotel group. It is modern and friendly with a cosy bar and a pool room. Rooms are spacious with all mod cons. Complimentary buffet breakfast. **www.thewhitehotel.be**

Leopold
🔲 P 🍴 🟦 €€€

Rue de Luxembourg 35, 1050 Brussels **Tel** *(02) 511 1828* **Fax** *(02) 514 1939* **Rooms** *111*   **Map** *3 A4*

An elegant four-star hotel near the European Parliament and Parc Leopold, Hotel Leopold also has a well-reputed gourmet restaurant. Rooms are designed for tourists and business travellers, with half-board and self-catering apartments available for longer-term visitors. The price includes breakfast. **www.hotel-leopold.be**

Four Points Sheraton
🔲 P 🍴 📺 🟦 €€€€

Rue Paul Spaak 15, 1000 Brussels **Tel** *(02) 645 6111* **Fax** *(02) 646 6344* **Rooms** *128*

The deluxe Four Points is a Sheraton hotel just off Avenue Louise. It has luxurious rooms, as well as a fitness room with indoor "whirlpool" and a gourmet restaurant. Popular with business travellers for its conference facilities. Paid parking. **www.fourpointsbrussels.com**

New Hotel Charlemagne
🔲 P 🍴 €€€€

Boulevard Charlemagne 25–27, 1000 Brussels **Tel** *(02) 230 2135* **Fax** *(02) 230 2510* **Rooms** *68*   **Map** *3 B2*

In the heart of the European district (next to the headquarters of the EU Commission), New Hotel Charlemagne is slightly distant from the historical centre, but well connected by metro. Close to the Parc du Cinquantenaire. Rooms are modern and comfortably furnished. A good choice for business travellers. **www.new-hotel.com**

The Hotel Brussels
🔲 P 🍴 📺 🟦 €€€€

Boulevard de Waterloo 38, 1000 Brussels **Tel** *(02) 504 1111* **Fax** *(02) 504 3350* **Rooms** *434*   **Map** *2 E5*

This five-star hotel offers luxury facilities and efficient service in a central location. Rooms are spacious and comfortable, and many have superb city views. The lobby is decorated with a frieze of the Grand Place. The hotel offers sightseeing tours as well as conference facilities. **www.thehotel-brussels.be**

Hotel Eurostars Sablon
🔲 📺 🟦 €€€€€

Rue de la Paille 2–8, 1000 Brussels **Tel** *(02) 513 6040* **Fax** *(02) 511 8141* **Rooms** *32*   **Map** *2 D4*

A friendly boutique hotel with sauna and relaxation centre, the Sablon boasts a fantastic location beside the city's main art galleries and is within walking distance of the characterful cafés on Place du Grand Sablon. Rooms are large with split-level suites and plenty of facilities. The staff are particularly helpful. **www.eurostarshotels.com**

Stanhope
🔲 P 🍴 📺 🟦 €€€€€

Rue du Commerce 9, 1000 Brussels **Tel** *(02) 506 9111* **Fax** *(02) 512 1708* **Rooms** *125*   **Map** *2 F4*

Providing deluxe Belgian hospitality in three converted townhouses, the five-star boutique Hotel Stanhope is decorated in English country style and delivers old-fashioned service that even stretches to chauffeur-driven cars. Elegant rooms, beautiful interior garden and gourmet restaurant. Extensive conference facilities. **www.stanhope.be**

GREATER BRUSSELS

Alliance Hotel
🔲 P 🍴 €

Avenue Imperatrice Charlotte 6, 1020 Brussels **Tel** *(02) 478 7080* **Fax** *(02) 478 1000* **Rooms** *79*

This hotel near the Brussels Exhibition Centre is well-located for reaching central Brussels thanks to the nearby metro station. Rooms are basic but comfortable. The well-equipped business centre includes meeting and conference facilities. Hotel restaurant and bar. Complimentary breakfast and parking.

Key to Price Guide *see p136* **Key to Symbols** *see back cover flap*

Gresham Belson

Chaussee de Louvain 805, 1140 Brussels **Tel** (02) 708 3100 **Fax** (02) 708 3166 **Rooms** 135

A welcoming hotel on the outskirts of central Brussels, the Belson offers standard and deluxe rooms with business amenities and a popular bar and restaurant. Small fitness centre. Close to Brussels airport. Meeting room and conference facilities. **www.gresham-hotels-brussels.com**

Husa President Park

Boulevard du Roi Albert II 44, 1000 Brussels **Tel** (02) 203 2020 **Fax** (02) 203 2440 **Rooms** 300

This modern but luxurious hotel next to a wide stretch of public park is a popular choice for business travellers and is within driving distance of central Brussels. The 300 rooms are spacious and family friendly. Delightful red-brick hotel restaurant. Impressive fitness centre. **www.husapresidentpark.com**

Les Tourelles

Winston Churchill Avenue 135, 1180 Brussels **Tel** (02) 344 9573 **Fax** (02) 346 4270 **Rooms** 21

A fantastically atmospheric hotel with fake medieval turrets and a faux rustic façade, the three-star Les Tourelles has an old-fashioned feel with old stone fireplaces and antique wooden furnishings. Located south of the centre, the hotel benefits from good transport links. Welcoming staff. **www.lestourelles.be**

Best Western County House

Square des Heros 2–4, 1180 Brussels **Tel** (02) 375 4420 **Fax** (02) 375 3122 **Rooms** 100

A comfortable and efficient hotel in a peaceful, park-side location south of central Brussels and close to the financial district. Rooms are spacious and modern with business-friendly facilities. Complimentary buffet breakfast. Meeting and conference centre. **www.bestwestern.be**

Eurostars Montgomery

Map 4 E4

Avenue de Tervueren 134, 1150 Brussels **Tel** (02) 741 8511 **Fax** (02) 741 8500 **Rooms** 63

A five-star hotel with a relaxed atmosphere and plenty of period furnishings, the elegant rooms in the Montgomery are individually decorated in diverse colours and styles. The restaurant is well-reputed and the staff are happy to provide sightseeing advice. **www.eurostarsmontgomery.com**

Hotel Capital

191 Chaussée de Vleurgat, 1050 Brussels **Tel** (02) 646 6420 **Fax** (02) 646 3314 **Rooms** 62

Located near Avenue Louise, Hotel Capital is just south of the historical centre of Brussels. Rooms are modern and comfortable with more luxurious suites also available, including longer-stay suites with kitchenettes. Breakfast can be taken on the terrace in the summer. Private underground parking. **www.hotelcapital.be**

Kasteel Gravenhof

Alsembergesteenweg 676, 1653 Dworp **Tel** (02) 380 4499 **Fax** (02) 380 4060 **Rooms** 26

The Kasteel Gravenhof is a stately castle hotel in the middle of a magnificent stretch of parkland, south of the city centre, that offers an elegant break in a peaceful setting. Built in 1649, the castle rooms have all the period fittings and luxurious furnishings you would expect from its genteel surroundings. **www.gravenhof.be**

Monty Hotel

Map 4 F3

101 Brand Whitlock Boulevard, 1200 Brussels **Tel** (02) 734 5636 **Fax** (02) 734 5005 **Rooms** 18

A small "design hotel" to the east of central Brussels, the Hotel Monty's rooms are carefully decorated to contemporary tastes with luxurious bathrooms and colourful, modern furnishings. Communal lounge, bar and private gardens. Breakfast is included. All furniture is individually produced by local designers. **www.monty-hotel.be**

Thon Hotel Bristol Stephanie

Map 2 D5

Avenue Louise 91–93, 1050 Brussels **Tel** (02) 543 3311 **Fax** (02) 538 0307 **Rooms** 142

The luxurious rooms in this five-star hotel on Brussels' fashionable Avenue Louise have been decorated in traditional Norwegian style – one even has its own private sauna! Suites have four-poster beds and dainty antique furnishings. Elegant restaurant serving tasty French cuisine. **www.thonhotels.be/bristolstephanie**

Marriott Courtyard

Avenue des Olympiades 6, 1140 Brussels **Tel** (02) 337 0808 **Fax** (02) 337 0800 **Rooms** 191

The Marriott Courtyard is a modern hotel in the city's financial district near Brussels airport, and is a good choice for business travellers. Built in 2004, rooms are comfortable and spacious with business amenities. Bar and brasserie serving Belgian and French fare. There is a 24-hour fitness centre. **www.courtyardbrussels.com**

Park Hotel

Map 4 D3

Avenue de L'Yser 21–22, 1040 Brussels **Tel** (02) 735 7400 **Fax** (02) 735 1967 **Rooms** 53

A Best Western hotel just in front of the Parc du Cinquantenaire, the Park Hotel occupies a renovated, 1903 mansion. Rooms are spacious and elegant with antique furnishings and modern facilities. The price includes breakfast. Health club and sauna. Business centre. Private garden. Transport network close by. **www.parkhotelbrussels.be**

Sofitel Louise

Map 2 D5

Avenue de la Toison d'Or 40, 1050 Brussels **Tel** (02) 514 2200 **Fax** (02) 514 5744 **Rooms** 170

South of the Grand Place, near Avenue Louise, the Sofitel Toison d'Or is well-placed for exploring the city's antique shops and museums. Rooms are modern and comfortable. Bar, four meeting rooms for up to 200 people and fitness centre. Baby-sitting service by request. Good transport links to centre of town. **www.sofitel.com**

Conrad International

Avenue Louise 71, 1050 Brussels **Tel** *(02) 542 4242* **Fax** *(02) 542 4200* **Rooms** *266*   **Map** *2 D5*

A grand hotel on Brussels' main shopping street, Avenue Louise, the Conrad Brussels has large, luxurious rooms, business-friendly facilities and extensive leisure facilities. Spa treatments are available at extra cost. The Grand Place is just a 20-minute walk away. Excellent restaurant and lounge bar. Baby-sitting service. **www.conradhotels.com**

Manos Premier

Chaussée de Charleroi 100–106, 1060 Brussels **Tel** *(02) 537 9682* **Fax** *(02) 539 3655* **Rooms** *53*

Close to its sister hotel, Manos Stephanie near Avenue Louise, the five-star Manos Premier is full of character and charm. Rooms and suites are individually decorated with elegant Louis XV and XVI period furniture. Spa and fitness centre. Peaceful private garden. Luxury restaurant. The price includes breakfast. **www.manoshotel.com**

Manos Stephanie

Chaussée de Charleroi 28, 1060 Brussels **Tel** *(02) 539 0250* **Fax** *(02) 537 5729* **Rooms** *56*

An elegant four-star hotel, Manos Stephanie is situated just south of the centre in a converted townhouse near Avenue Louise. The rooms are spacious with some charming features, including antique furnishings and marble bathrooms. The Duplex Suite has a circular wooden stairwell. Breakfast included. Meeting facilities. **www.manoshotel.com**

ANTWERP

Boulevard Leopold

Belgielei 135, 2018 Antwerp **Tel** *(03) 225 5218* **Rooms** *5*

Housed in a beautiful mansion in the atmospheric Jewish Quarter, this hotel offers grandeur without grand prices. It is the result of painstaking restoration by its friendly owners. As such, the high-ceilinged rooms, with large windows, original inlaid floors and works of art, ooze quality and charm. **www.boulevard-leopold.be**

Postiljon

Blauwmoezelstraat 6, 2000 Antwerp **Tel** *(03) 231 7575* **Fax** *(03) 226 8450* **Rooms** *21*

You can't get more central than this: the Postiljon is next to Antwerp's magnificent cathedral. Even better, it easily wins the contest for the city's best bargain hotel. The rooms are smart and comfortable; ask for one with a view of the cathedral. There is no breakfast, but that's not a problem given the number of excellent cafés in the area. **www.hotelpostiljon.be**

Antwerp Hilton

Groenplaats, 2000 Antwerp **Tel** *(03) 204 1212* **Fax** *(03) 204 8688* **Rooms** *210*

Well-located next to the historical cathedral, the Antwerp Hilton has some great views over the city's sights. An architectural landmark (it sits behind a listed Baroque façade), the hotel occupies part of the former Grand Bazar department store. Rooms are business-friendly with Wi-Fi Internet connections. **www.hilton.com**

Firean

Karel Oomsstraat 6, 2018 Antwerp **Tel** *(03) 237 0260* **Fax** *(03) 238 1168* **Rooms** *15*

A welcoming, four-star hotel in an early-20th century Art Deco mansion. With crystal chandeliers in the lounge, antique furnishings in the rooms and a secluded garden, the hotel offers its own unique version of luxury. Well-reputed hotel restaurant. Breakfast is included in the price. **www.hotelfirean.com**

Hotel O

Handschoenmarkt 3, 2000 Antwerp **Tel** *(03) 292 6510* **Fax** *(03) 292 6520* **Rooms** *37*

Situated opposite Antwerp Cathedral in the city's medieval centre, Hotel O is a state-of-the-art hotel offering spacious, well designed rooms with luxurious bathrooms. Ask for a room with a cathedral view. A buffet breakfast is available at an extra cost. **www.hotelhotelo.be**

Rubens Grote Markt

Oude Beurs 29, 2000 Antwerp **Tel** *(03) 226 9582* **Fax** *(03) 225 1940* **Rooms** *36*

This quietly-situated four-star hotel, just a short walk from the Grand Place, offers deluxe accommodation, including spacious double rooms and a romantic junior suite with private terrace. Rooms have views into the hotel garden or over to the city cathedral. Complimentary buffet breakfast. Paid parking. **www.hotelrubensantwerp.be**

Plaza

Charlottalei 49, 2018 Antwerp **Tel** *(03) 287 2870* **Fax** *(03) 287 2871* **Rooms** *81*

Priding itself on its personal touch, the four-star Plaza Hotel has rooms that have each been individually decorated by the owner – most even have a walk-in dressing room. Staff are on hand to offer tourist information and restaurant advice. Complimentary buffet breakfast. Paid parking. **www.plaza.be**

't Sandt

Zand 13–19, 2000 Antwerp **Tel** *(03) 232 9390* **Fax** *(03) 232 5613* **Rooms** *29*

A cosy four-star hotel in Antwerp's historical centre, 't Sandt occupies a protected Neo-Rococo building from the mid-19th century that was the site of the city's first customs duty office. The rooms and apartments are individually decorated. The Cathedral Penthouse has one of the city's best views. Breakfast included. **www.hotel-sandt.be**

Key to Price Guide *see p136* **Key to Symbols** *see back cover flap*

De Witte Lelie
P ©©©©©

Keizerstraat 16–18, 2000 Antwerp **Tel** *(03) 226 1966* **Fax** *(03) 234 0019* **Rooms** *10*

An atmospheric five-star B&B in Antwerp's historical core, the whitewashed De Witte Lelie ("The White Lily") is constructed out of three converted 17th-century canal houses. Rooms have great city views and a luxurious mix of white-linen sofas, antique furnishings and modern facilities. Breakfast buffet included. **www.dewittelelie.be**

BRUGES

de Pauw
P 11 ©

Sint Gilliskerkhof 8, 8000 Bruges **Tel** *(050) 33 7118* **Fax** *(050) 34 5140* **Rooms** *8*   **Map** *B2*

The welcoming de Pauw is a family-run two-star hotel in a quiet area just outside Bruges' historical centre. Rooms are basic, but spacious and comfortably furnished, with modern bathrooms. Breakfast included. Good restaurant serving traditional Belgian cuisine. Parking on the street beside the hotel. Half-board available. **www.hoteldepauw.be**

Bourgoensch Hof
P 11 ©©

Wollestraat 39, 8000 Bruges **Tel** *(050) 33 1645* **Fax** *(050) 34 6378* **Rooms** *25*   **Map** *B3*

Situated in Bruges' historical centre near the central market, this three-star hotel boasts some fabulous canal-side views. Rooms are simple, but well presented; most visitors to both the hotel and its bistro come for the views. Hotel bistro with outdoor terrace. The price includes breakfast. Paid parking available on request. **www.bourgoensch-hof.be**

Hotel Heritage
P ©©©

Niklaas Desparsstraat 11, 8000 Bruges **Tel** *(050) 44 4444* **Fax** *(050) 44 4440* **Rooms** *24*   **Map** *A3*

A four-star hotel which aims to pamper its visitors: some rooms have their own Jacuzzi baths; others are decorated with fine Italian fabrics. State-of-the-art technology in each room. Prices do not include breakfast, fitness facilities, Internet connection or underground parking. **www.hotel-heritage.com**

Ter Brughe
P ©©©

Oost Gistelhof 2, 8000 Bruges **Tel** *(050) 34 0324* **Fax** *(050) 33 8873* **Rooms** *46*   **Map** *B2*

This charming hotel in a converted 16th-century family home has luxury rooms with private terraces, antique furnishings and great canal views. Even the standard rooms have wood-beamed ceilings. Breakfast takes place in the hotel's medieval basement. Garage parking must be reserved in advance. **www.hotelterbrughe.com**

Hotel de Tuilerieën
P ©©©©©

Dyver 7, 8000 Bruges **Tel** *(050) 34 3691* **Fax** *(050) 34 0400* **Rooms** *45*   **Map** *B4*

A luxurious four-star hotel with indoor pool, the Hotel de Tuilerieën offers a deluxe break in the heart of Bruges' medieval centre. Rooms are spacious and elegantly decorated with four-poster beds and antique furnishings. Stately breakfast dining room with banquet tables and crystal chandeliers. **www.hoteltuilerieen.com**

GHENT

Cour St Georges
P ©©

Hoogpoort 75–77, 9000 Ghent **Tel** *(09) 224 2424* **Fax** *(09) 224 2640* **Rooms** *31*   **Map** *F2*

This well-priced and superbly-located Best Western hotel in the centre of Ghent occupies a historic building, which explains the establishment's unique décor (including painted panels in the breakfast room). The rooms in the attic have great views over the historical centre. (Note: there is no lift). Breakfast included. **www.bestwestern.be**

Gravensteen
P ©©

Jan Breydelstraat 35, 9000 Ghent **Tel** *(09) 225 1150* **Fax** *(09) 225 1850* **Rooms** *49*   **Map** *E1*

An elegant hotel in a converted 19th-century mansion, the Gravensteen has been decorated in keeping with its stately exterior, including an impressive marble stairwell. Rooms are simple but comfortable with modern facilities. Fitness room with sauna. Dinner for groups (but not individuals) by request. **www.gravensteen.be**

The Boatel
P ©©

Voorhoutkaai 44, 9000 Ghent **Tel** *(09) 267 1030* **Fax** *(09) 267 1039* **Rooms** *5*

The two-star Boatel is a floating hotel constructed from a converted canal boat! Moored in Portus Ganda, a short walk from the centre of town, its five cosy rooms (three standard and two luxury) are carefully decorated in various styles. Great river views. Breakfast is included. Evening entertainment with barbecue in good weather. **www.theboatel.com**

Ghent River Hotel
©©©

Waaistraat 5+, 9000 Ghent **Tel** *(09) 266 1010* **Fax** *(09) 266 1015* **Rooms** *77*   **Map** *F1*

This four-star riverside hotel occupies a mid-19th century rice mill on the banks of the River Leie. Although the entrance is modern, the rooms are more in keeping with the building's rich history, including wood-beamed ceilings and wooden floors. Fitness room with sauna. **www.ghent-river-hotel.be**

For Bruges and Ghent map references *refer to the inside back cover*

WHERE TO EAT

It is almost impossible to eat badly in Brussels. Some say one can eat better here than in Paris, and even meals in the lower- to mid-price bracket are always carefully prepared and often innovative. Venues range from top gastronomic restaurants to unpretentious local taverns where you can find generous

Thai chef in Brussels

servings of local specialities such as *moules-frites* (mussels and French fries). If you tire of Belgian fare, try the variety of excellent local seafood and the range of ethnic cuisine that reflects the city's lively cultural diversity. The listings on pp152–61 give recommendations on where to eat in Antwerp, Bruges and Ghent.

Brasserie Horta in Centre Belge de la Bande Dessinée *(see p152)*

WHERE TO EAT

The Belgian love affair with dining out makes for an astonishing concentration of restaurants and eateries: a 10-minute stroll from almost anywhere in Brussels should bring you to a decent, and often almost undiscovered, tavern or brasserie. However, superb dining is to be had without leaving the Ilôt Sacré, the area around the central Grand Place, where many very good and surprisingly reasonable restaurants abound. Beware the tourist traps around the Grand Place that make their living from gulling unwary visitors into spending far more than they intended to. The bill for a seemingly cheap meal may soar once expensive drinks have been added. The impressive displays of seafood adorning the pavements of Rue des Bouchers northwest of the Grand Place and Petite Rue des Bouchers can promote rather touristy restaurants, but those on p154 are recommended.

TYPES OF CUISINE

Elsewhere in the city centre is a wealth of quality fish restaurants, especially around the former fish market at Place Ste-Catherine, while the city's trendiest eateries can be found on Rue Dansaert and in the Place Saint-Géry district. If you are planning to explore other parts of Brussels, or if you are staying outside the city centre, you will find plenty of good Belgian fare on offer in the southern communes of Ixelles and Saint-Gilles, and in Etterbeek, where the European Commission buildings are located. Ixelles also boasts the largest concentration of Vietnamese and Southeast Asian restaurants, especially around Chaussée de Boondael. This student area in the Matonge district is also home to several African restaurants, serving food from the Congo (formerly Zaire), Senegal and Rwanda.

North of the city centre, in the communes of Schaerbeek and Saint-Josse, Turkish and North African communities have sprung up, and excellent Moroccan and Tunisian cuisine is commonplace. There is also a growing trend for "designer couscous", with Belgian restaurateurs exploiting the popularity of North African food in spectacularly ornate venues, often featuring ethnic music in the evenings.

Spanish and Portuguese restaurants can be found in the Marolles district and in Saint-Gilles, reflecting the wave of immigration in the 1950s and 1960s when many southern Europeans chose to settle in Brussels. The city is also liberally sprinkled with Greek restaurants, although

many veer on the over-touristy side. A better bet are the modern Latin American eateries.

VEGETARIANS

Despite a marked upturn in recent years, Brussels is far from being a vegetarian-friendly city, since there are only a handful of specialist vegetarian restaurants. However, those who eat fish will find mainstream restaurants cater generously to their needs; Brussels is very strong on fish and seafood. Also, the traditional dish, *stoemp*, mashed potatoes mixed with root vegetables, is a classic vegetarian speciality. North African restaurants usually offer vegetarian couscous courses, and there are plenty of Italian options. Indian restaurants are few and far between, but most offer vegetable curries. Vegans may struggle, particularly in European restaurants. Some health food shops have a café serving vegan dishes.

Place settings at the restaurant La Truffe Noire *(see p158)*

The opulent Belle Epoque dining room of the Belga Queen *(see p153)*

HOW MUCH TO PAY

Most restaurants, taverns and cafés display a menu in the window and the majority take credit cards. Prices usually include VAT (21 per cent) and service (16 per cent), although it is worth checking the latter before you tip. In tourist and shopping districts, visitors should also check that menu prices inside match those shown as special menu deals in the window.

A meal at the city's most luxurious restaurants can cost up to €150 per head, but you can eat superbly for around €50 per head (including wine) and a hearty snack in a tavern should cost no more than €15. The mark-up level on wine can be very high, especially in most Mediterranean restaurants and in obviously touristic areas, but most taverns do a reasonable *vin maison* and serve myriad varieties of beer.

Service in all but the most expensive restaurants can be erratic by British and US standards. But beneath the sometimes grumpy exterior, you will often find warmth and an earthy, cheerfully self-deprecating sense of humour that is unique to Belgium. There are no hard and fast rules, but some diners leave an additional tip of up to 10 per cent if they are especially satisfied with the quality of the meal and the service. Note that some restaurants cannot take service on a credit card slip, and this, plus the tip, will have to be paid in cash, as do other gratuities in the city.

DINING ON A BUDGET

Many restaurants offer bargain, fixed-price or rapid lunchtime menus for under €12.50, plus a selection of reasonably priced dishes of the day. Even when dining at

Stall selling freshly made snacks in Saint-Gilles at the weekend

the city's most expensive eateries you can find similar deals, meaning you can sample haute cuisine for less than €37. In the evening, look out for set menus with *vin compris* (wine included),

which are often a way to save a significant part of the dining bill. If wine is not included, opting to have a beer or a single glass of wine rather than a bottle can keep drinks costs down.

At the other end of the scale, Brussels has most of the usual fast-food outlets, and sandwiches are sold at most butchers or delicatessens *(traiteurs)*, usually with tuna, cheese or cold meat fillings. Some of the latter offer sit-down snacks too. Alternatively, take advantage of Belgium's national dish, *frites/frieten* (French fries, hand-cut and double-fried to ensure an even crispiness). There are *Friteries/Frituurs* all over town, serving enormous portions of French fries (traditionally in a paper cone) with mayonnaise and dozens of other sauces, plus *fricadelles* (sausages in batter), lamb kebabs, fish cakes or meatballs. Inevitably, these establishments vary in quality; one sure bet is Maison Antoine on Place Jourdan in Etterbeek, where they have been frying for over half a century.

Most cafés and taverns offer *petite restauration* (light meals) on top or instead of a regular menu. These simple, traditional snacks include croque monsieur, shrimp croquettes, chicory baked with ham and cheese, salads, spaghetti bolognaise and *américain* (raw minced beef with seasoning). Do not be fooled by the word "light" – most of these dishes will keep you going from lunchtime well into the evening.

The contemporary interior of Lola, a fashionable Brussels brasserie *(see p155)*

Entrance of the historic tavern
In 't Spinnekopke *(see p153)*

BUDGET FOOD

Brussels is home to a sizeable
Turkish community which
means that kebab, gyros and
pitta restaurants are
ubiquitous, especially in the
busy Saint-Josse neighbourhood and on the gaudy Rue
du Marché aux Fromages, just
off the Grand Place. The
nearby L'Express, a Lebanese
takeaway specializing in
chicken and felafel pittas,
generously crammed with
fresh salad, is perhaps a
better bet.
    Ethnic food can work out at
a very reasonable price; large
portions of couscous, pizzas
and African specialities are
often to be found at good
rates in student areas to the
south and at stands throughout the city. There are also
numerous Indian and Chinese
restaurants, which offer
decent takeaway food at an
affordable price.

BREAKFAST AND SNACKS

Especially good breakfasts –
as well as inventive light
lunches and snacks – with an
emphasis on vegetarian
dishes are the staple of
L'Ultime Atome *(see p157)*, a
bustling brasserie situated in
the St Boniface quarter of the
city. Breakfasting in a café or
brasserie, such as the Belgian
chain, Le Pain Quotidien (Het
Dagelijks Brood in Dutch), is
recommended if breakfast is
not included in your hotel
accommodation. For snackers
who are sweet-toothed, waffle
stands or vans appear on
almost every street corner,

Open-air tables outside fish
restaurants in Rue des Bouchers

while cafés and taverns offer
a tempting variety of waffles
(which can be topped with
jam, cream or chocolate).
Sweet pancakes *(crêpes/
pannekoeken)*, with lemon
and sugar or chocolate, are
just as popular – and filling –
although you can cut down
on the number of calories
with a savoury wholewheat
pancake at one of the city's
many crêperies.

OPENING TIMES

Time-consuming business
lunches are still part of the
culture in Belgium and most
restaurants serve lunch from
noon until 2 or 3pm. Dinner
is generally served from 7pm
onwards and last orders are
taken as late as 10pm. Late-
night restaurants, serving until
midnight, can be found in the
side streets of downtown
Brussels and a handful
provide meals after 1am.
Breakfast bars usually open
around 7am. For details of
café and bar opening times,
see pp162–7.

MAKING A RESERVATION

When visiting one of the
more celebrated restaurants, it
is always wise to book in
advance. The listings indicate
where booking is advisable. If
you plan on going to the
legendary Comme Chez Soi
(see p154), you should
reserve weeks ahead rather
than hope for a last-minute
cancellation. Trendy designer
restaurants are often crowded
but usually take reservations
well in advance. If you
change your mind, make sure
you cancel the reservation.

READING THE MENU

Menus at most restaurants are
written in French, sometimes
in Dutch and French. Some,
especially in tourist areas, may
have explanations in English.
Dishes of the day or suggestions are often illegibly
scribbled on black-
boards. Fortunately,
most waiters speak
some English and
should be able to help.
You may find a food
dictionary useful. For
details of some of the
most popular Belgian
specialities, see pp148–
9. The phrasebook on
pp205–208 also gives
translations of many
menu items.

ORDERING FOOD

On the whole, Belgians
like to eat beef fairly
rare. If you ask for a

The elegant interior of La Rose Blanche in the Upper Town *(see p155)*

The 16th-century cellar of 't Kelderke in the Grand Place *(see p153)*

medium-rare steak, it is likely to be cooked more rare than medium. The quality of the beef usually justifies light cooking, but if you want your meat well done, insist on it, and ignore any raised eyebrows. Lamb is also served rare; if you don't like it that way, ask for it to be well done when you order. Use the phrase-book at the back of this guide to help you when ordering food.

The logo of a Latin American restaurant

ETIQUETTE

Brussels is less relaxed than, say, Amsterdam and, although casual or smart-casual dress is acceptable in most restaurants, you will probably feel more at home dressing up for upmarket places. A few formal restaurants will insist on a jacket and tie for men. The dress code for women is more flexible, but smartness is appreciated.

PETS

Do not be surprised to see a dog sat beneath the next-door table. The Belgians are great dog lovers and many bars and cafés have a relaxed attitude to clients bringing their pets.

CHILDREN

In general, Brussels is child-friendly, perhaps because Belgian children tend to be well behaved in restaurants.

Many establishments have children's menus, although they are not always a bargain, and several offer free meals for children under 12. High-chairs should be available on request, and some restaurants have inside play areas, including some of the big hotels, where children are usually welcome. On the outskirts of Brussels or near one of the parks, eateries can offer extensive outside playgrounds. Ethnic restaurants, in particular Vietnamese, Greek and the less formal Italian ones, tend to be especially accommodating. They do not always have children's menus, but are happy for adults to share their meal with youngsters. Children are usually allowed in cafés and bars although

they are forbidden to drink alcohol. Some restaurants may be too formal for children to feel comfortable.

SMOKING

Brussels is still very much a smokers' city, although smoking is forbidden inside restaurants, bars and cafés. Many bars and restaurants provide their customers with outdoor heated terraces where smoking is permitted. It is important, therefore, to make sure you ask about smoking arrangements when reserving, or before you take a seat. Smokers should know that most restaurants and cafés do not sell cigarettes.

DISABLED FACILITIES

Facilities for the disabled are poor in Brussels, although there have been some improvements. The cobbled streets and hilly areas may be difficult to negotiate, but most people will go out of their way to offer assistance. There is a limited number of restaurants with ramps and ground-floor bathrooms, so do check the extent of the access before making a reservation or taking a seat. A list of restaurants and cafés equipped with disabled facilities is published by a Walloon charity, contact AWIPH at Rue de la Rivelaine 11, 6061 Charleroi (071 205 711). www.awiph.be (website in French).

The Art Nouveau interior of Comme Chez Soi *(see p154)*

The Flavours of Brussels

Most Belgians are passionate about food and standards are generally very high. The many first-class grocers, greengrocers, butchers, fishmongers, bakers and pâtissiers, including Belgium's noted chocolatiers, are held in high public esteem, alongside the nation's top chefs and restauranteurs. In Brussels, the culinary heart of the country, there are a wide range of fine eateries to suit all budgets, serving both sophisticated Walloon (Belgian-French) dishes alongside more basic, hearty Flemish fare. A history of invasion has also added a dash of other European culinary traditions, particularly those of Spain and Austria.

Belgian chocolates

Bunches of white asparagus, some of Belgium's finest produce

THE NORTH SEA

Brussels, being only 60 km (40 miles) from the North Sea, has a good supply of really fresh fish and seafood. In Place Sainte-Catherine, just to the west of the Grand Place, there used to be a bustling fish market and the area remains a centre for fish restaurants. The best sole, cod, turbot, skate, hake and monkfish, simply grilled or fried in butter, or swathed in a well-judged sauce, are always on the menu, along with huge platters of *fruits de mer* (mixed seafood).

A uniquely Belgian fish dish that is well worth seeking out and is *anguilles au vert (paling in't groen)*, which consists of large chunks of eel, cooked with a mass of finely chopped, fresh herbs.

PASTURE AND WOODLAND

The flat, reclaimed land of northern Belgium and the hills of the south are home to herds of cattle. Quality beef is the stock-in-trade of any Belgian butcher, and *steak-frites* (steak and chips) is a classic dish on bistro menus. Belgians are so confident in their beef that they are happy to eat it raw: minced

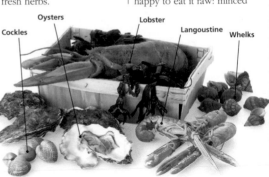

Oysters

Cockles

Lobster

Langoustine

Whelks

Selection of fine quality North-Sea seafood

LOCAL DISHES AND SPECIALITIES

Although Belgian chefs produce some of the world's most complex and sophisticated cooking, many of Belgium's great classic dishes are relatively simple, striking a healthy balance between nourishment and pleasure. Fine examples include steaming platefuls of *moules-frites* and warming stews such as *carbonnade flamades* and *waterzooï* (which is made with either fish or chicken) all dishes that might well be labelled as "comfort" food. However, the quality of the ingredients and the skill put into the making of such dishes in Belgium invariably turns such homely fare into a feast. Desserts include a host of sweet tarts and the ever-popular waffles. Endive, almost the national vegetable, gets in here too, as a flavouring for ice cream.

Endives

Moules-frites *Mussels, steamed in their own juices with onion and white wine, are served with chips and mayonnaise.*

Fish restaurant in the elegant Galéries St-Hubert shopping arcade

must be the potato, in the form of chips (French fries). *Frites* (*frietjes*), served with a dollop of mayonnaise, are a favourite street-food.

THE PÂTISSIER

No Belgian community is without a pâtisserie, selling superlative tarts, cakes and biscuits, and many pâtissiers double-up as chocolatiers. *Gaufres* (waffles) are another great sweet treat, sold at specialist shops and street stalls. Enjoyed freshly made, topped with knobs of butter and a sprinkling of sugar, they may be raised to perfection with spoonfuls of jam or fruit and fresh cream.

in *steak à l'américaine* (or *steak tartare*) and on toast as the snack, *toast cannibale*. Dairy cattle are the source of fine cheeses, such as Herve, Chimay and Maredsous.

Pork products include a range of sausages, patés and the noted Ardennes ham. In autumn and winter, look out for game, such as wild boar, pheasant and venison, often served in a rich fruity sauce. Quail, guinea fowl, pigeon and rabbit are also popular.

THE VEGETABLE PATCH

Not long ago, most Belgian householders toiled to fill their gardens with tightly-packed rows of top-class vegetables – beans, leeks, lettuces, carrots, potatoes and onions. This tradition may be waning, but the same quest for quality lives

on in commercial market-gardens. In the 1840s, Belgian gardeners created *chicon* (*witloof*) by forcing the roots of the chicorée lettuce. It is now one of Belgium's most widely used vegetables, although the most popular

Freshly made waffles on a street stall, a familiar sight in the city

ON THE MENU

White asparagus An early summer speciality, it is usually served with melted butter or hard-boiled egg and parsley.

Jets d'houblon Spring menus feature this dish of young hop shoots in a creamy sauce.

Crevettes grises Tiny but big on flavour, these "grey" shrimps are a popular snack.

Stoemp Mashed potato, with flecks of vegetables or meat, make up this pub favourite.

Garnaalkroketten Deep-fried croquettes, filled with shrimp.

Speculoos These buttery, spicy biscuits are available in festive shapes for Christmas.

Carbonnades flamandes *Beef is cooked in Belgian beer, with a touch of sugar, to make this hearty casserole.*

Waterzooî *This classic stew from Ghent consists of fish or chicken and vegetables, poached in a creamy broth.*

Flamiche aux Poireaux *Leeks, fried in butter and whisked with cream and eggs, are baked in a crisp pastry shell.*

Belgian Beer

Belgium makes more beers, in a greater mix of styles and flavours, than any other country in the world. The Belgian citizen drinks on average 100 litres (200 pints) a year, and even small bars will stock at least 20 varieties. The nation's breweries produce over 400 different beers.

Gambrinus, legendary Beer King

The cheerful peasants in Brueghel the Elder's 16th-century medieval village scenes would have been drinking beer from their local brewery, many of which had been active since the 11th century, as every small town and community produced its own beer. By 1900 there remained 3,000 private breweries throughout Belgium. Today, more than 100 still operate, with experts agreeing that even large industrial concerns produce a fine quality beer.

Detail from *The Wedding Dance* by Pieter Brueghel the Elder

TRAPPIST BEERS

Chimay label with authentic Trappist mark

Label for Westmalle Trappist beer

The most revered of refreshments, Belgium's Trappist beers have been highly rated since the Middle Ages when monks began brewing them. The drink originated in Roman times when Belgium was a province of Gaul, Gallia Belgica. Beer was a private domestic product until the monasteries took over and introduced hops to the process. Today's production is still controlled solely by the five Trappist monasteries, although the brewers are mostly laymen. Trappist beers are characterized by their rich, yeasty flavour. They are very strong, ranging from 6.2 to 11 per cent in alcohol content by volume. The most celebrated of the 20 brands is Chimay, brewed at Belgium's largest monastic brewery in Hainaut. This delicate but potent bottled beer has three different strengths, and is best kept for many years before drinking. The strongest Trappist beer is Westvleteren, from Ypres.

Chimay served in its correct glass

LAMBIC BEERS

Made for centuries in the Senne Valley around Brussels, the unique family of lambic beers are made using yeasts naturally present in the air to ferment the beer, rather than being added separately to the water and grain mix. Containers of unfermented wort (water, wheat and barley) are left under a half-open roof in the brewery and wild airborne yeasts, only present in the atmosphere of this region of Belgium, descend to ferment it. Unlike the sterility of many breweries and officially exempt from EU hygiene regulations, lambic cellars are deliberately left dusty and uncleaned in order for the necessary fungal activity to thrive. Matured in untreated wooden casks for up to five years, the lambic is deliciously sour to drink, with a moderate strength of 5 per cent alcohol.

Young and old lambic beers are blended together to produce the variant of gueuze. A tiny bead, distinctive champagne mousse and a toasty, slightly acid flavour, are its main characteristics. Bars and restaurants lay down their gueuze for up to 2 years before it is drunk.

Lambic cherry beer

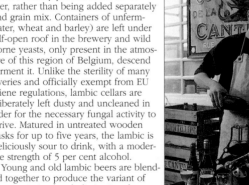

Brewer sampling beer from the vat at a brewery outside Brussels

SPECIALITY BELGIAN BEERS

Duvel

Chimay

Brugse Tripel

De Verboden Frucht

Kwak

Speciality beers are common in Belgium, where the huge variety of brands includes unusual tastes and flavours. Fruit beers are a Brussels speciality but are available throughout the country. The most popular, kriek, is traditionally made with bitter cherries grown in the Brussels suburb of Schaerbeek; picked annually, these are added to the lambic and allowed to macerate, or steep. The distinctive almond tang comes from the cherry stone. Raspberries are also used to make a framboise beer, or frambozen.

For a characterful amber ale, Kwak is good choice. Strong beers are also popular; apart from the Trappist beers, of which

Fruit beer mat of Chapeau brewery

Chimay is a popular variety, the pilseners De Verboden Frucht (meaning "forbidden fruit") and Duvel ("devil") are almost as strong as red wine. Brugse Tripel, from Bruges, is also popular. Even Belgium's best-sellers, Jupiler and Stella Artois, are good quality beers.

The façade of a beer emporium in Brussels

BLANCHE BEERS

Belgium's refreshing wheat beers are known as "blanche", or white beers, because of the cloudy sediment that forms when they ferment. Sour, crisp and light, they are relatively low in alcohol at 5 per cent. Blanche is produced in the western region of Hoegaarden, after which the best-known blanche is named. Many people now serve them with a slice of lemon to add to the refreshing taste, especially on warm summer evenings.

Hoegaarden

HOW TO DRINK BELGIAN BEER

There are no snobbish distinctions made in Belgium between bottled and casked beer. Some of the most prestigious brews are served in bottles, and, as with casks, bottles are often laid down to mature. The choice of drinking glass, however, is a vital part of the beer-drinking ritual. Many beers must be drunk in a particular glass, which the barman will supply, ranging from goblets to long thin drinking tubes. Beers are often served with a complementary snack; cream cheese on rye bread and radishes are a popular accompaniment.

The traditional drinkers' snack of *fromage blanc* on rye bread

Choosing a Restaurant

The restaurants in this guide have been selected for their good value, food, character and location. Restaurants in Brussels are listed by area, followed by a selection in Antwerp, Bruges, and Ghent. Restaurants within the same price category are listed alphabetically. For map references see pp190–93.

PRICE CATEGORIES
The following price ranges are for a three-course evening meal for one, including a half-bottle of house wine, tax and service.

€ under €30
€€ €30–€40
€€€ €40–€50
€€€€ €50–€60
€€€€€ over €60

LOWER TOWN

Comocomo €
Rue Antoine Dansaert 19, 1000 **Tel** *(02) 503 0330* **Map** *1 C2*

In the middle of downtown Brussels, a stone's throw from trendy St Géry, Comocomo combines a Basque tapas restaurant with a sushi-bar-style conveyor belt. After shopping on Rue Antoine Dansaert, retire to this modern establishment and pick out generously portioned *pintxos* (pronounced "pintchos") as they slowly pass you by.

Den Teepot €
Rue des Chartreux 66, 1000 **Tel** *(02) 511 9402* **Map** *1 B2*

In a town not famed for its vegetarian options this Flemish vegetarian restaurant is a welcome addition. Located above its sister health-food shop, although not completely vegan, the owners try to minimize the amount of animal products used. Many of the dishes feature beans and pulses. Open for lunch only, noon–2pm, Monday to Saturday.

Le Pain Quotidien €
Rue Antoine Dansaert 16A, 1000 **Tel** *(02) 502 2361* **Map** *1 C2*

This is the original branch of the successful café chain, now found all over the city and throughout Belgium. Famed for its large communal tables and what are quite simply the best croissants and pain au chocolat in Brussels, it's also very good for delicious and inventive lunchtime salads. Products are 100% organic and there's free Wi-Fi as well.

Nüetnigenough €
Rue du Lombard 25, 1000 **Tel** *(02) 513 7884* **Map** *1 C3*

A Nüetnigenough, in Brussels dialect, means the type of person who can never have enough of anything. This Art Nouveau-style brasserie aims to offer more than enough in terms of food choice, quality, prices and service, and largely succeeds. The decor has Bauhaus and 1940s touches.

Arcadi €€
Rue d'Arenberg 1B, 1000 **Tel** *(02) 511 3343* **Map** *2 D2*

Producing arguably the best quiches in a city that has some outstanding quiche-making outlets, Arcadi has an enormous selection of these egg flans, although the salmon and broccoli variety is the most popular. The rochefort and broccoli quiche is spectacular among the vegetarian options, and they don't skimp on portions. Great cakes too.

Bifanas €€
Rue des Dominicains 30, 1000 **Tel** *(02) 502 2548*

If you've missed the numerous Portuguese-run street markets in the commune of St Gilles during August weekends, the inexpensive Bifanas serves a cheerful representation of the cuisine of the city's large Portuguese community. Fish is the order of the day, above all, the *bacalhau* (salt cod).

Bonsoir Clara €€
Rue Antoine Dansaert 22, 1000 **Tel** *(02) 502 0990* **Map** *1 C2*

From the same stable as the collection of hip bars in St Géry owned by Brussels' famed impresario, Frederic Nicolay, Bonsoir Clara is situated right in the middle of the fashion district. One of the prettiest restaurants in town, Clara is high on style and a honeypot for fashionistas. Closed Saturday and Sunday lunch.

Brasserie Horta €€
Rue des Sables 20, 1000 **Tel** *(02) 217 7271* **Map** *2 E2*

This brasserie doubles as the cafeteria in the lobby of the Centre Belge de Bande Desinée, yet its cuisine is as strong as any of Brussels' best restaurants. The building itself is a spectacular example of Art Nouveau architecture. If you tire of the comic book exhibits before the youngsters, there's also a bar, designed by Victor Horta himself.

Brussels Resto €€
Place St Catherine 3, 1000 **Tel** *(02) 502 3573* **Map** *1 C2*

This restaurant is located in the seafood restaurant quarter of Ste-Catherine and specializes in lobster and fish dishes, such as *bouillebaisse* from the North Sea, salmon with a béarnaise sauce and a whole selection of mussel dishes. There's a charming outside terrace, and prices are reasonable and service attentive.

Key to Symbols *see back cover flap*

Chez Léon

⚐ ☰ ♿ ▦   €€

Rue des Bouchers 18, 1000 **Tel** *(02) 511 1415*   **Map** *2 D2*

Founded in 1893, Chez Léon is a stalwart of traditional Belgian culinary standards among the generally mediocre restaurants of the Rue des Bouchers. There are several versions of the classic *moules et frites* on offer along with other Belgian staples like *lapin à la kriek* (rabbit in kriek beer) and *stoemp* (mashed potato).The children's menu is excellent.

Chez Patrick

⚐ ♿ ▦   €€

Rue des Chapeliers 6, 1000 **Tel** *(02) 511 9815*   **Map** *2 D3*

Located just off the Grand Place, Chéz Patrick is as warm and inviting as one of the plates of *carbonade a la flamande* they serve with such care and attention. It's a great place for sampling traditional Belgian cuisine in a relaxed setting, and the hearty lunchtime *plats du jour* are always excellent value.

In 't Spinnekopke

♿   €€

Place du Jardin aux Fleurs 1, 1000 **Tel** *(02) 511 8695*

A superb example of quality Belgian food can be found in this intimate former 17th-century coaching inn. In 't Spinnekopke (In the Spider's Head) has a strong range of unusual local brews and items on the menu that are cooked in them. Friendly service and a lovely terrace in an area that's off the beaten track. Closed Saturday lunch, Sunday.

L'Achepot

▦   €€

Place Ste-Catherine 1, 1000 **Tel** *(02) 511 6221*   **Map** *1 C2*

This small, family-run tavern with contemporary decor, which is located off the *Vismarkt* (fish market), serves seasonal fresh food, including oysters. The cuisine is French/Belgian, and the veal liver and meatballs are recommended. The lunch set menu is in €16. Closed Sunday and Monday.

La Cantina

▤ ⚐ ♿   €€

Rue du Jardin des Olives 13–15, 1000 **Tel** *(02) 513 4276*

Customers to La Cantina come for the restaurant's *feijoada*, the rather heavy Brazilian national dish of rice, red beans, pork, smoked bacon and spicy sausage. In fact, just about every last part of the pig is thrown in the pot, along with oranges and a traditional sauce. Closed Sunday.

La Kasbah

♿   €€

Rue Antoine Dansaert 20, 1000 **Tel** *(02) 502 4026*   **Map** *1 C2*

Next door to achingly cool Bonsoir Clara, La Kasbah is another of Frederic Nicolay's stylish dining projects. This time, however, the food really is something to write home about. The interior is dark and decked out with North African knick-knacks, and the attentive service and decent Moroccan wines ensure that it is always busy but intimate.

L'Element Terre

▦   €€

Chaussée de Waterloo 465, 1050

This little vegetarian restaurant aims to convert even the fiercest of carnivores by offering a mouth-watering array of world cuisine from Brazil to Senegal and Japan to Greece. There is a great selection of home-made patisserie to top it off. Their exotic fish and scampi is a treat. Closed Sunday and Monday.

Le Paon Royal

⚐ ♿ ▦   €€

Rue du Vieux Marché-aux-grains 6, 1000 **Tel** *(02) 513 0868*   **Map** *1 C2*

This handsome 17th-century house encloses a temple to traditional Belgian cuisine without pretensions or faddish fusion twists. In particular, the customers roll in for the veal in *kriek* (cherry) beer with Belgian endive. Good wine list, but a superb beer list.

Strofilia

▤ ⚐   €€

Rue du Marché aux Porcs 11–13, 1000 **Tel** *(02) 512 3293*

One of the best Greek restaurants in town also happens to be one of the most atmospheric of Brussels' many eateries. Amid candlelight and brick walls, try the Strofilia salad, which includes spinach, capers, scampi and calamari. Mains include aubergine (eggplant) minced-meat roulade and suckling pig. Closed Saturday lunch and Sunday.

't Kelderke

€€

Grand Place 15, 1000 **Tel** *(02) 513 7344*   **Map** *2 D3*

On the Grand Place, this vaulted cellar restaurant is as busy as you may expect but the feel is decidedly genuine as both locals and visitors dine here. *Moules-frites* (mussels and French fries) are served in their traditional, huge black pails at a fast and furious pace.

Belga Queen

♿   €€€

Rue Fossé aux Loups 32, 1000 **Tel** *(02) 217 2187*   **Map** *2 D2*

The chic Belga Queen, with its two bars – one for fancy beverages, the other for oysters – and cigar lounge, is located in the completely transformed former Hôtel de la Poste, a cavernous Belle Epoque bank. A special beer and tasting menu is available. The toilet cubicle doors are transparent, but go opaque as soon as you lock the door.

Big Mama

⚐ ▦   €€€

Place de la Vieille Halle aux Blés 41, 1000 **Tel** *(02) 513 3659*

Just a short walk from Grand Place is Big Mama. The warm and cosy decor adds to the friendly atmosphere and children are well catered for with their own menu. The monthly changing four-course set menu with an aperitif offers great value at €35. Closed Monday and Tuesday in winter; open daily April to October.

La Manufacture
Rue Notre-Dame du Sommeil 12, 1000 **Tel** *(02) 502 2525* **Map** *1 B2*

A hundred years ago, this venue northwest of the city was a printer's workshop, replaced 40 years later by the Delvaux leather factory. Now it is a very 21st-century dining establishment complete with polished wood and iron pillars. Cuisine leans towards the international with a French base. Good value two-course set lunch served Monday to Friday.

Le Variétés
Place Ste-Croix 4, 1050 **Tel** *(02) 647 0436*

Located on the ground floor of a magnificent Art Deco building, Le Variétés has totally recreated the atmosphere of a 1930s brasserie. The centrepiece of the dining room is the open kitchen complete with an impressive grill, hence the wide range of rotisserie and grilled dishes. The beef tartare with fresh herbs is particularly recommended.

Vismet
Place Sainte-Catherine 23, 1000 **Tel** *(02) 218 8545* **Map** *1 C2*

Wood panelling, old-school green-stemmed wine glasses and paper tablecloths give Vismet a 1970s Germanic feel, but the open concept kitchen is of a more contemporary era. Seafood specialist head chef and owner Tom Decroos is known to wander the dining room. Closed Sunday, Monday.

Aux Armes de Bruxelles
Rue des Bouchers 13, 1000 **Tel** *(02) 511 5550* **Map** *2 D2*

In the heart of the Ilôt Sacré restaurant area, Aux Armes de Bruxelles was a favourite haunt of Brussels' most famous *chanteur*, Jacques Brel, and remains popular for its seafood. The lobster, mussels and game are the key recommendations. Try the Belgian endive salad to start.

Jaloa
Place Ste-Catherine 5–7, 1000 **Tel** *(02) 512 1831*

Located near the charming *Vismarkt* area, site of the former fish market, in an 18th-century house once inhabited by Vincent van Gogh is Jaloa. The restaurant serves modern European cuisine, offering both à la carte dishes and a wide range of monthly changing set menus.

Comme Chez Soi
Place Rouppe 23, 1000 **Tel** *(02) 512 2921* **Map** *1 C4*

Widely regarded as the city's best restaurant, Comme Chez Soi, with its two Michelin stars, is particularly strong in the game department. A mahogany bar, a bookcase and over-stuffed leather couches all feature in the lounge area. The dessert trilogy is unmissable. Book well in advance. Closed Sunday, Monday, Wednesday lunch.

L'Alban Chambon
Hotel Métropole, Place de Brouckère, 31 1000 **Tel** *(02) 218 0220* **Map** *2 D2*

If your budget allows it, a meal at the award-winning restaurant of the grand Hotel Métropole *(see p138)*, with its luxurious Baroque decor and classic French cuisine is not to be missed. The diverse menu feaures lobster, *foie gras*, game, meat and fish dishes, all made with the finest ingredients. Closed Saturday lunchtime, Sunday, Monday, public holidays.

L'Ogenblik
Galeries des Princes 1, 1000 **Tel** *(02) 511 6151* **Map** *2 D2*

In the centre of the stunning Saint Hubert's Galleries, this established Parisian-style bistro with a relaxed ambience is a gastronomic wonder. Dishes such as salmon and crayfish cake, or carpaccio of scallops are a gourmand's delight. Closed Sunday.

Vincent
Rue des Dominicains 8–10, 1000 **Tel** *(02) 511 2607*

Brussels may be landlocked, but that hasn't stopped the proprietors of Vincent from indulging their maritime fantasies in the decoration of their restaurant. With a surfeit of dark-wood panelling and sea-themed murals, it is no surprise that their speciality is turbot served in a mousseline sauce. Closed first two weeks in August and January.

UPPER TOWN

Het Warm Water
Rue des Renards 25, 1000 **Tel** *(02) 513 9159.* **Map** *1 C5*

A pleasant little Flemish café at the top of the narrow Rue des Renards, this is the perfect rendezvous point at the end of an afternoon of antique hunting in the shops and centuries-old *marché aux puces* (flea market). Relax with some cake and a glass of gueuze while the antique dealers pack up their wares. Closed Monday–Wednesday.

La Grande Porte
Rue Notre-Seigneur 9, 1000 **Tel** *(02) 512 8998* **Map** *1 C4*

The Marolles district, where the old but dying Bruxelaire patois can still occasionally be heard, is often described as the most Bruxellois of Brussels districts. The convivial La Grande Porte offers mostly regional specialities such as *jambonneau* (pig's knuckle), *waterzooi* (stew) and *stoemp* (mashed potato) in huge portions. Closed Saturday lunch and Sunday.

Key to Price Guide *see p152* **Key to Symbols** *see back cover flap*

L'Entrée des Artistes
Place du Grand Sablon 42, 1000 **Tel** *02 502 3161* **Map** *2 D4*

The laid-back, understated approach at the Entrée des Artistes is a welcome antidote to some of the Sablon's glitzier eateries. The cuisine is Franco-Belgian with a good selection of classic dishes, including a fine house steak *tartare* and *chicons* (endives) *au gratin*. It's also a good place to go for late night snacking, as it's open every day till midnight.

Les Larmes du Tigre
Rue de Wynants 21, 1000 **Tel** *(02) 512 1877*

The peaceful, elegant surroundings of Les Larmes du Tigre (The Tears of the Tiger) stand in a marked contrast to the rather explosive variety of flavours found in one of the city's most impressive Asian restaurants. As is usually the case for a Thai eaterie, Les Larmes offers extremely friendly service. Closed Saturday lunch and all day Monday.

Tutto Bene
Rue Joseph Stevens 28, 1000 **Tel** *(02) 512 4095* **Map** *2 D4*

In a rustic interior, to the sound of contemporary music and jazz, a friendly Italian family serve a changing menu of simple, Italian staples, including pasta, pizza and risotto. The prices are reasonable for the Sablon and there is a separate children's menu. Closed Tuesday, Wednesday.

Au Stekerlapatte
Rue des Pretres 4, 1000 **Tel** *(02) 512 8681* **Map** *1 C5*

This unpretentious yet high-quality brasserie near the Palais de Justice is owned by a film producer and attracts a mixture of business types as well as tourists. The tasty fare leans towards Belgian favourites such as grilled fish and chicken dishes as well as steaks and ribs. Friendly atmosphere with a wide selection of beers and wines.

Au Vieux Saint-Martin
Place du Grand Sablon 38, 1000 **Tel** *(02) 512 6476* **Map** *2 D4*

Another sharp, modernist eatery on the Sablon, Au Vieux Saint-Martin is also a gallery for contemporary painters, a number of whose works hang on the walls. Whether you come here for a coffee and a read of the trilingual magazines or to ingest in something more substantial, you'll definitely be made very welcome.

Havana
Rue de l'Epée 4, 1000 **Tel** *(02) 502 1224*

For dinner and dancing with a Latin flavour, take the outside lift that descends from Avenue Louise to Marolles. Here you will find Havana, a colourful establishment that is very welcoming during the grey northern European winter, but just as enticing on one of Belgium's long summer evenings. Open Thursday, Friday and Saturday only.

L'Atelier Europeen
Rue Franklin 28, 1000 **Tel** *(02) 734 9140* **Map** *3 C2*

In 1980, owner Michel Prévot gave up journalism and opened a restaurant. Situated in the European quarter, L'Atelier is a favourite for those who remain in his former profession. It has large but welcoming rooms, and highlights of the Belgian-inflected French cuisine include the veal escalope with Roquefort butter.

La Rose Blanche
Grand Place 11, 1000 **Tel** *(02) 53 6479* **Map** *2 D3*

Founded in 1905, this authentic brasserie on Grand Place serves traditional Belgian dishes, with many of the specialities cooked in beer – try the duck cooked in kriek. With its open fire, medieval feel and friendly staff, the restaurant is popular with both locals and visitors alike. La Rose Blanche is reasonably priced for a great location.

Le Cap
Place de la Vieille Halle aux Blés 28, 1000 **Tel** *(02) 512 9342*

A jazzy, lofty brasserie in the heart of Brussels with a good selection of old and new world wines at decent prices, Le Cap is perhaps more a place for friends to meet for drinks than one of Brussels' top dinner venues. The daily suggestions are more than substantial, however – the knuckle of ham is particularly recommended.

Le Loup Voyant
Avenue de la Couronne 562, 1050 **Tel** *(02) 640 0208*

This restaurant in the student area offers a wide variety of Belgian favourites as well as a good selection of Italian pasta dishes. Smaller snacks, such as *croque monsieur* (toasted cheese and ham) are also available for those in need of a quick pit-stop. Children are warmly received and well catered for.

L'Estrille du Vieux Bruxelles
Rue de Rollebeek 7, 1000 **Tel** *(02) 512 5857*

This old establishment just off the Place du Grand Sablon has something of a venerable literary pedigree: La Tribune Poétique (the Poetic Tribune) once held their meetings here. The eaterie specializes in traditional, substantial, beer-soaked Belgian cuisine. Try the eel or game when in season. Closed Tuesday.

Lola
Place du Grand Sablon 33, 1000 **Tel** *(02) 514 2460* **Map** *2 D4*

A brasserie so fashionably and contemporarily fitted out in white wood, stone and glass that the place would seem cold were it not for the warmth and open friendliness of the staff. Expect seasonal ingredients on a changing menu of healthy, light fusion dishes such as pea and bean risotto or fried scampi with espelette spices.

Orphyse Chaussette

Rue Charles Hanssens, 5, 1000 **Tel** *(02) 502 7581*

€€€

Orphyse Chausette's chef crosses the cuisine of the Languedoc-Roussillon in the south of France with that of Catalonia. He uses only seasonal regional produce, although the menu always carries its most popular dish, Indian-style red tuna tartare. A strong wine list of some 250 French wines. Closed Sunday, Monday.

La Tortue du Zoute

Rue de Rollebeek 31, 1000 **Tel** *(02) 513 1062*

€€€€

While the menu at the Tortue is solidly based around the lobster – for which the chefs offer 10 different preparations – other wonders of the sea receive no less consideration. The bistro is located on a delightful, descending cobbled pedestrian street filled with boutiques and other restaurants. Go for one of the alfresco tables in the summer.

Les Petits Oignons

Rue de la Régence 25, 1000 **Tel** *(02) 511 7615*   **Map** *2 D4*

€€€€

Close to Grand Place du Sablon, family-friendly Les Petits Oignons offers up French and Belgian brasserie-style cuisine in a relaxed and welcoming atmosphere. There are fixed price menus and a wide range of *à la carte* choices. The fried goose liver with caramelized onions is recommended. Closed Sunday.

L'Esprit de Sel Brasserie

Place Jourdan 52–54, 1000 **Tel** *(02) 230 6040*   **Map** *3 B4*

€€€€

The beef, stewed in Belgian beer, is as warming as the soft wood and velvet decor. The walls are partly but deliberately left unfinished, while elsewhere bear a message written in over-size copperplate from the Marquise de Sévigné, describing the restaurateur's art form.

L'Idiot du Village

Rue Notre-Seigneur 19, 1000 **Tel** *(02) 502 5582*   **Map** *1 C4*

€€€€

The Village Idiot is reportedly a favoured establishment of foreign ministers and even Belgian royalty. No wonder, with such intriguing concoctions as the escalope of hot *foie gras*, pepper and vanilla, served on the earthy crockery. Reservations are recommended at this extremely popular eatery. Closed Saturday and Sunday.

Tour d'y Voir

Place du Grand Sablon 8/9 B6, 1000 **Tel** *(02) 511 4043*   **Map** *2 D4*

€€€€

This calm and serene little restaurant is located on the first floor of an art gallery, Les Vieux Sablons. An unusual approach is taken; choose from a Surprise (€40) or Prestige (€60) menu and the chef will surprise you with the food, either on a fish, meat or vegetarian theme, although you will be given a card with the ingredients that will be used.

Kwint

Mont des Arts 1, 1000 **Tel** *(02) 505 9595*   **Map** *2 D3*

€€€€€

Designed by leading Belgian conceptual artist Arne Quinze, the dazzling Kwint is part of the major Mont des Arts renovation project and provides a top-quality restaurant in this otherwise poorly served area of the city. A luxurious flavour is added to traditional Belgian cuisine by the use of truffles and caviar. Closed Sunday.

L'Ecailler du Palais Royal

Rue Bodenbroek 18, 1000 **Tel** *02 512 8751*   **Map** *2 D4*

€€€€€

Housed in a 17th century mansion, this restaurant exudes the style and elegance of a different age. There's a meticulous attention to detail and an emphasis on freshness in the presentation of fish and seafood specialities. It's particularly strong on the range and quality of its oysters. Closed Sunday, public holidays and the whole of August.

GREATER BRUSSELS

Amazone

Rue du Méridien 10, 1210 **Tel** *(02) 229 3800*

€

Amazone is a Flemish non-profit association founded in 1995 aimed at establishing equality between the sexes. Its restaurant is situated in a grand 19th-century townhouse where you can have possibly the cheapest quality meal in Brussels. Booking advisable. Open Monday–Friday lunch only.

Maison Antoine

Place Jourdan, 1040 **Tel** *(02) 230 5456*   **Map** *3 B4*

€

Founded in 1948, this is the best-loved *friterie* in Brussels, its delicious double-fried *frites* have been devoured by everyone from the King of Belgium to Johnny Hallyday, the king of French rock music. It's open every day till 1am, Friday and Saturday till 2am, and you can eat your cone of fries at one of the many cafés that line Place Jourdan.

Tout Près, Tout Prêt

Chaussée de Boondael 413, 1050 **Tel** *(02) 640 8080*

€

Between the twin universities of the ULB and VUB, this sandwich bar offers quick, inventive snacks to a largely student crowd. The variety of freshly baked pies and brownies also bring in the crowds as does the fact this is one of the few outlets in town that sells bagels. Closed Sunday.

Key to Price Guide *see p152* **Key to Symbols** *see back cover flap*

Café des Spores
Chaussée d'Alsemberg 103, 1060 **Tel** *(02) 534 13 03*

If you don't like mushrooms, Café des Spores is not for you – the entire cuisine is based around fungus. The café is also an example of the gentrification that is slowly taking hold of St Gilles, with its stylish interior, blackboards instead of menus and downtown prices. An exciting wine list. Closed Saturday lunch, Sunday, Monday lunch.

La Buvette
Chaussée d'Alsemberg 108, 1060 **Tel** *(02) 534 1303*

Opposite Café des Spores lies its twin wine bar, La Buvette. The focus, is on the quality wine list, but the rustic dishes that accompany your degustation are more than generous, especially the *table d'hôte*. The venue is a transformed 1930s' Art Deco butcher's shop, with original hooks, tiles, mirrors and steel shelving serving as decor.

La Fin de Siècle
Rue des Chartreux 9, 1000

Located in a side street near the Bourse, this cosy Belgian restaurant in a 19th century building is well worth seeking out. The atmosphere is lively and friendly, with diners sitting on canteen-style tables to enjoy generous portions of traditional dishes – the *stoemp* is particularly good. Closed Saturday lunchtime, Sunday.

Le Bonnet d'Ane
Avenue Brugmann 522, 1180 **Tel** *(02) 345 6105*

The "Donkey Bonnet" (a dunce's cap) is adorned like a schoolroom from the 1900s. While reading the menu, bread and butter appears in a lunchbox. But it is no theme restaurant, as illustrated by the hearty servings of caramelized spare ribs or the knuckle of ham in mustard sauce and rich desserts. Closed Saturday lunch, Sunday, Monday evening.

Le Rubis
Avenue de Terveuren 22, 1040 **Tel** *(02) 733 05 49*   **Map** *4 E4*

Le Rubis serves excellent Chinese food, though it's the Cambodian owner's homegrown cuisine that makes this a real find. Among an eye-catching collection of Khmer art, you can try lightly spiced, aromatic dishes such as fish cooked in herbs and coconut milk, and *poulet oeuk*, chicken in khmer spices and grilled peanuts. Closed Sunday.

L'Ultime Atome
Rue St Boniface 14, 1050 **Tel** *(02) 511 1367*

The key venue in the gentrified St Boniface quarter, L'Ultime Atome is popular amongst the young Euro-set. Cavernous, bustling and noisy, this busy brasserie serves fantastic crêpes at breakfast, and there is a good range of vegetarian options.

Mille-et-une Nuits
Rue de Moscou 7, 1060 **Tel** *(02) 537 4127*

This undiscovered gem – decorated to give the impression of the inside of a Bedouin tent – lies hidden away in bohemian St Gilles, and has friendly service and reasonable prices. If one person at your table orders the lamb tagine with prunes and almonds, everybody else will wish they had as well.

Musical Instruments Museum
Rue Montagne de la Cour 2, 1000 **Tel** *(02) 502 95 08*   **Map** *2 E4*

On the top floor of the magnificent Art Nouveau Old England building, this restaurant has superb views of the city. The menu offers Belgian cuisine and a Sunday brunch that's famed throughout the city. You can take the lift up without a ticket to the museum, though it does keep to museum opening hours, closing on Mondays and in the evening.

Brasserie Georges
Avenue Churchill 259, 1180 **Tel** *(02) 347 2100*

Gorgeous Parisian-style seafood brasserie with numerous waiters in floor-length aprons and a conspicuous, showy shellfish stall at the front doors. The terrace overlooks the entrance to the Bois de la Cambre park (but also the number 23 tramline). The *fruits du mer* (seafood) platter is the restaurant's showpiece. Immaculate customer service.

Le Fils de Jules
Rue du Page 35, 1050 **Tel** *(02) 534 0057*

An Art Deco Basque bistro off Ixelles' happening Place du Châtelain. The well-heeled clientele come here for the house *foie gras*, tartare of tuna, spicy squid and the rest of the menu's resolutely Basque repetoire. If the Basque country had an ambassador to Belgium, it would be Le Fils de Jules. Closed Saturday lunch, Sunday lunch, Monday.

Les Fils à Papa
Chaussée de Waterloo 1484, 1180 **Tel** *(02) 374 4144*

It is worth the 15-minute drive from the city centre to Uccle to dine at this restaurant in a charming old renovated house. There are several seating areas, including a comfortable lounge for pre-meal drinks and a delightful terrace. The menu features French cuisine, sometimes with a twist of Asian flavour. Closed Saturday lunch, Sunday.

Relais St-Job
Place Saint-Job 1, 1180 **Tel** *(02) 375 5724*

It really is so much quieter, greener and more relaxed out in suburban Uccle, where you'll find the Relais just off the St-Job tram stop. If you want to get away from the bustle of the city, sit on the roof of the Relais in August, with your chilled rosé and awaiting your knuckle of ham and creamy mustard sauce. Have the nougat glacé for dessert.

Café Maris

Chaussée de Waterloo 1260, 1180 **Tel** *(02) 374 8834*

This splendid Parisian-style brasserie complete with an Art Deco interior and a warm atmosphere has a strong following. Fish and seafood dishes are the order of the day with a variety of oyster platters available. Carnivores will be satisfied with the wide choice of meat dishes as well.

En Face de Parachute

Chaussée de Waterloo 578, 1050 **Tel** *(02) 346 4741*

Mainly navy-blue and brown decor envelopes this Corsican-Marseillaise fusion establishment that sits across the road from Parachute, a men's clothing outlet (that also sells Vespa scooters). Presented on a blackboard, the Mediterranean menu changes every ten days and includes vegetarian options. Closed Monday, Saturday lunchtime, Sunday.

La Quincaillerie

Rue du Page 45, 1050 **Tel** *(02) 533 9833*

From the moment you enter this hardware store from the 1900s you know you're in for a treat; the restaurant is visually stunning, with metalwork galleries and a huge period clock. There are excellent steaks and a host of Bresse chicken dishes on the menu, while the seafood counter is one of the best in Brussels. Closed Sunday lunchtime.

Salon 58

Avenue de l'Atomium 6, 1020 **Tel** *(02) 479 8400*

The "vision-of-the-future" building of Salon 58 was originally called the Tuilier Pavillion when it was built for the 1958 Brussels Universal Exhibition. It was constructed by the same architect as the Atomium and its renovation in 2002 set it out in retro-futuristic pink and gold. An extraordinary dining experience. Closed Saturday lunch and Sunday.

Touareg

Chaussée de Charleroi 80, 1060 **Tel** *(02) 534 5400*

Touareg offers the traditional Moroccan mix of Berber, Arab and Andalousian cuisines, concocted from ancient recipes. A short walk up from boutique-filled Avenue Louise, this refined establishment offers a smart welcome to those made weary and, most especially, hungry from a hard day's shopping. Closed Saturday lunch and Sunday lunch.

Bouchéry

Chaussée d'Alsemberg 812a, 1180 **Tel** *(02) 332 3774*

Elegant, understated decor, excellent service and outstanding French gastronomic cuisine make for an exquisite dining experience. Chef Damien Bouchery uses the finest ingredients to create innovative dishes such as turbot poached in bergamot-infused veal stock. The three-course lunch offers excellent value. Closed Saturday lunch, Sunday, Monday.

La Truffe Noire

Boulevard de la Cambre 12, 1050 **Tel** *(02) 640 4422*

The menu at this renowned truffle restaurant is extravagant, with prices to match. It includes such items as a Périgord truffle cooked in a Porto jus, or warm duck foie gras with honey-roasted carrots. In summer, guests can eat in the garden. Closed Saturday lunch, Sunday.

Rouge Tomate

Avenue Louise 190, 1050 **Tel** *(02) 647 7044*

If you were in London or New York, you would feel at home with Rouge Tomate's health-conscious philosophy (only two meat dishes on the menu) and high prices. The restaurant prides itself on the quality of its produce and its seasonal menu. Not the place for a hearty stew, but you will go away satisfied that you have eaten exceptional food.

ANTWERP

De Groote Witte Arend

Reyndersstraat 18, 2000 **Tel** *(03) 233 5033*

In a fine building dating from the 15th century, there's nothing fancy about the food here, just good, hearty Flemish fare. The *"grote hunger"* part of the menu has steaks and pasta dishes, though you'll still need a healthy appetite to get through the omelettes and *uitsmijters* (eggs and ham on bread).

Amadeus

Sint-Paulusplaats 20, 2000 **Tel** *(03) 232 25 87*

This former glass-factory mecca for spare rib fans is extremely good value. The Art Nouveau interior, with glasswork and wooden carvings, creates a traditional brasserie atmosphere. Drink as much or as little of the litre of red wine that is plonked atop the table in advance of your sitting there – you only pay for what you consume.

Ciro's

Amerikalei 6, 2000 **Tel** *(03) 238 1147*

The best steaks in Antwerp, along with the rest of the traditional Belgian menu, are served up at Ciro's with little regard for pretence, fashion, or ambience – which is perhaps its most endearing quality. The last redecoration happened in 1962. It's rough and ready, but ever popular.

Key to Price Guide *see p152* **Key to Symbols** *see back cover flap*

De Foyer €€

Komedieplaats 18, 2000 **Tel** *(03) 233 5517*

This opulent space is in the foyer of the 19th-century Bourla Theatre. Red velvet drapes and marble columns add to the sumptuous feel. Prices are reasonable however, making this one of Antwerp's most popular venues, particularly for Sunday brunch and afternoon tea. Closed Sunday evening.

Mie Katoen €€

Kleine Kraaiwijk, 2000 **Tel** *(03) 231 1309*

Mie Katoen is a popular little fondue house located in a farm in central Antwerp. Choose a traditional fondue or try something different – the Japanese fondue served with tempura. Grilled dishes are also available. The inner courtyard is perfect for a summer's evening. Open for dinner only, closed Tuesday, Wednesday.

Hippodroom €€€

Leopold De Waelplaats 10, 2000 **Tel** *(03) 248 5252*

Across from the Musées Royaux des Beaux-Arts, the early 20th-century building that houses the Hippodroom is itself home to an enviable collection of art and photography. The restaurant's menu is as modern as its contemporary fittings, offering traditional French-Belgian cuisine with a hint of global influence. Closed Saturday lunch, Sunday.

De Kleine Zavel €€€€

Stoofstraat 2, 2000 **Tel** *(03) 231 9691*

The old furniture and the wooden crates filled with bottles remind customers that this was once a hotel for shipping industry workers. The bistro's affordable inventions has made the site popular with both travellers and locals, who appreciate such creations as the seven preparations of tuna in one dish. Closed Saturday lunch and all day Monday.

The Glorious €€€€

De Burburestraat 4a, 2000 **Tel** *(03) 237 0613*

South of the city centre, close to the Koninklijk Museum voor Schone Kunsten, is The Glorious, a Belgian take on an upscale New York bistro. Top chef Johan van Raes cooks up fine bistro dining, while sommelier and host Jurgen Lijcops offers a warm welcome and wine expertise. Boutique accommodation available. Closed Sunday, Monday.

Het Pomphuis €€€€€€

Droogdok, Siberiastraat 7, 2030 **Tel** *(03) 770 8625*

The Antwerp docklands drydock pumphouse was remade as Het Pomphuis in 2003, a Pacific Rim bistro that is in keeping with the city's appetite for industrial resto-bar conversions. The large, very dramatic restaurant has kept much of the original hydraulic machinery. Rare for Belgium, it also offers Wi-Fi access.

InVINcible €€€€€

Haarstraat 9, 2000 **Tel** *(03) 231 3207*

Located over two floors, InVINcible is undoubtedly one of Antwerp's finest seafood restaurants. Many of the items on the menu are based on that morning's catch from the North Sea, and the open kitchen allows diners to see the chef at work. Advance booking is essential. Open evenings only. Closed Saturday, Sunday

Pazzo €€€€€

Oudeleeuwenrui 12, 2000 **Tel** *(03) 232 8682*

This old warehouse has been updated with contemporary decoration but has still retained much of its original character, especially the wood beams and intimate cavern beneath the main floor. This wine bar offers most wines by the glass, each intended to match the various tapenades, stir-fries, tempuras and risottos. Closed Saturday, Sunday.

Rooden Hoed €€€€€

Oude Koornmarkt 25, 2000 **Tel** *(03) 233 2844*

As the oldest restaurant in Antwerp – it first served food back in around 1750 – the Rooden Hoed is one of the city's most renowned eateries. It specializes in seafood, especially mussels, of which there are at least half a dozen ways of having them cooked. You can have a pre-dinner drink in the restaurant's medieval cellar.

BRUGES

Sacré Coeur €

Langestraat 137, 8000 **Tel** *(050) 341093*   **Map** *C3*

With a menu featuring local meat and fish specialities along with a wide choice of pizza and pasta dishes, Sacré Coeur caters for everyone. Alternatively, you can opt for a light snack accompanied by one of the many Belgian beers on offer, while enjoying one of the restaurant's live music nights.

Bhavani €€

Simon Stevinplein 5, 8000 **Tel** *(050) 339025*   **Map** *A4*

Bruges may not be the most cosmopolitan of places, but it does at least have a decent Indian restaurant. Moreover the pleasant contemporary decor is quite a change to the typical Bruges brown café. Cosy but colonial Bhavani serves a wide range of Indian dishes and the Kashmiri Rogan Josh is one of its best. Closed Wednesday.

For Bruges map references *refer to the inside back cover*

Lotus
Wapenmakersstraat 5, 8000 **Tel** *(050) 331078*

€€

Map *B3*

On any given day, there will be just two options on the menu at this vegetarian café. These two dishes come in three sizes – small, medium and large – but lunch (the only meal served) is hearty no matter what size chosen. The value for money is the real attraction. There's a minimum spend of €35 per person. Closed Sunday.

Cafedraal
Zilverstraat 38, 8000 **Tel** *(050) 340845*

€€€

Map *4A*

The Cafedraal is one of the most attractive restaurants in Bruges. Its medieval setting is a delight and provides a highly atmospheric backdrop to inventive dishes based around meat, shellfish and local specialities, such as grilled sole with Zeebrugge grey shrimps. It's also very child-friendly. Closed on Sunday.

De Gouden Meermin
Markt 31, 8000 **Tel** *(050) 331805*

€€€

Map *A3*

Perhaps the best café in the Grote Markt. Because the square is so beautiful and such a tourist honeypot, few establishments on the Markt do right by their customers, but not here at the Golden Mermaid with its mainly Italian menu. The service is attentive and the café's mussels and frites are excellent.

Brasserie Erasmus
Wollestraat 35, 8000 **Tel** *(050) 335781*

€€€€

Map *B3*

The modern Brasserie Erasmus is found in the centrally located hotel of the same name and stocks over 150 beers – 10 on draught. What's more, every single dish on the menu is made with the stuff. Try the rabbit in beer sauce or the fish *waterzooi*. Save room for one of the decadent desserts.

De Stove
Kleine Sint-Amandsstraat 4, 8000 **Tel** *(050) 337835*

€€€€

Map *A3*

The very intimate De Stove has room for just 20 patrons, so with its simple furnishings and eponymous iron stove, is the perfect place for a romantic evening. The *foie gras* and duck are exceptional, but don't miss the fresh North Sea fish, supplied daily – particularly the breaded cod in butter sauce. Open Tuesday evening, Friday evening to Sunday.

De Karmeliet
Langestraat 19, 8000 **Tel** *(050) 338259*

€€€€€

Map *B3*

Regarded as the best restaurant in Bruges. In 1996 chef Geert Van Hecke became the first Flemish chef to be awarded three Michelin stars. The servings are substantial, as is common in Flanders. Many dishes are made with Belgian genever, and the roasted French scallops and marinated sea urchin is a favourite dish. Closed Sunday, Monday.

De Visscherie
Vismarkt 8, 8000 **Tel** *(050) 330212*

€€€€€

Map *B3*

De Visscherie is a seafood restaurant overlooking the centuries-old Vismarkt (fish market). The house's signature dish is the monkfish waterzooi with saffron, but try any of the turbot variations. The establishment is a popular destination for locals, so book ahead. Closed Tuesday.

Den Dijver
Dijver 5, 8000 **Tel** *(050) 336069.*

€€€€€

Map *B4*

Opened in 1992, this stylish restaurant makes creative use of regional Belgian beers in many of its dishes, which are served in cosy surroundings. Three-, four- or five-course set menus are available in addition to a sophisticated, locally-sourced à la carte selection. Booking is essential. Closed Wednesday, Thursday lunch.

Den Gouden Harynck
Groeninge 25, 8000 **Tel** *(050) 337637*

€€€€€

Map *B4*

Chef Philippe Serruys and his wife run this restaurant located in a 17th-century building in the museum district. The sea bass with coarse sea salt and rosemary for two people is a must. Alternatively, try other creative concoctions such as pigeon with apples or lobster with fig chutney. Closed Saturday lunch, Sunday, Monday.

Duc de Bourgogne
Huidenvettersplein 12, 8000 **Tel** *(050) 332038*

€€€€€

Map *B3*

As it overlooks a canal in the historical city centre, the Duc may be heaving with customers, but the service is friendly and the menu is more than passable, with a *bouillabaisse* made with local sea fish being the house speciality. The charming interior is decorated with tapestries and linen tablecloths.

GHENT

Groot Vleeshuis
Groentenmarkt 7, 9000 **Tel** *(09) 233 2324*

€

Map *E 1*

This medieval butcher's hall makes a spectacular setting for a meaty lunchtime sandwich or even meatier tourist "formule", and the *gentse waterzooi* (chicken stew) is particularly recommended. There's also an impressive list of Belgian beers to choose from, or else you can try *jenever* (gin) or apple wine. Closed Monday.

Key to Price Guide see p152 **Key to Symbols** see back cover flap

Kapittelhuis

🏛♿🍴 €

Lange Kruisstraat 4, 9000 **Tel** *(09) 336 8519*

Located in the heart of Ghent near St Baafskathedraal, Kapittelhuis offers a wide choice of dishes, ranging from steaks to pasta. Children are well catered for, with their own menu and play corner. The lunch menu is good value with a daily special. The adjoining tea room serves great waffles and pancakes. Closed Wednesday evening, Sunday.

Amadeus

🏛🍴 €€

Patershol-Plotersgracht 8–10, 9000 **Tel** *(09) 225 1385*

Vegetarian and fish dishes are served at Amadeus, but the main attraction here is the all-you-can-eat spare ribs meal, served with a choice of sauces and a baked potato. Pay for what you drink from the bottle of wine on the table. A Ghent institution with an Art Nouveau interior. Open for dinner only; there's an outdoor menu and wine option for €21.50.

Chef Liontine

€€

Groentenmarkt 10–11, 9000 **Tel** *(09) 225 9256* **Map** *E2*

A friendly little restaurant where you can savour fresh Flemish specialities, some of which are made with beer. The rustic setting with its four separate rooms enhances the unique atmosphere. Enjoy the restaurant's hearty meals with relatives, friends or business relations. Closed Monday evening, Tuesday and Wednesday.

Keizershof

🏛♿🍴 €€

Vrijdagmarkt 47, 9000 **Tel** *(09) 223 4466* **Map** *F1*

Located in a narrow, 17th-century building on the market square. The exposed beams and plain wood tables play as humble backdrop to a local lunchtime work crowd, who consume well-priced Belgian staples and salads. A convivial atmosphere. Paintings by local artists line the walls. Closed Sunday, Monday.

Brasserie Pakhuis

🏛📋♿🍴 €€€

Schuurkenstraat 4, 9000 **Tel** *(09) 223 5555* **Map** *E2*

Antwerp's obsession with industrial resto-bar conversions seems to have infected Ghent somewhat too, judging by this ultra-hip renovated 19th-century warehouse. Sit on oak and marble tables amongst exposed giant cast-iron pillars, pipes and tubing. The menu features seafood platters and Flemish favourites. Closed Sunday.

Coeur d'Artichaut

♿🍴 €€€

Onderbergen 6, 9000 **Tel** *(09) 225 3318* **Map** *E2*

A renowned restaurant in the centre of Ghent, Coeur d'Artichaut has a menu that changes every month. Featuring classic European dishes with a twist in addition to inventive Asian selections, it is housed in an impressive mansion building that also incorporates a patio area. A lunch menu is also available. Closed on Sundays and Mondays.

La Malcontenta

🏛♿🍴 €€€

Haringsteeg 7–9, 9000 **Tel** *(09) 224 1801* **Map** *E1*

Despite its name, you'll not walk away from this Spanish eatery that offers specialities from the Canary Isles and Latin America feeling anything but content. The seafood pancake is recommended, but their best item is the paella. Popular with students. Closed lunchtime, Sunday, Monday, Tuesday.

Nestor

🏛🍴 €€€

Kraanlei 17, 9000 **Tel** *(09) 225 1880* **Map** *E1*

One of the city's best mid-range bistros, Nestor has a friendly atmosphere and a dark, modern decor. The restaurant specializes in charcoal-grilled meat and fish dishes, with specialities including rib-eye steaks and beef tenderloin. Stylish and sometimes humorous food presentation. Closed Monday and Tuesday afternoon.

Valentijn

€€€

Rodekoningstraat 1, 9000 **Tel** *(09) 225 0429* **Map** *E1*

A feature of Ghent's restaurant scene since 1996, Valentijn is a favourite with the city's locals, who enjoy the value-for-money four-course menu in a building situated down a cobbled street next to the River Leie. Priding itself on always using the freshest ingredients, the eaterie serves dishes with a French bias. Closed lunch, Thursday, Sunday eve.

Georges

🏛📋♿ €€€€

Donkersteeg 23–27, 9000 **Tel** *(09) 225 1918* **Map** *E2*

A Ghent institution, this friendly seafood restaurant is now over 80 years old, having remained in the same family the whole time. Georges, a father-and-son operation, is one of Ghent's pricier addresses, but offers superior, far from indifferent service. The oysters, crab and mussels of Lélande are the main attraction here. Closed Monday, Tuesday.

Korenlei Twee

♿🍴 €€€€

Korenlei 2, 9000 **Tel** *(09) 234 0073* **Map** *E1*

The emphasis at this chic but intimate restaurant, located in an 18th-century building with superb views of the Korenlei and Graslei, is on top-notch ingredients and taking time to enjoy them to the full. The menu changes each month, though fish dishes always feature prominently. Closed Sunday and Monday.

De Blauwe Zalm

🏛♿🍴 €€€€€

Vrouwebroersstraat 2, 9000 **Tel** *(09) 224 0852* **Map** *E1*

With the kitchen visible from the street, it's no wonder De Blauwe Zalm ("The Blue Salmon"), in the Patershol district, has quickly made a local name for itself for its atypical way of doing things. Chef Daniel de Cleyn is responsible for one of the best fish and shellfish menus in town. Closed Saturday lunch, Sunday.

For Ghent map references *refer to the inside back cover*

Cafés and Bars

This section lists the best and most colourful cafés and bars in Brussels, Antwerp, Bruges and Ghent, including both the traditional and the new. Most cafés serve a small selection of alcoholic drinks as well as soft drinks, and most bars offer coffee in addition to alcohol. Light snacks and even larger meals can be found at both.

PRICE CATEGORIES
The following price ranges are for a three-course evening meal for one, including a half-bottle of house wine, tax and service.
€ under €30
€€ €30–€40
€€€ €40–€50
€€€€ €50–€60
€€€€€ over €60

LOWER TOWN

A La Mort Subite

€

Rue Montagne aux Herbes Potagères 7, 1000 **Tel** *(02) 513 1318*   **Map** *2 D2*

Cavernous former old haunt of Brussels' favourite son, Jacques Brel, and origin of the Mort Subite brand, "To the Sudden Death" is an Art Deco wonder. However, its proximity to the Grand Place means that prices are extortionate, with some of the most expensive beers in Brussels. Snacks on offer here include sandwiches, salads and omelettes.

Café Metropole

€

Place de Brouckère 31, 1000 **Tel** *(02) 219 2384*   **Map** *2 D2*

Located at the Hotel Metropole, this slightly pricey café has a beautiful Belle Epoque interior and an enormous terrace. Here, locals and hotel guests sit, facing the street, surveying Place de Brouckère and the shoppers descending on the escalators to the metro station that lies beneath. Open daily until 1am.

Delirium

€

Impasse de La Fidélité 4A, 1000 **Tel** *(02) 514 4434*

Down the narrow lane by the Grand Place, where Manneken Pis' lesser known little sister statue resides, lies Delirium, a subterranean tourist magnet that claims to carry over 2,000 beers. These can be enjoyed with a selection of meats or cheeses. Beautifully decorated and a cosy place for a beer or glass of wine, though slightly on the expensive side.

Gecko

€

Place St Gery 16, 1000 **Tel** *(02) 502 2999*   **Map** *1 C2*

Although not particualry trendy in comparison to the "fashionable" end of St Gery, Gecko successfully teams a calm and relaxed atmosphere with great and charming service. Very reasonable, hot sandwiches are available, as well as larger dishes such as quiche, lasagne and stoemp. The Lindemans draught is the drink of choice.

Kafka

€

Rue de la Vierge Noire 15, 1000 **Tel** *(02) 513 5489*   **Map** *1 C2*

Where other Belgian cafés have extensive beer lists, Kafka, which is just around the corner from the seafood restaurant alley of Ste-Catherine, also has a directory of vodkas, genevers and other spirits. The atmosphere here is unpretentious and mellow.

L'Archiduc

€

Rue Antoine Dansaert 6, 1000 **Tel** *(02) 512 0652*

L'Archiduc is conveniently located on one of the hippest shopping streets in Brussels. The bar staff here know their music as well as they do their cocktails. Live jazz acts play every weekend in this beautiful Art Deco room with high ceilings, complete with a grand piano. Rumour has it that Miles Davis used to come here to jam. No snacks available.

Le Cirio

€

Rue de la Bourse 22, 1000 **Tel** *(02) 512 1395*   **Map** *1 C2*

In the shadow of La Bourse, the interior of Le Cirio is a marvel of Art Nouveau ostentatiousness. It was formerly an Italian delicatessen and its location, right in the middle of town, makes it a perfect meeting place to start, or end, the day. Simple dishes on offer include pasta and *waterzooï*.

Le Greenwich

€

Rue des Chartreux 7, 1000   **Map** *1 C2*

Le Greenwich was once a legendary chess venue where the town's players gathered to battle it out over the board. The bar has been renovated but this Art Nouveau gem, which was once a favourite of René Magritte, has retained its charm and is a good choice for a quiet beer.

Le Roy d'Espagne

€

Grand Place 1, 1000 **Tel** *(02) 513 0807*   **Map** *2 D3*

A drink on the Grand Place is an essential part of any visit to Brussels. One of the best places to visit, and one of the best priced, is Le Roy d'Espagne, a huge two-tiered bar housed in the bakers' guildhouse with prime views from its terrace.

Key to Symbols *see back cover flap*

Mappa Mundo

Rue du Pont de la Carpe 2–6, 1000 **Tel** *(02) 513 5116*

Map *1 C2*

This Latin-flavoured hangout is arguably the best café, with the best terrace, in St Géry. It has its bars spread over three floors and the seating booths are actually old wooden train seats. They serve some of the best mojitos you are likely to find this side of Havana. Open daily until 2am.

Monk

Rue Ste-Catherine 42, 1000 **Tel** *(02) 503 0880*

Map *1 C2*

Monk is a relatively large, Flemish-language café in what is otherwise a French-speaking quarter. Step off the Francophone street and into a dark-wood-panelled Fleming stronghold. Although mixed, the crowd here tends to be mainly younger. One of the few cafés in town to sell the superb Mort Subite Kriek Extreme on tap. No food here.

Plattesteen

Rue du Marché au Charbon 41, 1000 **Tel** *(02) 512 8203*

Map *1 C3*

The Plattesteen sits at the heart of the St Jacques district behind the Grand Place. It has one of the most popular terraces in town and, with its loyal mix of gay, boho and locals, it's a chilled out microcosm of the trendiest area of the city centre. There's a decent menu offering Belgian classics, a good range of beers and a great atmosphere day or night.

UPPER TOWN

La Fleur en Papier Doré

Rue des Alexiens 55, 1000 **Tel** *(02) 511 1659*

Map *1 C4*

This legendary 18th-century *estaminet* was the preferred drinking place of Brussels' Surrealist artists. The walls are covered in their drawings and graffiti, but far from being a tourist haunt, it still attracts a colourful local crowd, many of whom look like they've been here since the days of Magritte. Closed Monday.

Le Bier Circus

Rue de l'Enseignement 57, 1000 **Tel** *(02) 218 0034*

Map *2 D3*

This bar is famous for its fabulous menu; the beer menu, that is. They have dozens of different brews, such as Lambic, Trappist, vintage and seasonal, from the €25 *Oude Kriek*, made with cherries from the Brussels commune of Schaerbeek, to the exotic *Cuvée des Trolls*. Wholesome Belgian dishes are also served. Closed Sunday and Monday.

Le Perroquet

Rue Watteau 31, 1000 **Tel** *(02) 512 9922*

Map *2 D4*

This classic Brussels Art Nouveau bar at the bottom of the Sablon has a terrace that is popular in summer. Serving a variety of beers as well as an assortment of bar snacks and salads, it is one of the more inexpensive hostelries in the dearest area of the city.

The Old Hack

Rue Joseph II 176,1000 **Tel** *(02) 230 0118*

Map *3 B2*

The Old Hack lies in the shadow of the Berlaymont EU Parliament building. Although it is rather small it does seem to have been around forever. A reasonably-priced lunch is available, offering a choice of seven main dishes including vegetarian options, but note that it is closed at weekends and throughout August.

Café Wittamer

Place du Grand Sablon 6, 1000 **Tel** *(02) 512 3742*

Map *2 D4*

Treat yourself to a pastry, slice of gateau or dessert fit for a king at Wittamer's, suppliers of chocolates and wedding cakes to the Belgian Royal Family for the past century. The café itself is as elaborately decorated as the heavenly creations it serves, with a terrace on the Sablon that's perfectly located for people-watching.

De Skieven Architek

Place du Jeu de Balle 50, 1000 **Tel** *(02) 514 43 69*

Map *1 C5*

The architect in question is Joseph Poelaert, whose nearby Palais de Justice caused half the Marolles to be knocked down, while "Skieven" is a Marolles dialect word that is less than complimentary. Fortunately there's little bitterness at this restaurant, just a relaxed atmosphere, tasty Belgian food, and a good beer list.

Falstaff

Rue Henri Maus 19, 1000 **Tel** *(02) 511 8789*

With its beautiful Art Nouveau interior and Neo-Classical detailing, the Falstaff is something of a Brussels' institution. As well as a wide range of beers, the bar-café also serves food ranging from omelettes to steaks and a selection of Belgian meat and fish specialities.

Le Grain de Sable

Place du Grand Sablon 15–16, 1000 **Tel** *(02) 514 0583*

Map *3 D4*

Regarded as having one of the best terraces in Brussels, the Sablon's Grain de Sable ("Grain of Sand") is a popular coffee-spot among the city's young and well-to-do. It is also a good place for brunch, a meal that is otherwise quite hard to locate in the city. Essentially, though, it's all about the terrace.

The James Joyce
Rue Archimede 34, 1000   🖼️♿🎵   €€
Map *3 B2*

A few paces away from the Old Hack is the The James Joyce. It is an Irish pub that plays host to quiz nights. The interior is more authentic than most Irish theme establishments and it serves the traditional Irish Guinness, Beamish and Murphys.

GREATER BRUSSELS

Brasserie de L'Union
Parvis de St Gilles 55, 1060 **Tel** *(02) 538 15 79*   🖼️🚹♿🎵🚇   €

Cornerstone of St Gilles bohwemia, L'Union is the place to waste a lazy Sunday reading and listening to some of the best, more experienced, accordion buskers in the business. The kitchen produces a really rather good lasagne, but the service can be questionable.

Brasserie Verscheuren
Parvis St Gilles 11–13, 1060 **Tel** *(02) 539 4068*   🖼️🚹♿🚇   €

Brasserie Verscheuren could possibly be described by some as the Art Deco headquarters of Brussels' down-and-out intellectual left. However, it is worth a visit as here you can find the rare Mort Subite Faro, as well as Affligem beer. Light meals are available.

Café Belga
Place Flagey 18, 1050 **Tel** *(02) 640 3508*   🖼️♿🎵🚇   €

On the corner of the popular Place Flagey, Café Belga is located in an Art Deco building complex, which also houses a cinema. It has a similar bohemian feel to St Gery favourite Mappa Mundo and Le Roi des Belges. Provides a good place to choose which films to see at any of the numerous film festivals held in the cinema. Serves light meals.

Chez Moeder Lambic
Rue de Savoie 68, 1060   🖼️♿🚇   €

Although Chez Moeder Lambic's stock of 800 beers is impressive, it is considerably less than downtown's more famous Delirium, which stocks 2,000. "Mother" Lambic makes up for this with its array of deadly house beer cocktails that are also on offer.

Le Tavernier
Chausée de Boondael 445, 1050 **Tel** *(02) 640 7191*   🖼️♿🎵🚇   €

Between the VUB and ULB twin universities, Le Tavernier is often busy with students. Although no meals are available and there is not much of a selection of beers, the Vedett lager is cheap and keeps you cool while dancing along to the musical selection of house-jazz and world beats.

Michael Collins
Rue de Bailli 1, 1050 **Tel** *(02) 644 6121*   🖼️♿🎵🚇   €

Michael Collins is an Irish pub, named after the infamous Irish revolutionary leader. It has none of the Emerald Isle kitsch you usually expect to find in such venues and is a smart and relaxed pub. There are performances of live music on Thursday and Friday.

The Bank
Rue de Bailli 79, 1050 **Tel** *(02) 537 5265*   🎵🚇   €

Down the road from the Michael Collins is The Bank. It attracts many different nationalities and is actually a converted bank – the toilets have been carved out of the old vault and original features (such as the numbered brass lock-boxes above the urinals) still remain. The Bank serves brasserie-style food and grilled dishes.

La Terrasse
Avenue des Celtes 1, 1040 **Tel** *(02) 732 28 51*   🚹♿🚇   €€
Map *4 E4*

A lovely old brasserie, where EU journalists, MEPs and Commission *fonctionnaires* sit cheek by jowl munching on huge plates of steak *americain* and quaffing delicious beers. In winter, its wooden benches and booths give it a cozy old-fashioned feel; in summer, you need to get there early to grab a table on its very popular eponymous terrace.

ANTWERP

Bar Tabac
Waalse Kaai 43, 2000   🖼️♿🎵   €

Bar Tabac is a favourite retro hangout in the trendy, redeveloped Zuid district. The music played here ranges from 1980s new wave to electro and back again. It is famous for its strawberry margaritas and is an extremely popular venue for New Year's Eve celebrations. Bar Tabac doesn't serve meals.

Key to Price Guide *see p162* **Key to Symbols** *see back cover flap*

Billenkletser
Hoogstraat 22, 2000

Billenkletser is a tiny brown café at the crossroads of Hoogstraat and Haarstraat. There is a bar window from which terrace-dwellers can order their next round of *witbiers met citroen* (white beer with lemon) in the summer, without having to squeeze themselves inside.

Café Beveren
Vlasmarkt 2, 2000

The Beveren organ was built by the Decap brothers in 1937 and this café is home to one of only two Decap organs that are still actually played in a bar (with all other remaining examples being found only in museums). As well as a selection of drinks, you can also purchase Decap organ CDs.

Cocktails at Nine
Lijnwaadmarkt 9, 2000 **Tel** *(03) 707 1007*

Choose your cocktail from the extensive list then relax on leather couches, with the fire crackling, lights dimmed and the sound of lounge music, while the friendly bartender prepares your drinks using fresh ingredients. There is also a good range of whiskies. In warmer weather, enjoy your drinks on one of two enclosed terraces. Closed Monday.

De Volle Maan
Oude Koornmarkt 7

Just off the Grote Markt, De Volle Maan ("The Full Moon") is a lively place to hangout throughout the week. Though not overtly fashionable, it's a perfect place to have a quiet sit-down, a snack and a read of the newspapers. Thursday is a dedicated student night.

Den Engel
Grote Markt 3, 2000 **Tel** *(03) 233 1252*

The city's most famous tavern, and one of the oldest cafés in Antwerp, Den Engel ("The Angel") is extremely popular with local business regulars from the town hall, just across on the Grote Markt. It is also more than welcoming to new guests. Try the De Koninck beer served in the famous *Bolleke* (bowl-shaped) glass. Snacks are available.

Kulminator
Vleminckveld 32, 2000 **Tel** *(03) 232 4538*

A classic old Antwerp brown café, with one of the best selections of beers in town – some 750 Belgian and 80 foreign bottles are available from 4pm. The draught beers change regularly and the staff are knowledgeable. Widely regarded as the best specialist beer bar in the city and, some would argue, the country. Closed Sunday.

't Elfde Gebod
Torfbrug 10, 2000 **Tel** *(03) 289 3466*

A stone's throw from the cathedral, 't Elfde Gebod ("The Eleventh Commandment") is a mandatory pit-stop on any wander through town. However, the kitsch displays of saint figurines, angels and pictures of Jesus – along with the classical music – may dissuade you from ordering a Lucifer or a Duvel ("devil"). Good value three-course set lunch.

Berlin
Kleine Markt 1-3, 2000 **Tel** *(03) 227 1101*

Extremely hip Berlin is located in the Sint-Andries neighbourhood. The soundtrack here leans towards the jazzy-house end of the music spectrum. However, if you are not in the mood for dancing, you can make use of the bar's Wi-Fi connection instead. Berlin serves brasserie-style dishes.

De Vagant
Reyndersstraat 25, 2000 **Tel** *(03) 233 1538*

De Vagant is a jenever bar just off the Groenplaats, with a terrace and over 200 varieties of Dutch gin, including walnut, vanilla and chocolate. (You can buy a copy of the jenever menu for €1.25; the free version used to be regularly stolen.) They don't serve food here, but the sister restaurant across the street serves typical Belgian fare.

Hangar 41
Sint-Michielskaai 41, 2000 **Tel** *(03) 257 0918*

Massively popular venue that serves as a hangout for Antwerp's "fashionable" crowd. Its features include a cool, industrial interior and a terrace. Here the drink of choice for most are the stiff cocktails, of which there are many to choose from. Hangar 41 also serves Belgian cuisine.

't Karveel
Vlaamse Kaai 11, 2000 **Tel** *(03) 237 3623*

This theme bar is styled on a 16th-century ship and includes portholes, ropes, barrels, rigging and cannon. The beer is ordered at the rudder, as are any of the 15 different whiskys that 't Karveel stocks. Bar food is available, and the menu changes monthly. There's also a children's menu.

Flamant Dining
Lange Gasthuisstraat 12, 2000 **Tel** *(03) 227 7441*

Located on the first floor of the Flamant Concept Store, this is the lounge bar of Les Nuits, a trendy boutique hotel. With its comfortable seating, it makes a good spot for a relaxed drink. If you are hungry, try the restaurant for a delicious breakfast, lunch or dinner. If you like the decor, you can buy furniture and homewares in the shop.

BRUGES

Café Vlissinghe
Blekerstraat 2, 8000 **Tel** *(050) 343737*   €

Map *B2*

The genuinely medieval Vlissinghe dates back to 1515 and is the city's oldest hostellery. At the turn of the 20th-century, the building was the meeting place for a number of different artist groups, not least of which was the Kunstgenegen. The interior is an historical marvel and there's a beautiful beer garden. Closed Monday, Tuesday.

De Halve Maan
Walplein 26, 8000 **Tel** *(050) 444222*   €

Map *A4*

In the heart of the old town, The De Halve Maan home-brewery is the only remaining family brewery still operating in the centre of Bruges. The current favourite brew is the Brugse Zot ("Bruges Lunatic"), named after the celebration organized by locals to welcome Maximilian of Austria to their city. Open until 6pm.

De Republiek
St Jacobsstraat 36, 8000 **Tel** *(050) 340229*   €

Map *A3*

A medium-sized brown café, popular with students and artists who drink in the courtyard at night, De Republiek is also part of a cinema and theatre complex. It has live music late at night and is a good location to find out what's going on in town after the sun sets.

Le Comptoir des Arts
Vlamingstraat 53, 8000 **Tel** *(0494) 387961*   €

Map *A3*

Le Comptoir des Arts is an actual cellar, windowless and dark, but it is all the more cosy for it. Watch your head on the steps on the way down and have a seat on one of the mismatched wooden chairs with their decades-old wax patina, perhaps next to the massive stone fireplace. They offer 90 Belgian beers and a fine selection of whiskeys.

Lokkedize
Korte Vuldestraat 33, 8000 **Tel** *(050) 334450*   €

Map *A4*

Offering live music in the form of jazz and rhythm 'n' blues nights – with an occasional dose of rock 'n' roll thrown in – Lokkedize is a great place to spend an evening. With a range of beers on tap and light snacks available, the bare-brick and open-fire surroundings create a lovely, relaxed ambience. Closed Monday and Tuesday.

Staminee de Garre
De Garre 1, 8000 **Tel** *(050) 341029*   €

Map *B3*

Down a narrow lane off the Breidelstraat, this quaint pub is rather easy to miss and remains a real bar for locals. Worth a visit for cheese lovers, as it stocks many of the regional cheeses with an accompanying beer made in the same area.

't Brugs Beertje
Kemelstraat 5, 8000 **Tel** *(050) 339616*   €

Map *A4*

Attracting locals and tourists alike, 't Brugs Beertje is a great red-brick beerhouse located in central Bruges that is renowned for its friendly atmosphere. Choose from 300 different Belgian beers, including five on tap. Belgian cheese plates are also served to keep hunger at bay. Closed on Wednesday.

't Poatersgat
Vlaminstraat 82, 8000 **Tel** *(050) 330431*   €

Map *B3*

't Poatersgat, "The Monk's Hole", is an excellent Flemish bar in an atmospheric, candle-lit cellar. It serves more than 120 beers, including a wide Trappist selection. If you want a quiet beer aim to arrive when it opens at 5pm or head there later in the evening for a livelier time. Service is friendly.

Wijnbar Est
Braamsbergstraat 7, 8000 **Tel** *(050) 333839*   €

Map *A3*

A wine bar with the atmosphere of a brown café, Est has a range of more than 90 different wines, specializing in New World wines from Chile, South Africa and California, all of which can be ordered by the glass. Also try the melted cheese *raclette*. Free blues and jazz music on Sunday evening. Closed Monday, Wednesday.

Café Craenenburg
Markt 16, 8000 **Tel** *(050) 333402*   €€

Map *A3*

On the corner of Markt Square and St Amandstraat is this bar and brasserie with friendly waiters who are happy to make beer recommendations. Situated in the north-west of the square, this bar is a little away from the more tourist-heavy bars and therefore attracts locals too. A limited menu includes pasta dishes, salads and sandwiches.

De Versteende Nacht
Langestraat 11, 8000 **Tel** *(0496) 557398*   €€

Map *C3*

De Versteende Nacht ("The Petrified Night") is a downtown cafe whose walls are covered with jazz posters and comic strips. It has free concerts or jazz jam sessions every Wednesday night that last until the early hours and attract a mixed crowd.

For Bruges and Ghent map references *refer to the inside back cover*

GHENT

Café Fatima 🖻🖺🎵 €
Struifstraat 3, 9000 **Tel** *(09) 233 9333* **Map** *E2*

Situated near the university, Café Fatima is a student hangout and art space, complete with poetry readings, local bands and a gallery for Ghent artists and photographers to exhibit their work. Not pretentious, the café has a very relaxed ambience.

De Dulle Griet 🖻 €
Vrijdagmarkt 50, 9000 **Tel** *(09) 224 2455* **Map** *F1*

De Dulle Griet is heaven for a beer fan. One of the 250 beers available is the "Drink Max", an oversized, two-pint house beer served in an ornamental glass. But you must first hand over your shoes, which are then placed in a basket that is hoisted to the ceiling. When you return their glass, they return your shoes!

De Gentenaar 🖻 €
Vlaanderenstraat 68, 9000 **Tel** *(09) 233 4870* **Map** *F3*

There is no phone-book-thick extensive beer list at De Gentenaar, just a comfy old pub for the card-playing, blue-collar locals (one of the last of its kind left in the centre of Ghent). Juicy gossip, jokes and political opinions are served gratis.

Damherd Jazz Café 🖺 €
Korenmarkt 19, 9000 **Tel** *(09) 329 5337* **Map** *E1*

Rub shoulders with Ghent's cool crowd at this atmospheric bar in the heart of the city. Located in an ancient tavern, it's been serving up top quality live jazz music since 1978 and is an established part of Ghent's nightlife. During the day, it's a good place for a coffee.

Kinky Star 🖻🖺🎵 €
Vlasmarkt 9, 9000 **Tel** *(09) 223 4845* **Map** *F1*

This alternative music bar is the headquarters of the Ghent-based Kinky Star record label, which is home to Belgian groups such as Sexmachines, Little Troubled Kids and Starfighter. There are theme parties on several nights each week. There's no food available at this bar.

t' Dreupelkot 🖻 €
Groentenmarkt 12, 9000 **Tel** *09 221 2120* **Map** *E1*

This is the place to sample part of an older way of life in Ghent. Small, smoky and not for the faint-hearted, it specializes in jenever, a type of Belgian gin. There are more than 200 brands of jenever on the menu, made with everything from vanilla to banana and, this being Belgium, chocolate, and lovingly poured by the cigar-smoking owner.

't Gebed Zonder Eind 🖺🚋 €
Walpoortstraat 13, 9000 **Tel** *(09) 329 0397* **Map** *F3*

There's excellent food on offer at the "Prayer Without End", though it's equally popular with locals who want to chill out over a beer or coffee. Whether you're there for the food or the drink, the delightful old-style interior and cozy atmosphere are always inviting. Closed Sunday and Monday.

Trappistenhuis 🖻 €
Brabantdam 164, 9000 **Tel** *(09) 224 2937* **Map** *F3*

Trappistenhuis has 150 beers available including a blonde beer produced by the owner, who used to write a beer column for a Belgian weekly. You can read his framed articles on the walls of the pub. At Trappistenhuis, the beer menu comes with extensive descriptions for each item available. Snacks can be ordered to accompany the beers.

Hasta Mañana 🖻🖺 €€
Lammerstraat 19, 9000 **Tel** *(09) 233 5400* **Map** *F3*

A Spanish bar popular for its sangria and home-made tapas. The sangria is served in carafes that strike the right balance between alcohol and fruit, and there is also a wide variety of Spanish wines that can be tasted by the glass. It is just down the street from sister establishment Gringo Bar, a Mexican cantina.

Het Waterhuis aan de Bierkant 🖻🖺🚋 €€
Groentenmarkt 9, 9000 **Tel** *(09) 225 0680* **Map** *E1*

Het Waterhuis aan de Bierkant ("The Waterhouse at the Beerside") has more than 170 kinds of beer, 18 of which are on tap, and boasts one of the finest terraces in Ghent, stretching along the banks of the Leie. A lovely place to be in the summer when the terrace is lit up. Chez Leontine next door serves Belgian specialities.

Vooruit Café 🖺 €
Sint-Pietersnieuwstraat 23, 9000 **Tel** *(09) 267 2848* **Map** *F3*

A famous Ghent landmark, this café is situated in the stunning early 20th-century former HQ of the Vooruit socialist cooperative. It now shares the building with a theatre and concert hall, and has an artsy, intellectual feel, with a laid-back clientele that come to read the newspapers, discuss the latest plays and enjoy the historic surroundings.

Key to Price Guide *see p162* **Key to Symbols** *see back cover flap*

SHOPPING

Brussels may traditionally be known for its high-quality chocolate shops but this great shopping city has much more to offer. It is fast gaining on fashion capital Antwerp for its own collection of cutting-edge designers, and the city also happens to be the world capital of comic books, with almost as many shops selling comics as there are

Belgian chocolates

vending chocolate. Throw in department stores selling luxury goods and street markets for bargain-hunters and you have a city that caters for all shopping styles and budgets. Of the other cities, Antwerp is renowned for its diamond and fashion outlets, Ghent offers vibrant music and clothes shops, while you can find beer and classical music in Bruges.

Rue Neuve crowded with shoppers

WHERE TO SHOP

Brussels' Grand Place is surrounded by lace vendors, chocolate shops and souvenir outlets, but just one street south is Rue des Éperonniers, with shops selling vintage clothing, posters and specialist teas. North-west of the Grand Place is Avenue Antoine Dansaert, centre of the Bruxellois fashion scene.

To the south-west of the Grand Place is the Rue du Midi, where you can find shops selling second-hand records, clothing, comic books, stamps and coins. Between the Lower and Upper Towns lies the antiques district of Rue Haute and Rue Blaes, leading into the Place du Grand Sablon, where exquisite chocolate shops can be found alongside high-end florists and antique shops.

South of the Palais du Justice lies Avenue Louise and Boulevard de Waterloo, where you can find top boutiques such as Gucci and Louis Vuitton. Perpendicular to Avenue Louise is Rue du Bailli, with its art boutiques,

game shops and tea importers. To the west of the Avenue lies the Matonge, the city's most multi-cultural area, where street markets are held on some weekends, and where you can find skatewear, rare vinyl and vintage denim in the St Boniface area. It is a pleasant district to wander around on a Sunday afternoon.

For all the major high-street chains, head to pedestrianized Rue Neuve, a short walk from the Grand Place.

Renowned Dandoy biscuit shop on Rue au Beurre

OPENING HOURS

Most shops open from around 10am to 6pm, but at a few of the arcades, and in the Rue Neuve area, there is late-night shopping on Fridays until 8pm. Apart from the "night shops" (or corner stores), almost all shops are closed on Sundays (except for the shops in the Quartier Marolles) and many on Mondays. The night shop chain White Nights is the best option for Sunday and late-night convenience shopping.

Sales in Belgium are regulated, with summer sales running from 1 to 31 July, and winter sales taking place from the first weekday after New Year's Day through to the end January.

HOW TO PAY

There is a noticeable lack of ATMs in and around the Grand Place, and a number of the smaller shops, newsagents, supermarkets, cafés, and even some restaurants do not accept debit or credit cards. It is wise, therefore, to ensure that you always take out sufficient cash if you are planning to spend the day in the city centre.

Visitors from outside the EU are entitled to a refund on VAT of purchases of more than €125 in one store. As the sales tax on items can be as much as 21 per cent, this can be a considerable saving. Look out for the "Tax-Free Shopping" logo on a shop door and request a tax-free cheque, which you can redeem at customs on your way out of the EU.

Galéries Saint-Hubert historic 19th-century shopping arcade

DEPARTMENT STORES AND ARCADES

Brussels has a selection of shopping malls, though they differ little from those found in other cities. However, **City 2** at the northern end of Rue Neuve, is host to the exhaustive French book and CD emporium, **Fnac**, and the Belgian department store **Inno**. Further south on the same street lies **Hema**, a Dutch low-cost store, selling everything from clothes to kitchen utensils. Closer to the Grand Place is the **Centre Anspach**, which includes a casino, concert hall, restaurant, a hotel and upmarket shopping. Possibly the most impressive collection of shops is the delightful **Galéries Saint-Hubert**, an opulent 19th-century covered arcade – Europe's first – housing a selection of upscale outlets.

MARKETS AND ANTIQUES

Brussels is blessed with markets. Most weekends you can find a "brocante" – a glorified car boot sale combined with street party – somewhere in the city. These are listed in most of the city's free events magazines, as are the various farmers' markets found across the city where you can try some remarkable local breads and cheeses. Cheapest and most extensive

of the traditional markets is the **Marché du Midi** (Sundays 6am to 1pm) near the Gare du Midi that reflects the tastes of the area's North African community.

The eclectic **Marolles Marché aux Puces** (flea market) in Place du Jeu de Balles (daily 6am to 2pm, but best at weekends) dates back to 1873 and is the starting point for any antiques hunter. It can take time to sort through the various boxes of items but there are definitely bargains to be found. For pre-sorted antiques, head instead for the more expensive market in the Place du Grand Sablon (weekends only).

FASHION

Though Antwerp has long been regarded as Belgium's international fashion centre, these days it is the capital city itself that is creating a stir. Downtown's Rue Antoine Dansaert is at the heart of Brussels' thriving fashion industry, and the principal outlet remains **Stijl**. Since 1984 it has sold the work of fashion graduates from the Antwerp Art Academy such as Dries van Noten, and still offers the best wares – for males and females – produced by domestic talent. Further down the street, peruse the dresses and womenswear of **Nicolas Woit**,

A Dries van Noten design

the beautiful knitwear of **Annemie Verbeke**, and **Martin Margiela**'s shop in Rue de Flandre, which offers the apparel of one of Belgium's most talked about designers.

CHOCOLATES

There are 81 chocolatiers listed in the Brussels phone book – not including franchise outlets – almost all of high quality. The three biggest chains in Belgium are **Godiva, Neuhaus** and **Leonidas. Galler** and **Corné Port-Royal** are also excellent and have numerous outlets throughout the city.

While the area around the Grand Place has many chocolate shops – including the impressive **Dandoy** on Rue au Beurre – it is worth trekking to Rue des Minimes. There you will find **Pierre Marcolini** (who also happens to be a champion pastry-maker) and the **Wittamer** shop *(see p79)*, which are probably the best – and most expensive – in Brussels. **La Maison des Maîtres Cholatiers** is also worth a stop.

BEER

Having fallen in love with Belgium's beers, you may want to take a few bottles home with you. Most local supermarkets, such as **Delhaize**, GB and Match, have quite comprehensive selections of many of the country's finest beers. However, for rarer finds – as well as appropriate glasses for each beer, gift boxes and other beer paraphernalia – visit **Beer Mania** in Ixelles where you can try the beer before you buy it. Also recommended are **De Bier Tempel** and **Delices et Caprices**, both near the Grand Place.

Specialist beer glasses can be found at the Marolles flea market on Saturday mornings.

Browsers at the Marolles flea market

Brüsel, one of Brussels' many comic bookshops

COMICS

Brussels is the world capital for comic books, and the best of its many shops is **Brüsel**, which has a vast collection of comics in French, Dutch and English; it also has a gallery of framed original art for sale on the second floor. In Rue des Renards is **Utopia**, which leans towards American super-hero strips and science fiction but also has a selection of Japanese anime titles. **La Boutique Tintin** is a short walk from the Grand Place and offers a variety of Tintin-imprinted knick-knacks.

A more economical bet is the well-stocked comic shop on the ground floor of the **Centre Belge de la Bande Desinée** *(see pp50–1)*. Separate from the musuem itself, it is free to enter, and despite being a main tourist destination, is one of the better stocked comic shops in the city.

BOOKSHOPS

The Brussels outlet of the English bookstore, **Waterstone's**, and the friendly, independent store **Sterling Books** both have a wide selection of English-language books. Nestled among the high-fashion boutiques of Rue Antoine Dansaert is **Passa Porta**, which calls itself a trilingual bookstore and "International House of Literature". **Bibliopolis**, a popular and cheap French second-hand bookstore, has a number of outlets in the city.

ANTWERP

Apart from the city's diamond district – located west of the railway station – modern jewellery outlets can be found in Schutterhofstraat. Then try **Nadine Wijnants'** shops for clever but inexpensive contemporary pieces from one of the country's most exciting young jewellery designers. The Brussels-based **Christa Reniers**, regarded as Belgium's premier jeweller, has a shop at Vrijdagsmarkt.

Cutting-edge fashion can be found just a few streets away from Antwerp's main high-street shopping district, the Meir. **Ann Demeulemeester**, Dries van Noten's **Het Modepaleis** and Walter van Beirendonck and Dirk van Saene at **Walter** are all must-sees for fashionistas.

Bruges' Bottle Shop has a range of beers

Het Modepalis in Antwerp, housing Dries van Noten's collections

GHENT

Ghent is a university town, so it has a high number of hip record stores, streetwear outlets and second-hand shops to service the youthful population. The pedestrianized main shopping area, the Veldstraat, also has all the typical chain stores. For jumble-sale bargains, visit **N'Importe Quoi**; for more organized bargain-hunting, go to **De Kaft**, where you will find used CDs, vinyl and other second-hand goods. **Music Mania** covers three floors and specializes in drum 'n' bass, reggae and jazz. **Het Oorcussen** is another outlet for Antwerp's famed fashion designers, as is the men's boutique **Hot Couture**.

Ghent's quirkiest shop may be **Vve Tierenteijn-Verlent**, a mustard shop dating back to 1858. The recipe for the mustard sold here was first concocted by a Madame Tierenteijn-Verlent in 1790, and it remains a firm favourite over 200 years later.

BRUGES

While Bruges is considered less of a shopping destination than Belgium's other major cities, the main shopping thoroughfare of Steenstraat is a little quieter and less stressful than Brussels' Rue Neuve or Antwerp's Meir. What's more, the Belgian fashion scene has spilled over into this quaint city. There's the boutique of Brussels' designer **Olivier Strelli**, and L'Heroine, which sells works by a number of Antwerp's famed young designers and their contemporaries.

The Bottle Shop has a more comprehensive range of Belgian beer than its Brussels-based competitors, with an array of some 850 beers and genevers.

Medieval Bruges is the perfect setting for **Rombaux**, which has been selling classical records and sheet music for three generations.

DIRECTORY

DEPARTMENT STORES AND ARCADES

Centre Anspach
Boulevard Anspach 30–36.
Map 2 D2.

City 2
Rue Neuve 123. **Map** 2 D2. **Tel** *(02) 211 4060.*
www.city2.be

Fnac
City 2, Rue Neuve 123.
Map 2 D1.
Tel *(02) 275 1111.*
www.fnac.be

Galéries Saint-Hubert
Galérie de la Reine.
Map 2 D2

Hema
Rue Neuve 13. **Map** 2 D2.
Tel *(02) 227 5210.*
www.hema.be

Inno
Rue Neuve 111–123.
Map 2 D2.
Tel *(02) 211 2111.*

MARKETS AND ANTIQUES

Marché du Midi
Gare du Midi. **Map** 1 A5.

Marolles Marché aux Puces
Place du Jeu de Balle.
Map 1 C5.

FASHION

Annemie Verbeke
Rue des Liegeöls 47–49.
Map 1 C2.
Tel *(02) 646 1325.*
www.annemieverbeke.be

Martin Margiela
Rue de Flandre 114.
Map 1 B1.
Tel *(02) 223 7520.*
www.maisonmartin margiela.com

Nicolas Woit
Rue Antoine Dansaert 80.
Map 1 C2.
Tel *(02) 503 4832.*
www.nicolaswoit.com

Stijl
Rue Antoine Dansaert 74.
Map 1 C2.
Tel *(02) 512 0313.*

CHOCOLATES

Corné Port-Royal
Rue de la Madeleine 9.
Map 2 D3.
Tel *(02) 512 4314.*
www.corne-port-royal.be

Dandoy
Rue au Beurre 31.
Map 2 D3.
Tel *(02) 511 0326.*
www.biscuiteriedandoy.be

Galler
Rue au Beurre 44.
Map 2 D3.
Tel *(02) 502 0266.*
www.galler.com

Godiva
Grand Sablon 47–48.
Map 2 D4.
Tel *(02) 502 9906.*
www.godiva.be

La Maison des Maîtres Chocolatiers
Grand Place 4, Grote Markt. **Map** 2 D3.
Tel *(02) 888 6620.*

Leonidas
Rue au Beurre 34.
Map 2 D3.
Tel *(02) 512 8737.*
www.leonidas.com

Neuhaus
Galerie de la Reine 25–27.
Map 1 C3.
Tel *(02) 512 6359.*
www.neuhaus.be

Pierre Marcolini
Rue des Minimes 1.
Map 1 5C.
Tel *(02) 514 1206.*
www.marcolini.be

Wittamer
Place du Grand Sablon 6, 12 & 13. **Map** 2 D4.
Tel *(02) 512 3742.*
www.wittamer.com

BEER

Beer Mania
Chausée de Wavre 174–176. **Map** 2 F5.
Tel *(02) 512 1788.*
www.beermania.be

De Bier Tempel
Rue Marché aux Herbes 56. **Map** 2 D3.
Tel *(02) 502 1906.*

Delices et Caprices
Rue des Bouchers 68.
Map 2 D3.
Tel *(02) 512 1451.*

COMICS

Brüsel
Boulevard Anspach 100.
Map 1 C3.
Tel *(02) 511 0809.*

Centre Belge de la Bande Desinée
Rue des Sables 20.
Map 2 F5.
Tel *(02) 219 1980.*

La Boutique Tintin
Rue de la Colline 13.
Map 2 D3.
Tel *(02) 514 5152.*

Little Nemo
Boulevard Maurice Lemonnier 25. **Map** 1 C3.
Tel *(02) 514 6804.*

Utopia
Rue de Midi 39. **Map** 1 C5. **Tel** *(02) 514 0826.*

BOOKSHOPS

Bibliopolis
Rue du Midi 93.
Map 1 C3.
Tel *(02) 502 4676.*
www.bibliopolis.be

Passa Porta
Rue Antoine Dansaert 46.
Map 1 C2.
Tel *(02) 502 9460.*
www.passaporta.be

Sterling Books
Fossé aux Loups 38.
Map 2 D2.
Tel *(02) 223 6223.*
www.sterlingbooks.be

Waterstone's
Boulevard Adolphe Max 71–75. **Map** 2 D1.
Tel *(02) 219 2708.*

ANTWERP

Ann Demeulemeester
Verlatstraat 38.
Tel *(03) 216 0133.*

Christa Reniers
Drukkerigstraat 22B.
Tel *(03) 233 2602.*
www.christareniers.com

Het Modepaleis
Nationalestraat 16.
Tel *(03) 470 2510.*

Nadine Wijnants
Kloosterstraat 26.
Tel *(03) 226 4569.*
www.nadinewijnants.be

Walter
St Antoniusstraat 12.
Tel *(03) 213 2644.*
www.waltervan beirendonck.com

GHENT

De Kaft
Kortrijksepoortstraat 44.
Map E4.
Tel *(09) 329 6438.*

Het Oorcussen
Vrijdagmarkt 7.
Map F1.
Tel *(09) 233 0765.*

Hot Couture
Gouvernementstraat 34.
Tel *(09) 233 7407.*

Music Mania
Walpoortstraat 3.
Tel *(04) 7777 0743.*
www.musicmaniarecords.com

N'Importe Quoi
Burgstraat 11.
Map D/E1.
Tel *(09) 223 0617.*

Vve Tierenteijn-Verlent
Groentenmarkt 3.
Map E1.
Tel *(09) 225 8336.*

BRUGES

Olivier Strelli
Eiermarkt 3.
Map A3.
Tel *(050) 343837.*
www.strelli.be

The Bottle Shop
Wollestraat 13. **Map** B3.
Tel *(050) 349980.*

Rombaux
Mallebergplaats 13.
Tel *(050) 332575.*
www.rombaux.be

ENTERTAINMENT

Lying at at the crossroads of London, Paris, Amsterdam and Cologne, Brussels benefits from the best international touring groups passing through the city. In its own right, Brussels is one of the top destinations in Europe for modern dance and jazz, is host to a world-renown classical musical competition, and has a knowledgeable,

Ecran Total Cinema poster

cinephilic population. The visitor really is spoilt for entertainment choice. Knowingly hip Antwerp, the country's clubbing and fashion capital, offers a similar range of options, while Ghent's large student population gives the city a lively urban scene. Bruges, although quieter, is equipped with a clutch of cosy pubs and jazz bars to while away the evening.

The 19th-century interior of La Monnaie Opera House

LISTINGS AND TICKETS

Expatriates in the Belgian capital depend on the weekly English-language listings magazine *The Bulletin* costing around €2.70. The magazine's pull-out section, *What's On*, is distributed free to hotels. There is also a twin website, www.xpats.com which includes cultural information, news, weather reports and other useful information and links.

More up-to-date and in tune to the city's goings-on is *Agenda*, a trilingual listings magazine that can usually be found freely distributed in boxes outside supermarkets and in cafés. The French newspapers *La Libre Belgique* and *Le Soir* both publish their entertainment supplements every Wednesday. For cinema times online, check www.cinenews.be

Magazines on sale in Brussels

or www.cinebel.be. Visit www.jazzinbelgium.com for a trilingual schedule of jazz gigs throughout the country. If you are interested in reggae, ska and dancehall, visit www. irielion.com. The best online arts agenda is found at www.netevents.be (although the information is only available in French and Dutch).

On foot, head to the Tourist Information Office, which, as well as offering free maps and other information, will also help you book tickets.

OPERA AND CLASSICAL

Students from around the world come to study at the Royal Conservatory of Music, which is the site of the initial rounds of the Concours Musical International Reine Elisabeth de Belgique, one of the most challenging musical contests in the world, which instantly places its winners at the very height of their profession.

The **Théâtre Royal de la Monnaie** (*see p48*) is one of Europe's finest opera houses, and its season runs from September to June. Tickets can be cheap, but beware, many productions sell out months in advance. The **Palais des Beaux-Arts**, the country's most notable cultural venue, is home to the **Belgian National Orchestra** and site of the final rounds of the Concours Musical. Its Art Nouveau hall, Salle Henri LeBoeuf, has recently been renovated, vastly improving the building's acoustics. Its season also runs from September to June.

DANCE

For its size, Belgium is particularly strong in the field of modern dance, with its leading choreographers – above all Anne Teresa de Keersmaeker, Michèle Anne de Mey (www.madm.be) and Wim Vandekeybus (www. ultimavez.com) – having enormous influence internationally. De Keersmaeker is resident at the Brussels opera and director of the world-renowned Rosas company (www.rosas.be).

Venues naturally vary, but the **Théâtre Les Tanneurs**, tucked away in the cobbled streets of the Marolles district, puts dance at the centre of its programme. Another of Belgium's feted dance makers, Michèle Noiret, is its resident choreographer. Tickets prices are reasonable.

JAZZ

Brussels is one of the key cities in the world for jazz, and the leading soloists and groups are sure to include the town in their tour schedules.

Every May, jazz fans from around the world congregate for the **Brussels Jazz Marathon**, which hosts hundreds of gigs in all forms, many of them for free.

The quintessential Brussels Jazz venue is the venerable **L'Archiduc**, an Art Deco gem in the centre of town where Miles Davis once popped in to jam. There are regular concerts at weekends and occasionally in the week. For international acts head to **Athanor Studio**, in the basement of the Hotel Arlequin, or classy **Music Village**, which stretches across two 17th-century buildings close to the Grand Place, and features local and international names. Free Tuesday jam sessions pack out **L'Arts-Ô-Bases** across the canal in Molenbeek, and **Sounds** is another popular venue with a prolific agenda of concerts every day except Sunday.

ROCK, FOLK, WORLD AND REGGAE

Brussels is one of the best cities in Europe to catch up-and-coming acts, and ticket prices don't usually go much above €20 for a concert.

The **Forêt-National**, lying southeast of the city centre, is Belgium's top arena for big-name acts. Closer to the centre, Brussels' other venues tend to be more intimate

L'Archiduc, hosting regular jazz concerts in Art Deco surroundings

places, with their own favoured musical genres. **Café Central** favours R&B, blues, bossa nova and ambient. **Cirque Royale** leans towards indie rock, and has a reputation for booking rock and new-wave bands long before they are household names.

The downtown **Ancienne Belgique** has a similar line-up to Cirque Royale, if for more established acts. Flemish student venue **Kultuur Kaffee** at the Vrij Universiteit Brussel (the Dutch-language university) always has a strong line-up of bands and serves the cheapest beer in town. **Recyclart**, showcases avant-garde techno, hardcore, punk and a bit of world music in a refitted abandoned train station. Look out for the old wood-and-brass ticket windows which have been turned into the bar. **Magazin 4** is dedicated to the promotion of French punk and ska. Visit the **Halles de Schaerbeek**, a 19th-century former market,

Logo for rock venue
Ancienne Belgique

for a range of different groups, **Vaartkapoen** (also known as **VK Club**) for reggae, the **Beursschouwburg** – the Flemish Cultural Community centre – for Flemish acts, and **La Tentation** for flamenco, salsa and Flemish folk.

Although the city has few noted bands of its own, nearby Liège has quite a strong indie rock scene, centring around the Jaune-Orange label, whose acts often play in Brussels.

THEATRE

There is a substantial English-language theatre scene in Brussels. The city's five English-language troupes – the **American Theater Company**, the **Brussels Light Opera Company**, the **Brussels Shakespeare Society**, the **Irish Theatre Company** and the **English Comedy Club** – are an established part of the Brussels theatre society. Performances are far from amateur and all plays are advertised in the city's listings magazines.

The most important Belgian theatre is the **Théâtre National**, which stages high-quality productions of mainly French classics as well as welcoming visiting companies, such as the Royal Shakespeare Company. Young Belgian playwrights have the opportunity to be showcased at the private **Théâtre Public**, while French 20th-century and burlesque pieces are staged in the glorious and beautifully restored surrounds of the **Théâtre Royal du Parc**.

Le Botanique cultural centre, venue for Les Nuits Botanique festival

CINEMA

For the latest blockbuster films – always in their original language and never dubbed – head to the massive **Kinepolis Laeken**, boasting 28 screens (including IMAX) and free parking. Two central UGC cineplexes will also satisfy most mainstream tastes.

For more intriguing programmes and ambience, try the **Nova** for truly independent films, the **Actors Studio** for foreign and art films and **Arenberg-Galeries**, which has its own eclectically chosen, summer-long festival, "Ecran Total". For mainstream films in Art Deco movie palace surrounds go to **Movy Club**. Tickets cost from €6–7.50.

Brussels has a packed agenda of film festivals for all genres including fantasy (**Brussels International Festival of Fantastic Film**, April), animation (**Anima**, February) and gay (**Belgian Gay and Lesbian Film Festival**, January).

Poster for BIFFF film festival, held annually in April

CLUBS AND NIGHTLIFE

Brussels' bright young things start off their weekend in St Géry, a square of trendy cafés and clubs just off the fashion district of Rue Antoine Dansaert. Formerly a run-down quarter surrounding the old grain exchange, the area is now home to latin-flavoured **Mappa Mundo**, popular **Le Roi des Belges** and the elegant **Gecko** bar. The most renowned club in

Latin-inspired Brussels hot spot Mappa Mundo

Brussels, **The Fuse**, has earned a reputation for top-name techno and dance DJs. Once a month it becomes La Demence, a gay night that draws crowds from Germany, France and the Netherlands (www.lademence.com).

Ric's Boat, an actual boat turned nightclub, has a popular Single Friends night the first Friday of the month. **Les Jeux d'Hiver**, in the middle of the Bois de la Cambre woods, attracts an affluent crowd. The loungey Strictly Niceness, on the first Friday of the month at the **Athanor Studio**, is a Brussels institution. In the Marolles, Cuban disco **Havana** stays open until 7am at weekends.

Check www.noctis.com for up-to-date nightlife listings.

MUSIC FESTIVALS

A definite high point on the classical music calender is **Ars Musica**, a festival where composers often premiere their works. The festival takes place over several weeks, usually in March.

Les Nuits Botanique is a festival of over a hundred concerts, with indie rock, *chanson Française* and rap figuring prominently; it takes over the Botanique for the whole of May. In June, hundreds of free concerts are on offer during the **Fete de la Musique** festival. In the last weekend of the same month, the biggest pop and rock festival in the country comes to the village of Werchter (15 km/9 miles from Leuven) when the giant **Rock Werchter** festival takes place.

ANTWERP

Antwerp is home to Belgian ballet. The **Royal Ballet of Flanders**, founded in 1969, performs both classical and contemporary works. Tickets start at €15.

The city also claims two opera houses and some fine theatres and jazz venues. Try Art Deco wonder **Buster** for first-rate jazz and jam sessions.

Clubbers from across the country flock to **Café d'Anvers**. The former church, located in Antwerp's red light district, was turned into a house club in 1991. **Petrol Club**, meanwhile, blends electro, hip-hop and rock.

GHENT

For Ghent jazz, the mandatory visit is to Art Nouveau **Damberd Jazz Café**, which has live jazz on Tuesdays. Ghent's popular **Hotsy Totsy** jazz bar also offers occasional stand-up comedy.

The country's most warm-spirited festival, **De Gentse Feesten**, is a centuries-old celebration that lasts for ten days in July. Buskers, street perfomers, rock and jazz bands compete for the attention of a lively crowd.

BRUGES

Bruges is a real pub-goer's town more than anything, yet jazz lovers have plenty to choose from, notably the family-friendly art centre **De Werf** in Werfstraat and **De Versteende Nacht**. This friendly bar puts on live jazz every Wednesday evening and stays open until 4am.

DIRECTORY

OPERA & CLASSICAL

Belgian National Orchestra
Galeries Ravenstein 28.
Map 2 E3.
Tel (02) 552 0460.

Palais des Beaux-Arts
Rue Ravenstein 23.
Map 2 E3. Tel (02) 507 8200. www.bozar.be

Théâtre de la Monnaie
Place de la Monnaie.
Map 2 D2. Tel (02) 229 1200. www.lamonnaie.be

DANCE

Théâtre Les Tanneurs
Rue des Tanneurs 75.
Tel (02) 512 1784.
www.lestanneurs.be

JAZZ

Athanor Studio
Rue De La Fourche 17–19.
Tel (02) 514 1615.
Map 2 D2.
www.studio-athanor.be

Brussels Jazz Marathon
www.brusselsjazz
marathon.be

L'Archiduc
Rue Antoine-Dansaert 6.
Map 1 C2. Tel (02) 512 0652. www.archiduc.net

L'Arts-Ô-Bases
Rue Ulens 43.
Tel (048) 605 6015.

Sounds
Rue de la Tulipe 28.
Map 2 F5.
Tel (02) 512 9250.
www.soundsjazzclub.be

The Music Village
Rue des Pierres 50.
Map 1 C3.
Tel (02) 513 1345.
www.themusicvillage.com

ROCK, FOLK, WORLD & REGGAE

Ancienne Belgique
Boulevard Anspach 110.
Tel (02) 548 2424.
www.abconcerts.be

Beursschouwburg
A Ortsstraat 20–28.
Tel (02) 550 0350. www.
beursschouwburg.be

Café Central
Rue de Borgval 14.
www.lecafecentral.com

Cirque Royale
Rue de l'Enseignement 81.
Tel (02) 218 2015.
www.botanique.be

Forêt-National
Avenue Victor Rousseau 208. Tel (02) 340 2123.
www.forestnational.be

Halles de Schaerbeek
Rue Royale Sainte-Mairie 22a. Tel (02) 218 2107.
www.halles.be

Kultuur Kaffee
Boulevard Triomphe 6.
Tel (02) 629 2325.
www.kultuurkaffee.be

La Tentation
Rue de Laeken 28.
Tel (02) 223 2275.
www.latentation.org

Magasin 4
Avenue du Port 51B.
Tel (02) 223 3474.
www.magasin4.be

Recyclart
Rue des Ursulines 25.
Map 1 C4.
Tel (02) 502 5734.
www.recyclart.be

VK Club
Schoolstraat 76.
www.vkconcerts.be

THEATRE

American Theater Company
Rue Waelhem 73.
www.atc-brussels.com

Brussels Light Opera Company
Tel (02) 720 6729.
www.bloc-brussels.be

Brussels Shakespeare Society
Tel (02) 234 6510.
www.shaksoc.com

English Comedy Club
Rue Waelhem 73.
www.theatreinbrussels.com

Irish Theatre Co
www.irishtheatregroup.
be

Théâtre National
Boulevard Emile Jacqmain 111–115.
Tel (02) 203 4155.
www.theatrenational.be

Théâtre Le Public
Rue Braemt 64–70.
Tel 0800 94444.
www.theatrelepublic.be

Théâtre Royal du Parc
Rue de la Loi 3.
Tel (02) 505 3040.
www.theatreduparc.be

CINEMA

Actors Studio
Petite Rue des Bouchers 16. Tel (02) 512 1696.
www.cinenews.be

Anima
Tel (02) 534 4125.

Arenberg-Galeries
Galerie de la Reine 26.
Tel (02) 512 8063.
www.arenberg.be

Belgian Gay and Lesbian Film Festival
www.fglb.org

Brussels Intl Festival of Fantastic Film
www.bifff.org

Kinepolis Laeken
Bruparck, Boulevard du Centenaire 20.
www.kinepolis.com

Movy Club
Rue des Moines 21.
Tel (02) 537 6954.

Nova
Rue d'Arenberg 3.
Tel (02) 511 2477.
www.nova-cinema.com

CLUBS & NIGHTLIFE

Gecko Bar
Place Saint-Géry 16.
Map 1 C2.

Havana
Rue de l'Epée 4.
Tel (02) 502 1224.
www.havana-brussels.com

Le Roi des Belges
Rue Jules Van Praet 5.
Tel (02) 503 4300.

Les Jeux d'Hiver
Chemin du Croquet 1.
Tel (02) 649 0864.
www.jeuxdhiver.be.

Mappa Mundo
Rue du Pont de la Carpe 2.
Tel (02) 513 5116.

Ric's Boat
Quai des Péniches 44.
Tel (02) 203 6728.

The Fuse
Rue Blaes 208.
Tel (02) 511 9789.
www.fuse.be

MUSIC FESTIVALS

Ars Musica
www.arsmusica.be

Fete de la Musique
www.conseildelamusique.
be

Les Nuits Botanique
www.botanique.be

Rock Werchter
www.rockwerchter.be

ANTWERP

Buster
Kaasrui 1.
Tel (03) 232 5153.

Café d'Anvers
Verversrui 15.
Tel (03) 226 3870.
www.cafe-d-anvers.com

Petrol Club
D'Herbouvillekaai 25.
Tel (03) 226 4963.
www.petrolclub.be

Royal Ballet of Flanders
Kattendijkdok-Westkaai 16. Tel (03) 234 3438.
www.koninklijkballet
vanvlaanderen.be

GHENT

Damberd Jazz Café
Korenmarkt 19.
Map E2.
Tel (09) 329 5337.
www.damberd.be

De Gentse Feesten
Tel (09) 269 4600.
www.gentsefeesten.be

Hotsy Totsy
Hoogstraat 1. Map D1 2.
Tel (09) 224 2012.
www.hotsytotsy.be

BRUGES

De Versteende Nacht
Langestraat 11. Map C3.
Tel (049) 655 7398.
www.deversteendenacht.
com

De Werf
Werfstraat 108.
Tel (050) 330529.
www.dewerf.be

For Ghent and Bruges map references *refer to the inside back cover*

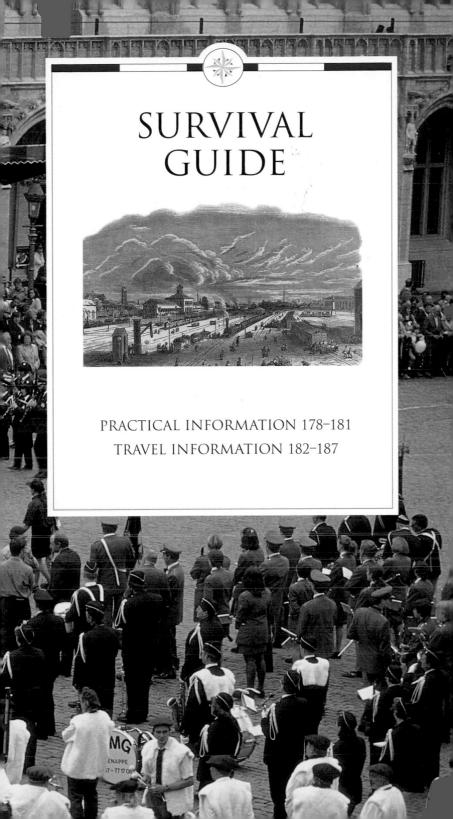

SURVIVAL GUIDE

PRACTICAL INFORMATION

Although comfortable with its status as a major political and business centre, Brussels has sometimes struggled with its role as a tourist destination. It can be hard to find all but the most obvious sights: the same goes for inexpensive hotels. The tourist office, however, goes out of its way to help travellers enjoy the city and provides help with everything from finding hidden sights to medical and financial information. Brussels is a very cosmopolitan city, and its residents, many of whom are foreigners themselves, are usually charming and friendly, with most speaking English. Both the Upper and Lower Town can be negotiated on foot, and although Brussels' reputation as a rainy city is overplayed, bring a raincoat in summer and warm clothing for winter.

Tourist information sign

CUSTOMS AND IMMIGRATION

Belgium is one of the signatories to the 1985 Schengen agreement, which means travellers moving from one Schengen country to another are not subject to border controls. However, carry your passport as there are occasional spot checks, and always carry ID with you in Belgium.

Britain does not belong to Schengen, so travellers coming from the UK must present a valid passport and hold proof of onward passage when entering Belgium. This also applies to US, Australian and Canadian citizens.

British travellers no longer benefit from duty-free goods, but visitors from non-EU countries are entitled to a VAT refund if they spend more than €125 in a single transaction.

TOURIST INFORMATION

The city is rarely crowded, so you should not have to wait at major attractions and museums unless a special event is taking place. If you are planning to do extensive sightseeing, the one-day tram and bus pass *(see p185)* is a must. Better still, pick up a Brussels Card from the Tourist and Information Office in Grand Place. The card costs €33 and includes a three-day travel pass, free access to 25 of the city's museums, discounts for some attractions, restaurants and shops, and a guide to the city. The tourist office also publishes a variety of maps, guides and tours.

LANGUAGE

Brussels is officially bilingual, which means that everything from street signs to bus destination boards must be in French and Dutch. Visitors will find that the locals are also remarkably adept at other languages too, and English in particular is spoken to an impressive level across much of the city.

Things become slightly more complicated outside Brussels, in part due to historical issues over language between the French and Flemish communities. Long-standing resentment at the dominance of French in Belgium means that initiating a conversation or ordering in a restaurant in French while you are in Flanders doesn't go down that well. A simple "*goed dag*" will do the trick, after which the conversation will almost certainly to revert to your own language.

In Wallonia, on the other hand, there will be almost no Dutch and little English spoken outside the main tourist areas. A useful start would be to look through the Phrase Book on p205.

OPENING HOURS

Most shops and businesses are open Monday to Saturday from 10am to 6pm. Supermarkets are usually open from 9am to 8pm. For late-night essentials and alcohol, "night shops" stay open until 1 or 2am. Banks are usually open weekdays from 9am to 1pm and 2 to 4pm.

Many sights are closed on Monday. Public museums are usually open Tuesday to Sunday from 10am to 5pm.

ADMISSION CHARGES

Most of Brussels' major attractions charge an entrance fee, currently around €6–8, though there are often reductions available for students, senior citizens and the unemployed, while children

The sculpture court in the Musées Royaux des Beaux-Arts in summer

◁ **Colourful festival parade in Grand Place, Brussels**

Visitors taking a break from sightseeing at a pavement café

under 12 usually get in free. Some museums, such as the Musées Royaux des Beaux-Arts de Belgique and the Musée des Instruments de Musique, have free entry for all visitors after 1pm on the first Wednesday of each month. There are still a few sights with no admission charge, including the Cathédrale des Sts Michel et Gudule and the Musée Royal de l'Armée et d'Histoire Militaire.

TIPPING

A service charge is included in all hotel and restaurant prices. A small tip for the chambermaid and porter should be given personally to them, or left in your vacated room. Most diners round up the bill or add about 10 per cent if the service has been particularly good. Service is also included in taxi fares, although a 10 per cent tip is customary.

TRAVELLERS WITH SPECIAL NEEDS

The Belgian capital is not the easiest city for the disabled traveller to negotiate, but the authorities have recognized that there is significant room for improvement. Most of the more expensive hotels have some rooms designed specifically for people with disabilities; there are designated parking spaces for disabled drivers and newer trams provide wheelchair access, through only 10 metro stations have lifts.

The **Brussels For All** website has information for travellers with reduced mobility on everything from transport to restaurants and exhibitions. The Tourist Office also provides information and advice about facilities within the city.

TRAVELLING WITH CHILDREN

Brussels is one of the most child-friendly cities in Europe. There are some excellent museums aimed specifically at younger children, such as the Musée du Jouet, packed with vintage toys, and the Musée des Enfants in Ixelles. Attractions like the Natural Science Museum, Bruparck and the Walibi theme park, just outside the city, will appeal to older kids. There are almost always discounts available for children: at the Musées Royaux des Beaux-Arts, under-18s are free if accompanied by an adult, and there are price reductions at Walibi for kids aged six to 11. Children under six have free entry to most museums, and they can travel for free on buses, trams and trains.

PUBLIC TOILETS

Many public toilets in Brussels, including those in bars, restaurants and even cinemas and railway stations, have attendants, who should be given 40–50 cents. If they are unmanned an honour system applies and you'll be expected to leave the money in a dish at the entrance.

RESPONSIBLE TOURISM

Awareness of the environment and local culture is subtly, yet powerfully felt in Brussels. Recycling has become second nature: public litter bins are colour-coded for different types of rubbish and supermarkets across the capital charge for using plastic bags.

Every commune has excellent weekly food markets offering the best in fresh, local produce. Two of these markets, at Place de la Monnaie and the Ateliers des Tanneurs in the Marolles, offer organic (or "bio") vegetables, cheese, bread, fruit, meat and charcuterie. Even the traditional Cantillon Brewery in Anderlecht uses cereal that is 100% organic for its beer.

Under the auspices of **Karikol**, a union of food-producers and restaurateurs founded in 2007, the week-long Goûter Bruxelles festival in late September celebrates the Slow Food movement. Events held at locations throughout the city are dedicated to savouring long, convivial meals and the ideals of "eco-gastronomy".

Personal Security and Health

Brussels is one of Europe's safest capitals, with street crime against visitors a relatively rare occurrence. The poorer areas west and north of the city centre, including Anderlecht, Molenbeek and parts of Schaerbeek and St-Josse, have quite a bad reputation, but these areas are perfectly safe during the daytime for everyone except those who flaunt their wealth. After dark, it is sensible not to walk around on your own in these areas. Public transport is usually safe at all hours.

POLICE

There are two levels of integrated police in Brussels. Major crimes and motorway offences are handled by the national gendarmerie. However, visitors are most likely to come across the communal police, who are responsible for law and order in each of the capital's 19 administrative districts. All Brussels police officers must speak French and Flemish, and many will be proficient in English too.
The main police station for central Brussels is on Rue du Marché au Charbon, close to the Grand Place. If stopped by the police, visitors will be asked for identification, so carry your passport on you at all times. Be aware that talking on a mobile phone while driving and possession of cannabis is illegal here; not using road crossings correctly is also illegal and may be subject to on-the-spot fines.

Police officer on patrol

WHAT TO BE AWARE OF

Most of Brussels' main tourist attractions are located in safe areas. When driving, make sure car doors are locked and any valuables are kept out of sight. If you are sightseeing, limit the amount of cash you carry. Handbags should be worn with the strap across the shoulder and the clasp facing towards the body. Wallets should be kept in a front, not back, pocket. Hotel rooms often come with a safe; if not, there should be one at reception to keep valuables locked up.

At night, avoid the city's parks, especially at Botanique and Parc Josaphat in Schaerbeek, both of which are favoured haunts of drug-dealers.

IN AN EMERGENCY

For emergencies requiring police assistance, call 101; for medical or fire services, phone 100. Hospitals with emergency departments include **Institut Edith Cavell** and **Hôpital Universitaire Saint Luc**. The **Community Help Service**'s (CHS) 24-hour English-language help line is for expatriates, but it may be able to assist tourists.

LOST PROPERTY

Your chance of retrieving property that was lost in the street is minimal. For insurance purposes, contact the police station for the commune in which the article disappeared. (If you are not sure where that is, contact the central police station on Rue du Marché au Charbon). The public transport authority **STIB/MIVB** operates a lost-and-found service for the metro, trams and buses. Report items lost in a taxi to the police station nearest your point of departure, and quote registration details and the taxi licence number.

TRAVEL AND HEALTH INSURANCE

Travellers from Britain and Ireland are entitled to free healthcare under reciprocal agreements within the EU. To obtain this, you must carry an EHIC (European health insurance card). Europeans should make it clear that they have state insurance, or they may end up with a large bill. State healthcare subsidies do not cover all problems and it is worth taking out full travel insurance. This can also cover lost property.

MEDICAL MATTERS

Whether or not you have insurance, doctors in Belgium will usually expect you to settle the bill on the spot – and in cash. Arrange to make a payment by bank transfer (most doctors will accept this if you insist).
Pharmacies are usually open Monday to Friday from 8:30am to 6:30pm and Saturday from 8:30am to noon, with each commune operating a rota system to cover holiday and other periods.

DIRECTORY

POLICE

Central Police Station
Rue du Marché au Charbon 30, 1000 Brussels. **Map** 1 C3.
Tel (02) 279 7979.

IN AN EMERGENCY

Ambulance and Fire Services
Tel 100.

Community Help Service
Tel (02) 647 6780.

Hôpital Universitaire Saint Luc
Ave Hippocrate 10, 1200 Brussels.
Tel (02) 764 1111.

Institut Edith Cavell
Rue Edith Cavell 32, 1180 Brussels.
Tel (02) 340 4001.

Police
Tel 101.

LOST PROPERTY

Central Police Station
Tel (02) 274 1699.

STIB/MIVB
Avenue de la Toison d'Or 15 1050 Brussels. **Map** 2 D5.
www.stib.be

Banking and Communications

Along with an array of banks and exchange bureaux in Brussels, there are hundreds of 24-hour cashpoints located around the city, and international credit and debit cards are widely accepted. The postal system is efficient and although Internet cafés are not common in Brussels, phone shops and Wi-Fi access in hotels, cafés and bars make up for this. As the capital of Europe, Brussels is a multilingual media hub; all aspects of publishing and broadcasting are available whatever your language.

BANKS AND BUREAUX DE CHANGE

Most banks in Brussels are open weekdays from 9am to 1pm and 2 to 4pm; some open late on Friday until 4:30 or 5pm, and a few on Saturday mornings.
Banks often offer very competitive exchange rates, and most will happily serve non-clients. Many transactions (especially money transfers) are liable to banking fees, so ask in advance what these rates might be. Most banks will be able to cash traveller's cheques with the signatory's passport or other form of photographic identification. Visitors are also usually able to exchange foreign currency, again with valid ID. You will find that many bank attendants speak good English.

There is a 24-hour automated exchange machine at Grand Place 7, while in the streets around the square there are several bureaux de change that are open until 7pm or later. Some of these charge no commission for exchanging cash, though it's always worth comparing prices between different bureaux. There are currency exchange booths at all of the city's major stations.

Red Belgian postbox

CREDIT CARDS

American Express, Diners Club, MasterCard and Visa are widely accepted in Brussels, although it is wise to check in advance if booking a hotel or restaurant. Most hotels will accept a credit card booking, and the cardholder may be asked for a credit card imprint at check-in. Check first in shops and super-markets whether they take credit cards, as some will only accept cards issued by Belgian banks, most notably the popular Mister Cash card.

ATMS

Almost all bank branches have 24-hour cashpoint facilities. Most ATMs will accept a wide range of credit or debit cards including those belonging to the Cirrus, Plus, Maestro and Star systems, as well as those from MasterCard and Visa.

POST AND COMMUNICATIONS

Brussels' central post office, 1 Boulevard Anspach, is open from 9am to 7pm Monday to Friday and from 10am to 4:30pm on Saturday.

Public payphones are run by Belgacom and accept both coins and telephone cards. The operator can be contacted by dialling 1380 or for directory enquiries in English dial 1405.

The ability to use your mobile phone in Belgium depends on your network and you should ask your provider whether this service is available to you before travelling.

There are almost no large Internet cafés, though in and around Boulevard Anspach in particular are phone shops and corner stores that have a few computers with Internet access. Instead, the city is especially big on Wi-Fi.

NEWSPAPERS, TV AND RADIO

Most British and American daily newspapers produce international editions, which are on sale along with English-language magazines at specialist bookshops and newsstands across the city.

Belgium has one of the world's most advanced cable TV networks, with access to more than 40 channels, including both BBC 1 and 2, CNN and Arte. TV listings can be found in *The Bulletin*.

Classical music radio stations include Musique 3 (91.2 FM) and Radio Klara (89.5 FM). Internet radio stations, such as StarRadio (www.star-radio. net), offer pop music, as well as news and chat in English.

A magazine stand

DIRECTORY

LOST CREDIT CARDS

American Express
Tel (02) 676 2121.

MasterCard
Tel 0800 1 5096.

Visa
Tel 0800 1 8397.

BOOKSHOPS

Librairie de Rome
Librairie de Rome.
Map 2 D5. *Tel (02) 511 7937.*

Sterling Books
Rue du Fossé-aux-Loups 38.
Map 2 D2. *Tel (02) 223 6223.*

Waterstone's
Boulevard Adolphe Max 71–75.
Map 2 D1. *Tel (02) 219 2708.*

TRAVEL INFORMATION

Brussels is well suited to both casual and business travellers, with excellent connections by air, rail and road. The increasing political significance of Brussels in its role as the heart of Europe has led to greater competition between airlines, with many operators offering discounted

High-speed Thalys train

fares. The Eurostar and Thalys high-speed trains link the city with London, Paris, Amsterdam and Germany, and compare favourably with flying in terms of time. British travellers can use the Channel Tunnel or a range of cross-Channel ferry services if they want to bring their car with them.

An aeroplane from Belgian carrier Brussels Airlines' fleet

ARRIVING BY AIR

Situated 14 km (9 miles) northeast of the city centre, **Brussels National Airport** is in the Flemish commune of Zaventem (the name by which it is known to most citizens, including taxi drivers). A centre for Belgian carrier **Brussels Airlines**, the airport is also served by major carriers such as **British Airways**, **American Airlines**, **KLM**, **Air Canada**, **Delta** and **Lufthansa** and low-cost operators like **Ryanair**. A typical journey from London takes around 45 minutes. A scheduled return flight can be as much as £270, though prices can be significantly reduced if you are flexible regarding dates and keep an eye on airline websites for offers.

Reaching Brussels from the US can be more expensive than reaching other European cities. Flights average US$1000 for a charter return from New York. Prices from Canada are comparable.

The best-value flights from Australia and New Zealand are usually found with **Singapore Airlines**.

Brussels **South-Charleroi** Airport has become a second hub since Ryanair began operating scheduled flights

from various European destinations (including Glasgow Prestwick and Edinburgh in the UK). The airport is located 55 km (34 miles) from the centre of Brussels and can be reached by train or coach.

GETTING INTO TOWN

The cheapest way of getting from Zaventem to the city centre is the express train from the airport to Gare du Nord, Gare Centrale or Gare du Midi. Tickets (about €3) are on sale in the airport complex or can be purchased there. Three trains run each hour between 5am and midnight; the journey to Gare Centrale takes 20 minutes. There is also an airport bus, Line 12, which runs hourly between 6am and 11pm. It stops at only the main train stations and Schuman metro stop, terminating at Place Luxembourg, near the European Parliament.

There is a taxi rank outside the arrivals hall. A one-way fare from the airport to the centre of Brussels will cost €30–35 and should take around 20 minutes (though

this may be longer at rush hour). If you plan to return by taxi, ask the driver about deals, as some companies offer discounts on return fares.

An SNCB/NMBS *(see p185)* train runs from Charleroi to Gare du Midi. The journey takes about 45 minutes to/from the station. Ryanair also operates a shuttle bus between Brussels South-Charleroi Airport and Gare du Midi, with a journey time of approximately 1 hour.

ARRIVING BY RAIL

Brussels is at the heart of Europe's high-speed train networks, connected to London by the **Eurostar** service and to Paris, Amsterdam and Cologne by the **Thalys** network. These trains have a top speed of 300 kph (186 mph) and have slashed journey times between northern Europe's major cities.

Eurostar passengers should book their tickets at least a week in advance, especially to take advantage of reduced fares; they should also arrive at the terminal a minimum of 20 minutes before departure to go through the check-in and customs procedures

Eurostar train at the Gare du Midi, Brussels

before boarding. It is possible that you may be refused access to the train if you arrive after this time, although you can often be transferred to the next service at no extra charge.

Trains run hourly between London's St Pancras International station and Brussels via the Channel Tunnel; the journey takes just under 2 hours and arrives at the Gare du Midi, which is served by metro trains, buses and trams. Taxis to the centre cost around €12.

Many visitors to Brussels arrive from mainland Europe. The high-speed train company **Thalys** also operates from the Gare du Midi and offers a comfortable journey, with Paris accessible in 1 hour and 25 minutes, Amsterdam in around 2 hours and Cologne in under 3 hours.

ARRIVING BY SEA

Belgium can easily be reached from the UK by ferries which arrive several times a day. Cross-Channel ferries run frequently from Dover to Calais and Dunkirk, Ramsgate to Ostend and Hull to Zeebrugge.

Services are offered by several companies, including **Norfolkline** and **P&O Ferries**. Foot passengers do not usually need to book, but those with vehicles should always reserve a space and arrive promptly.

ARRIVING BY CAR

Le Shuttle, operated by **Eurotunnel**, takes vehicles from the Channel Tunnel entrance near Folkestone direct to Calais, a journey of about 35 minutes. From there, Brussels is just a 2-hour drive via the A16 motorway, which becomes the E40 when you cross the Franco-Belgian border. Follow signs first to Brugge (Bruges), and then on to Brussels. Those planning to use the Eurotunnel should book tickets in advance and try to arrive early. Three trains per hour operate between 6:30am and midnight, with one train running hourly from midnight to 6:30am. There are a number of special offers that are intermittently available.

Eurolines coach running between London and Brussels

ARRIVING BY COACH

Eurolines, a group of coach companies forming Europe's largest coach network, operates daily bus services from Victoria Coach Station in London to Brussels' Gare du Nord, via the Channel Tunnel. Prices are extremely competitive compared to other forms of travel to Brussels, though this is offset by a journey time of around 7 hours. Note that coaches are sometimes checked at the border with France, so be sure to keep passports handy. From Gare du Nord, the centre can be reached either by mainline SNCB trains, prémetro trams or city buses. Small discounts are available for travellers aged under 26 and over 60.

DIRECTORY

ARRIVING BY AIR

Air Canada
Tel (0871) 220 1111 (UK).
www.aircanada.com

American Airlines
Tel (0845) 778 9789 (UK).
Tel (1 800) 433 7300 (US).
www.aa.com

British Airways
Tel (0870) 850 9850 (UK).
www.britishairways.com

Brussels Airlines
Tel (0902) 51600.
www.brusselsairlines.com

Brussels National Airport Information
www.brusselsairport.be
Flight Information
Tel 0900 70000.

Disabled Travellers and Special Needs
Tel (02) 753 2212.
Airport Police
Tel (02) 709 6666.
Customs
Tel (02) 753 2910.

Delta
Tel (0800) 414 767 (UK).
Tel (404) 765 5000 (US).
www.delta.com

KLM
Tel (0871) 222 740 (UK).
Tel (1 866) 434 0320 (US). Tel (61 1) 30 039 2192 (AUS).
www.klm.com

Lufthansa
Tel (0845) 773 7747 (UK).
www.lufthansa.com

Ryanair
Tel (08701) 569 569 (UK). www.ryanair.com

Singapore Airlines
Tel (0844) 800 2380 (UK).
www.singaporeair.com

South-Charleroi Airport
Tel (0)71 251 211.
www.charleroi-airport.com

ARRIVING BY RAIL

Belgian & International Railway Info
www.b-rail.be

Eurostar
Tel (0870) 535 3535 (UK).
www.eurostar.com

Thalys
Tel (07) 066 7788.
www.thayls.com

ARRIVING BY SEA

Norfolkline
Tel (0870) 870 1020.
www.norfolkline.com

P&O Ferries
Tel (0871) 664 5645.
www.poferries.com

ARRIVING BY CAR

Eurotunnel
Tel (0990) 535 3535 (UK).
www.eurotunnel.com

ARRIVING BY COACH

Eurolines
Tel (08717) 818181 (UK).
www.eurolines.com

Getting Around Brussels

Metro station street sign

Although its public transport system is clean, modern and efficient, Brussels is a city best explored on foot. Most of the key attractions for first-time visitors are within a short walk of the Grand Place, and the Art Nouveau architecture in Ixelles and Saint-Gilles is also best enjoyed on a leisurely stroll. For those anxious to see the main sights in limited time, the tram and metro network covers most of the city at speed, while buses are useful for reaching more out-of-the-way areas. Although expensive, taxis are recommended for late-night journeys. Cycling can be hazardous for the inexperienced.

Bus at a stop in Brussels city centre

GREEN TRAVEL

Brussels is the perfect place to reduce your carbon footprint. The centre is small enough to make walking around its ancient cobbled streets one of the highlights of any visit, while the use of bicycles is encouraged through the imaginative **Villo** rental scheme and kilometres of bicycle lanes. Each September a popular "car-free" day is held, when traffic is banned and pedestrians and cyclists take over the streets.

Brussels also has an excellent public transport system, with a highly integrated, affordable metro, tram and bus network. The city is committed to an Eco-drive scheme, reducing energy consumption by lowering speeds on all modes of public transport and accessing electricity from renewable sources for trams and metro trains, and the development of hybrid and fuel cell engines on its buses.

There's little need for a car even when you go beyond Brussels. The other main cities aren't that far away and are served by an excellent national train network.

Several special tariffs are available, including discounts for young adults aged under 26 and seniors, and weekend tickets, which reduce the price by up to 40 per cent.

PLANNING YOUR JOURNEY

If you are seeing Brussels by car, avoid its major roads during rush hours, which are weekdays from 8 to 9:30am and 5 to 7pm as well as Wednesday lunchtimes during the school year, when there is a half day. Tram and bus services run frequently at peak times and are usually not too crowded. However, the small size of Brussels means that walking is often a viable option.

WALKING IN BRUSSELS

The short distance between sights and the interest in every corner make central Brussels easy to negotiate on foot. Outside the city centre, walking is the only way to appreciate the concentration of Art Nouveau buildings on and around Square Ambiorix, around the district of Ixelles and near St-Gilles Town Hall.

Drivers in Brussels have a bad reputation, and it is important to be alert to traffic while crossing roads. Motorists are obliged to stop at pedestrian crossings but you will find that this rule is often ignored. At traffic lights, drivers turning right or left may pay no attention to the walker's priority. It is essential to be careful even in residential areas.

Blue or white street signs are placed on the walls of buildings at one corner of a street, and can be somewhat hard to locate. Street names are always in French first, then Flemish, with the name in capital letters and the street type in small letters to the top left and bottom right corners (for example, Rue STEVIN straat).

CYCLING

Car traffic can be fierce, but happily the number of cycle lanes is ever on the increase, as is the ease with which visitors can rent a bike. One of the most convenient ways is the Villo scheme. You can take a Villo unisex bike by the day or week, paying online or at one of the 180 cycle stations across the city. Use your credit card for the €150 deposit. The bike can be parked or returned to any of the stations. The current rental charge is €1.50 for a day and €7 for a week.

Children enjoying the sights of Brussels by bike

A city tram travelling down Rue Royale towards the city centre

TRAVELLING BY BUS, TRAM AND METRO

The authority governing Brussels' public transport is the bilingual **STIB/MVIB**, which runs buses, trams and metro services in the capital. Tickets are valid on all three services, which run between 5:30am and 12:30am on weekdays with shorter hours on Sundays and public holidays.

A single ticket, which allows unlimited changes within 1 hour (excluding the Nato-Brussels Airport Line 12), costs €1.80. You can also buy a five-ticket card at €7.30, a ten-ticket card at €12.30, or a one-day pass costing €4.50. Single tickets can be bought on buses and trams but cost €2. Tickets should be stamped in the machines next to the exits; you must restamp your ticket if the journey involves a change. A map of the whole network is available at most metro stations. STIB is gradually replacing transport tickets with a single pass, called MOBIB, which can store different travel options at the same time, such as a season ticket, a ten-day journey or a day pass, on an electronic chip.

At street level, metro stations are marked by a large white 'M' on a blue background. Tickets must be bought and stamped before you reach the platform. They can be obtained from metro ticket offices and automated machines inside

One-day travel pass

stations, as well as many newsagents. Metro stations in the city centre have electronic displays showing where each train is in the system and all the stops on the route.

The older yellow trams are slowly being phased out. Unlike newer models, these have no information on what the upcoming stop is so you need to have a copy of the tram network or ask the driver to call out the relevant stop.

As well as the main network, a few bus services in the capital are run by the Walloon transport group (TEC) and the Flemish operator De Lijn. These services have lettered rather than numbered codes, but most tickets are valid on all the services.

DRIVING IN BRUSSELS

Belgium drives on the right, and the *priorité à droite* rule – which means that the driver coming from the right at junctions has absolute priority to pull out unless otherwise indicated – is enforced with sometimes startling regularity. Always watch for vehicles coming from the right, no matter how small the road; some drivers have been known to take their priority even though it means a crash, secure in the knowledge that they are legally correct. Always give way to trams, who will ring their bells should a car be blocking their path. Street parking, usually by meter, is becoming increasingly difficult in the centre of the city.

Essential safety precautions should be adhered to at all times. Safety belts are obligatory in all seats, and children under 12 years old are not allowed to sit in the front. Drink-driving is illegal (the limit in Belgium is currently 0.5g/l) as is talking on a mobile while driving (though not on "hands free" phones so far). The Belgian police are notorious for suddenly target-ing an offence, so you might find one day they ignore you

DIRECTORY

USEFUL NUMBERS

STIB/MIVB
Avenue de la Toison d'Or 15
1050 Brussels. **Map** 2 D5.
Tel (02) 515 2000. **www**.stib.be

Villo
Tel 078 05 1110 (hotline).
www.villo.be

completely and the next give you a €50 on-the-spot fine.

Most international car rental agencies have branches in Brussels, many at the National Airport in Zaventem or at the Gare du Midi, where the Eurostar, Thalys and other main train services arrive. The success of the Belgian Mister Cash bank card means that many petrol stations, when unattended on Sundays and out of hours, only accept this card, so fill up during the week if possible.

TAKING A TAXI

Brussels' taxis are fairly expensive, but most journeys are short and cabs are the city's only 24-hour transport service. All taxis have a rooftop sign which is illuminated when the vehicle is vacant. Cabs are generally picked up at a taxi rank or ordered by phone rather than flagged down on the street. Tips are included in the fare, but an extra tip is usually expected. Give the taxi's registration number, its make and colour when making a complaint.

Traffic on a busy main street in central Brussels

Getting Around Belgium

Touring Club de Belgique logo

As you might expect from a country that is small, modern and predominantly flat, Belgium is an extremely easy place in which to travel. The toll-free motorways compare favourably with any in France, train travel is swift and there are good bus services in those areas not covered by the railway network. Intercity trains leave from all three of the city's main stations and take 40 minutes to Antwerp (for the section on getting around Antwerp *see p94*), 40 minutes to Ghent (*see p114*) and 50 minutes to Bruges (*see p120*). Public transport is clean and efficient and the range of touring tickets allows a great deal of freedom and the ability to see the whole country inexpensively. In the level Flemish countryside to the north, hiking and cycling are pleasant ways to get around.

Car travelling through Durbuy in the scenic Ardennes

TRAVELLING BY CAR

After the rather enervating traffic in Brussels, driving in the rest of Belgium comes as something of a relief. The motorways are fast, reasonably well maintained and toll-free, while major roads are also excellent. Drivers in cities outside the capital tend to be more relaxed, although the trend in Flanders for car-free city centres can make navigation through them demanding. The only difficulty most drivers come across is an occasional absence of clear signs for motorway exits and junctions, which can necessitate taking extra care when approaching junctions (in Flanders, many drivers are confused by signs for "Uitrit". It means exit).

Speed limits are 50 kph (30 mph) in built-up areas, 120 kph (75 mph) on motorways and dual carriageways and 90 kph (55 mph) on all other roads. If you break down, three motoring organizations should be able to provide assistance: **Touring Club de Belgique**, **Royal Automobile Club de Belgique** and **Vlaamse Automobilistenbond** in Flanders. It is worth getting breakdown coverage before you leave, and you must have a valid driving licence (from the EU, US, Australia or Canada) or an International Driving Licence on your person. It is also essential to have comprehensive insurance and/or a Green card. Visitors are expected to carry a first-aid kit, a reflective orange or yellow jacket and a warning triangle at all times.

All the major car rental agencies operate in Belgium, although renting one can be an expensive business. To hire a vehicle, you must be 21 or over, with a year's driving experience, and be in possession of a credit card. A week's rental with unlimited mileage will cost €370 or more but might be reduced as the big firms offer regular special deals. Local rental agencies may also be cheaper, but be sure to check the terms and conditions.

Bicycle hire is available in most Flemish towns with a modest deposit of €15.

TRAVELLING BY RAIL

Run by **Belgian National Railways** (Société Nationale Chemins de Fer Belges/Belgische Spoorwegen), Belgium's train network provides a fast and economical means of getting to and from major towns and cities. As most journeys are fairly short, only light refreshments, including good Belgian beers, are available on board.

FRENCH/DUTCH PLACE NAMES

One of the most confusing aspects of travel in Belgium is the variation between French and Dutch spellings of town names. On road signs in Brussels, both names are given, while in Flanders only the Dutch and in Wallonia only the French are shown. The following list gives main towns:

French	Dutch	French	Dutch
Anvers	Antwerpen	Malines	Mechelen
Ath	Aat	Mons	Bergen
Bruges	Brugge	Namur	Namen
Bruxelles	Brussel	Ostende	Oostende
Courtrai	Kortrijk	Saint-Trond	Sint-Truiden
Gand	Gent	Tongrès	Tongeren
Liège	Luik	Tournai	Doornik
Louvain	Leuven	Ypres	Ieper

Train travelling through Belgium on a spring evening

Fares for standard second-class tickets are calculated by distance, so return tickets generally offer no savings and are usually valid only until midnight. Children aged under six travel free, with a maximum of four children allowed per adult, and those aged between six and 11 receive a 50 per cent discount. A range of special tariffs are available for people under 26 and senior citizens.

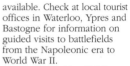

Belgian railway logo

A variety of rail passes are available for extensive travel. The Railpass costs €74 and allows ten trips within Belgium over one year, while the Benelux Pass costs €175 and offers unlimited travel on any five days within one month of purchase. The Benelux Pass can be used on trains in Belgium, the Netherlands and Luxembourg.

TRAVELLING BY BUS

While slower and less comfortable for travelling between major cities, buses come into their own in the more remote or rural areas of the rest of Belgium, as well as in city suburbs. In Flanders, buses are run by the **De Lijn** group; in Wallonia, the network is operated by **TEC**. Fares are calculated according to distance, and are bought from the driver. Bus stops and terminals are generally close to railway stations. Buses have priority on public roads, so journeys are often swift.

SPECIALIST TOURS

Brussels is a city rich in culture and there are many tours on offer to visitors. The Tourist and Information Centre (*see p178*) in the city centre runs over 40 walking, bus and car day tours that cover all of the capital with topics as diverse as "Humanist Brussels" and "Industrial Belgium". The focus is largely on the city's exceptional range of art and architecture, but many themes are covered. In each major regional city, detailed multi-lingual private tours are available in the historic town centre; you should contact the city's main tourist office for full information.

Belgium's position as one of Europe's most fought over territories is reflected in the range of battlefield tours available. Check at local tourist offices in Waterloo, Ypres and Bastogne for information on guided visits to battlefields from the Napoleonic era to World War II.

Away from cities, Belgium also offers hiking and cycling excursions, ranging from one-day adventures to five-day hikes. The Ardennes is a popular destination for hikers, who can appreciate the area's flora and fauna as well as its history. Contact the **Wallonia-Brussels** tourist office for more details.

DIRECTORY

TRAVELLING BY CAR

Tel Avis *(02) 730 6211.*
Tel Budget *(02) 646 5130.*
Tel Europcar *(02) 721 0592.*
Tel Hertz *(02) 513 288 6.*

Police Road Information
www.policefederale.be

Royal Automobile Club de Belgique
Rue d'Arlon 53, 1040 Brussels.
Map 3 A3. ***Tel*** *(02) 287 0911.*

Touring Club de Belgique
Rue de la Loi 44, 1040 Brussels.
Map 3 A2. ***Tel*** *(070) 344777*

Vlaamse Automobilistenbond
Pastoor Coplaan 100,
Zwijndrecht. ***Tel*** *(03) 253 6130.*

TRAVELLING BY RAIL AND BUS

De Lijn
Tel *(02) 526 2820.*

SNCB/BS (Belgian National Railways)
Tel *(02) 528 2828.*

TEC
Tel *(010) 235353*

SPECIALIST TOURS

Arau
Boulevard Adolphe Max 55.
Map 1 A2. ***Tel*** *(02) 219 3345.*

La Fonderie
Rue Ransfort 27. ***Tel*** *(02) 410 1080.* Industrial heritage, chocolate and beer walks.

Wallonia-Brussels Tourist Office
Tel *(070) 221 021.*

A long-distance bus in a city suburb in Belgium

BRUSSELS STREET FINDER

The page grid superimposed on the area by area grid below shows which parts of Brussels are covered in this *Street Finder*. The central Upper and Lower Town areas are marked in the colours that are also the thumbtab colours throughout the book. The map references for all sights, hotels, restaurants, shopping and entertainment venues

Nymph in Parc de Bruxelles

described in this guide refer to the maps in this section only. A street index follows on pp194–6. The key, set out below, indicates the scales of the maps and shows what other features are marked on them, including transport terminals, emergency services and information centres. All the major sights are clearly marked so they are easy to locate. The map on the inside back cover shows public transport routes.

KEY

◼	Major sight
◻	Other sight
◻	Other building
M	Metro station
🚆	Train station
🚊	Tram route
🚌	Bus station
🚖	Taxi rank
P	Parking
ℹ	Tourist information
✚	Hospital
🚔	Police station
✝	Church
⊠	Post office
═	Railway line
▬	Pedestrian street

SCALE OF MAPS   **1:11,500**

0 metres   250

0 yards   250

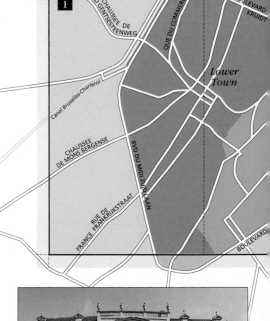

1

GAND CHAUSSEE DE
GENTSESTEENWEG

QUE DU COMMERCE

BOULEVARD KRUIDT

Lower Town

Canal Bruxelles Charleroi

CHAUSSEE DE MONS BERGENSE

BVD DU MIDI ZUIDLAAN

RUE DE FRANCE FRANKRIJKSTRAAT

BOULEVARD

Façade of La Maison des Ducs de Brabant, Grand Place *(see pp42–3)*

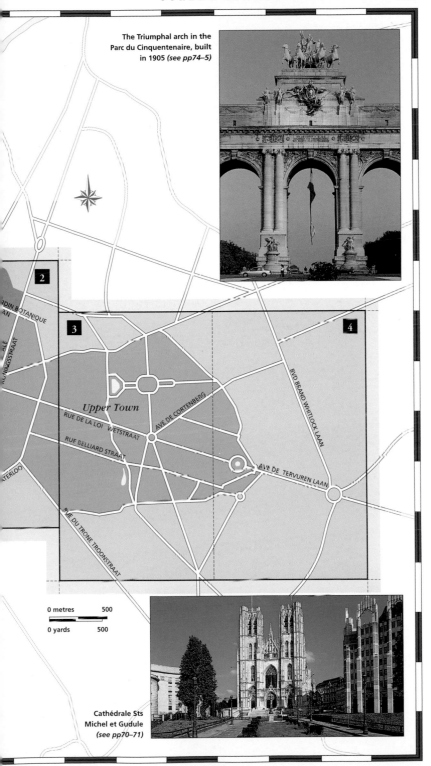

The Triumphal arch in the
Parc du Cinquentenaire, built
in 1905 *(see pp74–5)*

2

3

4

JARDIN BOTANIQUE
LAAN

KONINGSSTRAAT

ALE

Upper Town

RUE DE LA LOI WETSTRAAT

AVE DE CORTENBERG

BVD BRAND WHITLOCK LAAN

RUE BELLIARD STRAAT

AV. DE TERVUREN LAAN

WATERLOO

RUE DU TRONE TROONSTRAAT

0 metres 500

0 yards 500

Cathédrale Sts
Michel et Gudule
(see pp70–71)

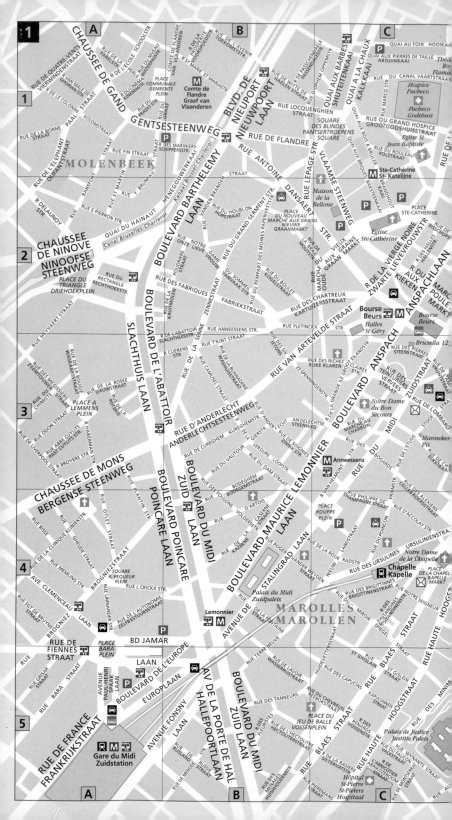

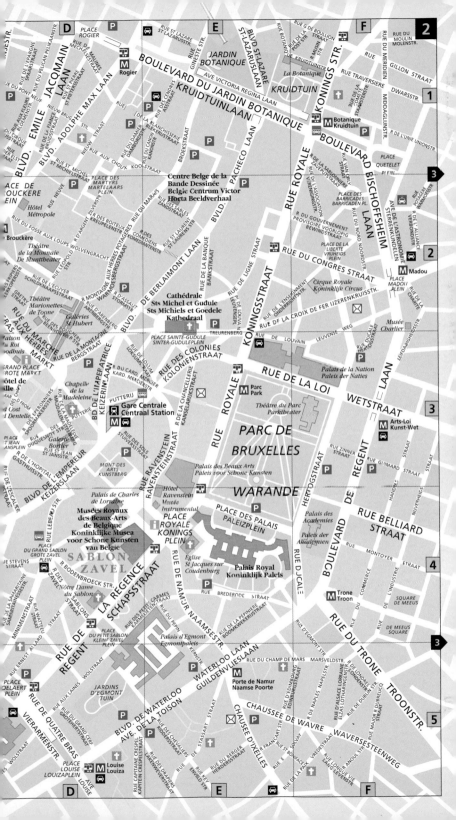

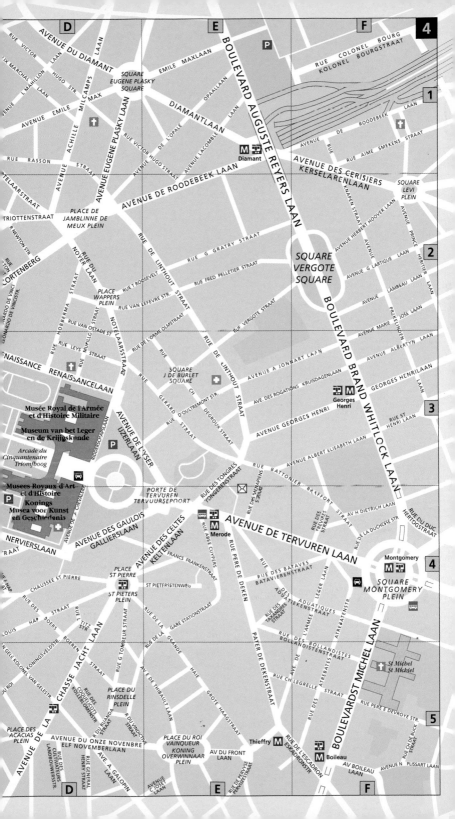

Street Finder Index

General Index

Page numbers in **bold** type refer to main entries

Acknowledgments

Dorling Kindersley would like to thank the following people whose assistance contributed to the preparation of this book:

Main Contributors
Zoë Hewetson is based in London but works in Brussels as a simultaneous translator for the European Commission. She is also a keen walker and has recently published a guide to walking in Turkey.

Philip Lee lives and works in Nottingham. A veteran travel writer, he has contributed to numerous *Rough Guide* and *Dorling Kindersley Travel Guide* publications, including the *Rough Guide to Belgium*. He frequently writes on travel for British newspapers and magazines.

Zoë Ross is a London-based writer and editor. She has worked on several Dorling Kindersley travel guides, and is now a freelance author.

Sarah Wolff has lived and worked in Brussels for several years. An editor and journalist, she is currently working for *The Bulletin*, Brussels' English-language newsweekly magazine.

Timothy Wright lived in Brussels for most of the 1990s. A successful journalist, he contributed to several English-language magazines published in Brussels and elsewhere in the Benelux countries.

Julia Zyrianova is a freelance journalist and translator. She lived in Brussels and Paris for several years and is now based in London.

Additional Contributors
Antony Mason, Emma Jones, Leigh Phillips.

For Dorling Kindersley
Gillian Allan, Douglas Amrine, Claire Baranowski, Marta Bescos Sanchez, Louise Bostock Lang, Dan Colwell, Paula da Costa, Vivien Crump, Simon Davis, Rhiannon Furbear, Donald Greig, Amy Harrison, Marie Ingledew, Jude Ledger, Carly Madden, Catherine Palmi, Lee Redmond, Marisa Renzullo, Ellen Root, Meredith Smith, Susana Smith, Lesley Joan Williamson.

Proofreader
Sam Merrell.

Indexer
Hilary Bird.

Additional Photography
Anthony Cassidy, Steve Gorton, Ian O'Leary, Roger Mapp, Neil Mersh, David Murray, Tim Ridely, Stuti Tiwari, Jules Selmes, Anthony Souter, Clive Streeter, Matthew Ward, Lesley Joan Williamson.

Special Assistance
Many thanks for the invaluable help of the following individuals: Joanna at Belgo; Derek Blyth; Christiana Ceulemans at Institut Royal Du Patrimonie Artistique; Charles Dierick at Centre Belge de la Bande Dessinée; Anne at Gaspard de Wit; Elsge Ganssen and Georges Delcart at Rubenshuis; Doctor Janssens at the Domaine de Laeken; Leen de Jong at Koninklijk Museum Voor Schone Kunsten; Antwerpen; Noel at Leonidas; Chantal Pauwert at Stad Brugge Stedelijke Musea; Marie-Hélène van Schonbroek at Cathédrale Sts Michel et Gudule; Elaine de Wilde and Sophie van Vliet at Musées Royaux des Beaux-Arts.

Photography Permissions
Dorling Kindersley would like to thank all the cathedrals, churches, museums, hotels, restaurants, shops, galleries and sights too numerous to thank individually for their assistance and kind permission to photograph at their establishments.

Placement Key - a–above; b–below/bottom; c–centre; f–far; l–left; r–right; t–top.

Works of art have been produced with the permission of the following copyright holders: ©Casterman 20 br, Ted Benoit Berceuse Electrique 50clb; ©DACS 2011 18bl, 51t/cra/crb/b, 82tr/cl/cr; ©Dupuis 1999 20tr, 21ca; Sofa Kandissy ©Alessandro Medini 115c; Lucky Luke Licensing ©MORRIS 20br; @Moulinsart SA 4, 20tl/cr/cl/bl, 50tl/tr/cra/crb, 51cla/clb; ©Peyo 1999 - Licensed through I.M.P.S. (Brussels) 21bc; 50cla;

The publishers would like to thank the following individuals, companies, and picture libraries for their kind permission to reproduce their photographs:

ACCUEIL ET TRADITION: 146; AKG, LONDON: 31b, 34t, 36b, 37bl, 37br, 150tr; Galleria Nazdi Cupodimonte 22-3; Erich Lessing 28, / Kunsthistoriches Museum 31t; Musée du Louvre 29b; Musée Royaux d'Arts et d'Histoire, Brussels 35c; Museo de Santa Cruz, Toledo 29t; Museum Deutsche Geschichte, Berlin 31c; Private Collection 150tl; Pushkin Museum 30c; Victoria and Albert Museum, London 32c; Ancienne Belgique: 173c; ALAMY IMAGES: Pat Dehnke 149tl, 99bl; Gary Cook 128cl; Ian Dagnall 116cl, 116br; Richard Wayman 181cr; INSADCO Photography/Martin Bobrovsky 148cl; Andre Jenny 78cla; Art Kowalsky 8bl; Angus McComiskey 9br; mediacolor's 78br; Paul Thompson Images/Chris Ballentine 128bc; pictureofeurope.co.uk 149c; Ray Roberts 105br; Joern Sackermann 79br; L'ARCHIDUC: Antoine Huart 173tr; ART ARCHIVE: Imperial War Museum, London 109b.

DUNCAN BAIRD PUBLISHERS: Alan Williams 151br. CH. BASTIN & J. EVRARD: 18tr/cb/hr, 19tr/hr, 76br; 86bl/br; 97t, 107t, 118b, 121br; WWW.BRIDGEMAN.CO.UK: Christie's Images, London Peter Paul Rubens (1557–1640) *Self Portrait* 17t; Musée Crozatier, Le Puy-en-Velay, France designed by Bernin (c 1725–1730) *Dawn*, Brussels lace 23bl; Private Collection/ Marie-Victoire Jaquotot (1778–1855) *Portrait of the Duke of Wellington* 35b./Max Silbert (b.1871) *The Lacemakers of Ghent* 1913 23t; Private Collection French School (19th century) Louis XIV (1638–1715) of France in the costume of the Sun King in the ballet 'La Nuit' c.1665 (litho) 32br; Private Collection/ Bonhams, London/Robert Alexander Hillingford (1825–1904) *The Turning Point at Waterloo* (oil on canvas) 34bl; St. Bavo Cathedral, Ghent Hubert Eyck (c.1370–1426) & Jan van Eyck (1390–1441), *Adoration of the Mystic Lamb*, Oil on panel 114bl; Stad Brugge Stedelijke Musea: Groeningemuseum 124ca/cb/b, 125bl; Paul Delveaux *Serenity*, 1970 ©Foundation P. Delveaux – St Idesbald, Belgium 125b; Gruithuis 122t/cb/b, 123c; Gruuthusemuseum 30t; BRÜSEL: 170tl; BRUSSELS AIRLINES: 182cla; BRUSSELS INTERNATIONAL FESTIVAL OF FANTASTIC FILM: 174clb.

CAFE COULEUR: 25t; CEPHAS: Nigel Blythe 130-1; TOP/ A. Riviere-Lecoeur 150bl; CHIMAY: 150cr; DEMETRIO CARRASCO: 145b; ALAN COPSON: 15bl, 37c; CORBIS: David Bartruff 21cb, 148tr; Jon Hicks 105tr; Wolfgang Kaehler 182br; Ludovic Maisant 145tr; Patrick Ward 25b.

DAS PHOTO: 172c, 180c, 182t, 186; DRIES VAN NOTEN: 8cr, 169c, 170bc.

ECRAN TOTAL©CINEDIT: 172t; EUROLINES: 183tr.

GETTY IMAGES: AFP/Getty Images / Dominique Faget 184br.

ROBERT HARDING PICTURE LIBRARY: Charles Bowman 93tr; Julian Pottage 81t, 185b; Roger Somvi 17b, 24t/c; HAVANA: 147c; HEMISPHERES IMAGES: Monde/Suetone Emilio 168bc; HOLLANDSE HOOGTE: 116clb, 117tr; HOTEL BLOOM: 133tr; HOTEL MARIVAUX: 135bl; HULTON GETTY COLLECTION: 33t, 34c, 36c, 97b; Keytone 37t.

INSTITUT ROYAL DU PATRIMOINE ARTISTIQUE/
KONINKLIJK INSTITUUT VOOR HET
KUNSTPATRIMONIUM: 22tr, Societé des Expositions du
Palais des Beaux-Arts de Bruxelles 53tr.

GLENDA KAPSALIS/www.photographersdirect.com: 129bl;
KONINKLIJK MUSEUM VOOR SCHONE KUNSTEN,
ANTWERP: Delvaux *Pink's Bow* ©Foundation P. Delveaux
– St Idesbald, Belgium/DACS, London 2006 100br; J.
Jordaens *As the old sang, the young ones play pipes* 100clb;
R. Magritte *Madame Recamier* ©ADAGP, Paris and DACS,
London 2006 100bl; P.P. Rubens *Adoration of the Magi*
101c; J. Van Eyck *Saint Barbara* 101t; R. Wouters *Woman
Ironing* 101cb.

LEONARDO MEDIABANK: 104tr, 133bl, 135cr;
LONELY PLANET IMAGES: Martin Moos 104cb, 104bl;
Rockoxhuis, Frans Snijders, Fishmarket Antwerp, detail
99ca.

MAPPA MUNDO: 174tr; MODEMUSEUM, Antwerp: 98cl;
MUSEA BRUGGE: Museum of Folklore 129cr; MUSÉE DE
L'ART WALLON DE LA VILLE DE LIÈGE: Legs M. Aristide
Cralle (1884) 35tl; MUSÉES ROYAUX DES BEAUX-ARTS
DE BELGIQUE, BRUXELLES-KONINKLIJKE MUSEA VOOR
SCHONE KUNSTEN VAN BELGIË, Brussel: photo Cussac
6–7, 16t, 34–5, 62clb, 63crb/bl, 66t, 67tr, 67b, /©ADAGP,
Paris and DACS, London 2011 64bl; photo Speltdoorn 16b,
17c, 22c, 63cr, 65br, 65cra,/©ADAGP, PARIS AND DACS,
London 2006 64cl.

DOCUMENT POT: Alain Mathieu 187t. P&O FERRIES LTD:
183bl; PHOTOSHOT: Michael Owston 181bl; PICTOR: 93t;
ROBBIE POLLEY: 118b, 122ca, 123b, 124tr, 184c/b, 187b;

PRIVATE COLLECTION: 7, 34, 39, 89, 131, 177.

REX FEATURES: 24b, 26c, Action Press 36t.

SCIENCE PHOTO LIBRARY: CNES 1992 Distribution Spot
Image 10; ©STANDAARD STRIPS: 21bl; Sensum.be: 145bl;
NEIL SETCHFIELD: 22tl, 92t, 148c, 169b; SUNDANCER: ©
Moulinsart 20cl.

TELEGRAPH COLOUR LIBRARY: Ian McKinnell 88-9;
ARCHIVES DU THEATRE ROYAL DE LA MONNAIE: 35tr;
TONY STONE IMAGES: Richard Elliott 27; Hideo Kurihara
2–3; ©TOERISME OOOST-VLAANDEREN: 107br;
TOURING CLUB DE BELGIQUE: 186tl; TOURISM
ANTWERP: 95cr; 96clb; 117cl; LA TRUFFE NOIRE: 144br;
SERVICE RELATIONS EXTERIEURES CITY OF TOURNAI:
22b.

ROGER VIOLLET: 32t; Musee San Martino, Naples 33b.

WORLD PICTURES: 26b, 109b.

Map Cover
PHOTO LIBRARY: Reso/Kouprianoff Kouprianoff.

Jacket
Front - PHOTO LIBRARY: Reso/Kouprianoff Kouprianoff.
Back - DORLING KINDERSLEY: Demetrio Carrasco cla, clb,
tl; Paul Kenward bl. Spine - PHOTO LIBRARY: Reso/
Kouprianoff Kouprianoff t.

All other images ©Dorling Kindersley.
For further information see: www.dkimages.com

Phrase Book

Tips for Pronouncing French

French-speaking Belgians, or Walloons, have a throaty, deep accent noticeably different from French spoken in France. Despite this, there are few changes in the vocabulary used in spoken and written language.

Consonants at the end of words are mostly silent and not pronounced. *Ch* is pronounced *sh*; *th* is *t*; *w* is *v*; and *r* is rolled gutturally. *Ç* is pronounced *s*.

In Emergency

Help!	Au secours!	oh sek**oor**
Stop!	Arrêtez!	aret-**ay**
Call a doctor!	Appelez un medecin	apuh-**lay**un meds**añ**
Call the police!	Appelez la police	apuh-**lay** lah pol-**ees**
Call the fire brigade!	Appelez les pompiers	apuh-**lay** leh poñ-peey**ay**
Where is the nearest telephone?	Où est le téléphone le plus proche	oo ay luh tehleh**fon** luh ploo prosh
Where is the nearest hospital?	Où est l'hôpital le plus proche	oo ay l'opeetal luh ploo prosh

Communication Essentials

Yes	Oui	wee
No	Non	noñ
Please	S'il vous plaît	seel voo **play**
Thank you	Merci	mer-**see**
Excuse me	Excusez-moi	exkoo-**zay** mwah
Hello	Bonjour	boñzhoor
Goodbye	Au revoir	oh ruh-**vwar**
Good night	Bonne nuit	bon-**swar**
morning	Le matin	mat**añ**
afternoon	L'après-midi	l'apreh-**meedee**
evening	Le soir	swah
yesterday	Hier	eeyehr
today	Aujourd'hui	oh-zhoor-**dwee**
tomorrow	Demain	duhm**añ**
here	Ici	ee-**see**
there	Là bas	lah bah
What?	Quel/quelle?	kel, kel
When?	Quand?	koñ
Why?	Pourquoi?	poor-**kwah**
Where?	Où?	oo
How?	Comment?	kom-**moñ**

Useful Phrases

How are you?	Comment allez vous?	kom-moñ ta**lay** voo
Very well, thank you.	Très bien, merci.	treh byañ, mer see
How do you do?	Comment ça va?	kom-moñ sah **vah**
See you soon.	A bientôt.	byañ-toh
That's fine.	Ça va bien.	Sah vah byañ
Where is/are...?	Où est/sont...?	ooh ay/soñ
How far is it to...?	Combien de kilomètres d'ici à...?	kom-byañ duh keelo-**metr** d'ee-**see** ah
Which way to...?	Quelle est la direction pour...?	kel ay lah deer-ek-**syoñ** poor
Do you speak English?	Parlez-vous Anglais?	par-**lay** voo oñg-**lay**
I don't understand.	Je ne comprends pas.	zhuh nuh kom-**proñ** pah
Could you speak slowly?	Pouvez-vous parlez plus lentement?	voo pwee-say par-lay ploos **loñ**tuh-moñ
I'm sorry.	Excusez-moi.	exkoo-**zay** mwah

Useful Words

big	grand	groñ
small	petit	puh-**tee**
hot	chaud	show
cold	froid	frwah
good	bon	boñ
bad	mauvais	moh-**veh**
enough	assez	as**say**
well	bien	byañ
open	ouvert	oo-**ver**
closed	fermé	fer-**meh**
left	gauche	gohsh
right	droite	drawht
straight on	tout droit	too drwaht
near	près	preh
far	loin	lwañ
up	en haut	oñ oh
down	en bas	oñbah
early	tôt	toh

late	tard	tar
entrance	l'entrée	l'on-**tray**
exit	la sortie	sor-**tee**
toilet	toilette	twah-let
occupied	occupé	o-koo-**pay**
free (vacant)	libre	leebr
free (no charge)	gratuit	grah-**twee**

Making a Telephone Call

I would like to place a long-distance telephone call	Je voudrais faire un Interurbain	zhuh voo-dreh faire uñ añter-oorbañ
I'd like to call collect	Je voudrais faire un communication PCV	zhuh voo-**dreh** faire oon kom-oonikah-**syoñ** peh-seh-veh
I will try again later	Je vais essayer plus tard	zhuh vay ess-ay-eh ploo tar
Can I leave a message?	Est-ce que je peux laisser un message?	es-**keh** zhuh puh les-**say** uñ meh-**sazh**
Could you speak up a little please?	Pouvez-vous parler un peu plus fort?	poo-**vay** voo par-**lay** uñ puh ploo for
Local call	Communication local	komoonikah-**syoñ** low-kal

Shopping

How much does this cost?	C'est combien?	say kom-**byañ**
I would like....	Je voudrais	zhuh voo-**dray**
Do you have...	Est-ce que vous avez...	es-kuh voo zavay
I'm just looking	Je regarde seulement	zhuh ruh**gar** suhl moñ
Do you take credit cards?	Est-ce que vous acceptez les cartes de crédit	es-**kuh** voo zaksept-**ay** leh kart duh kreh-**dee**
Do you take travellers' cheques?	Est-ce que vous acceptez les chèques de voyage	es-**kuh** voo zak-sept-**ay** lay shek duh vwayazh
What time do you open?	A quelle heure vous êtes ouvert	ah kel urr voo zet oo-**ver**
What time do you close?	A quelle heure vous êtes fermé	ah kel urr voo zet fer-**may**
This one	Celui-ci	suhl-wee **see**
That one	Celui-là	suhl wee lah
expensive	cher	shehr
cheap	pas cher, bon marché	pah shehr, boñ mar-shay
size, clothes	la taille	tye
white	blanc	bloñ
black	noir	nwahr
red	rouge	roozh
yellow	jaune	zhownh
green	vert	vehr
blue	bleu	bluh

Types of Shops

shop	le magasin	le maga-**zañ**
bakery	la boulangerie	booloñ-zhuree
bank	la banque	boñk
bookshop	la librairie	lee brehree
butcher	la boucherie	boo-shehree
cake shop	la pâtisserie	patee-**sree**
chocolate shop	le chocolatier	shok-oh-lah-tyeh
chip stop/stand	la friterie	free-tuh-ree
chemist	la pharmacie	farmah-**see**
delicatessen	la charcuterie	shah-koo-tuh-**ree**
department store	le grand magasin	groñ maga-**zañ**
fishmonger	la poissonerie	pwasson-ree
greengrocer	le marchand des légumes	mar-**shoñ** duh lay-goom
hairdresser	le coiffeur	kwa**fuhr**
market	le marché	marsh **ay**
newsagent	le magasin de journaux/tabac	maga-**zañ** duh zhoor-**no**
post office	le bureau de poste	boo-**roh** duh pohst
supermarket	le supermarché	soo-pehr-**marshay**
travel agent	l'agence de voyage	azhons duh vwayazh

Sightseeing

art gallery	la galérie d'art	galer-**ree** dart
bus station	la gare routière	gahr roo-tee-yehr

cathedral	la cathédrale	katay-dral
church	l'église	aygleez
closed on public holidays	fermeture jour ferié	fehrmeh-tur zhoor fehree-ay
garden	le jardin	zhah-dañ
library	la bibliothèque	beebleeo-tek
museum	le musée	moo-zay
railway station	la gare (SNCF)	gahr (es-en-say-ef)
tourist office	les informations	layz uñ-for-mah-syoñ
town hall	l'hôtel de ville	ohtel duh vil
train	le train	trañ

Staying in a Hotel

Do you have a vacant room?	est-ce que vous avez une chambre?	es-kuh voo zavay oon shambr
double room with double bed	la chambre à deux personnes, avec un grand lit	la shambr uh duh per-son uh-vek uñ groñ lee
twin room	la chambre à deux lits	la shambr ah duh lee
single room	la chambre à une personne	la shambr ah oon pehr-son
room with a bath	la chambre avec salle de bain	shambr ah-vek sal duh bañ
shower	une douche	doosh
I have a reservation	J'ai fait une reservation	zhay fay oon ray-zehrva-syoñ

Eating Out

Have you got a table?	Avez vous une table libre?	avay-voo oon tahbl leebr
I would like to reserve a table.	Je voudrais réserver une table.	zhuh voo-dray rayzehr-vay oon tahbl
The bill, please.	L'addition, s'il vous plait.	l'adee-syoñ voo play
I am a vegetarian.	Je suis végétarien.	zhuh swee vezhay-tehryañ
waitress/waiter	Monsieur, Mademoiselle	gah-sohn/ mad-uh-mwah-zel
menu	le menu	men-oo
cover charge	le couvert	luh koo-vehr
wine list	la carte des vins	lah kart-deh vañ
glass	verre	vehr
bottle	la bouteille	boo-tay
knife	le couteau	koo-toh
fork	la fourchette	for-shet
spoon	la cuillère	kwee-yehr
breakfast	le petit déjeuner	puh-tee day-zhuh-nay
lunch	le déjeuner	day-zhuh-nay
dinner	le dîner	dee-nay
main course	le grand plat	groñ plah
starter	l'hors d'oeuvres	or duhvr
dessert	le dessert	duh-zehrt
dish of the day	le plat du jour	plah doo joor
bar	le bar	bah
cafe	le café	ka-fay
rare	saignant	say-nyoñ
medium	à point	ah pwañ
well done	bien cuit	byañ kwee

Numbers

0	zero	zeh-roh
1	un	uñ, oon
2	deux	duh
3	trois	trwah
4	quatre	katr
5	cinq	sañk
6	six	sees
7	sept	set
8	huit	weet
9	neuf	nerf
10	dix	dees
11	onze	oñz
12	douze	dooz
13	treize	trehz
14	quatorze	katorz
15	quinze	kañz
16	seize	sehz
17	dix-sept	dees-set
18	dix-huit	dees-zweet
19	dix-neuf	dees-znerf
20	vingt	vañ
21	vingt-et-un	vañ ay uhn
30	trente	tront
40	quarante	karoñt
50	cinquante	sañkoñt

60	soixante	swahsoñt
70	septante	septoñt
80	quatre-vingt	katr-vañ
90	quatre-vingt-dix/ nonante	katr vañ dees nonañ
100	cent	soñ
1000	mille	meel
1,000,000	million	miyoñ

Time

What is the time?	Quelle heure?	kel uhr
one minute	une minute	oon mee-noot
one hour	une heure	oon uhr
half an hour	une demi-heure	oon duh-mee uhr
half past one	une heure et demi	uhr ay duh-mee
a day	un jour	zhuhr
a week	une semaine	suh-mehn
a month	un mois	mwah
a year	une année	annay
Monday	lundi	luñ-dee
Tuesday	mardi	mah-dee
Wednesday	mercredi	mehrkruh-dee
Thursday	jeudi	zhuh-dee
Friday	vendredi	voñdruh-dee
Saturday	samedi	sam-dee
Sunday	dimanche	dee-moñsh

Belgian Beer and Food

fish	poisson	pwah-ssoñ
bass	bar/loup de mer	bah/loo duh mare
herring	hareng	ah-roñ
lobster	homard	oh-ma
monkfish	lotte	lot
mussel	moule	mool
oyster	huitre	weetr
pike	brochet	brosh-ay
salmon	saumon	soh-moñ
scallop	coquille Saint-Jacques	kok-eel sañ jak
sea bream	dorade/daurade	doh-rad
prawn	crevette	kreh-vet
skate	raie	ray
trout	truite	trweet
tuna	thon	toñ

Meat

meat	viande	vee-yand
beef	boeuf	buhf
chicken	poulet	poo-lay
duck	canard	kanar
lamb	agneau	ahyoh
pheasant	faisant	feh-zoñ
pork	porc	por
veal	veau	voh
venison	cerf/chevreuil	surf/shev-roy

Vegetables

vegetables	légumes	lay-goom
asparagus	asperges	ahs-pehrj
Belgian endive /chicory	chicon	shee-koñ
Brussels sprouts	choux de bruxelles	shoo duh broocksell
garlic	ail	eye
green beans	haricots verts	arrykoh vehr
haricot beans	haricots	arrykoh
potatoes	pommes de terre	pom-duh tehr
spinach	epinard	aypeenar
truffle	truffe	troof

Desserts

pancake	crêpe	crayp
waffle	gauffre	gohfr
fruit	fruits	frwee

Drinks

coffee	café	kah-fay
white coffee	café au lait	kah-fay oh lay
milky coffee	caffe latte	kah-fay lat-uh
hot chocolate	chocolat chaud	shok-oh-lah shoh
tea	thé	tay
water	l'eau	oh
mineral water	l'eau minérale	l'oh meenay-ral
lemonade	limonade	lee-moh-nad
orange juice	jus d'orange	zhoo doh-ronj
wine	le vin	vañ
house wine	vin maison	vañ may-sañ
beer	une bière	byahr

Tips for Pronouncing Dutch

The Dutch language is pronounced in largely the same way as English, although many vowels, particularly double vowels, are pronounced as long sounds. *J* is the equivalent of the English *y*, *v* is pronounced *f*, and *w* is *v*.

late	laat	laat
entrance	ingang	in-ghang
exit	uitgang	ouht-ghang
toilet	wc	vhay-say
occupied	bezet	buh-zett
free (vacant)	vrij	vraiy
free (no charge)	gratis	ghraah-tiss

In Emergency

Help!	Help!	help
Stop!	Stop!	stop
Call a doctor!	Haal een dokter!	Haal uhn **dok**-tur
Call the police!	Roep de politie!	Roop duh poe-**leet**-see
Call the fire brigade!	Roep de brandweer!	Roop duh **brahnt**-vheer
Where is the nearest telephone?	Waar ist de dichtsbijzijnde telefoon?	Vhaar iss duh **dikst**-baiy-zaiyn-duh-tay-luh-**foan**
Where is the nearest hospital?	Waar ist het dichtsbijzijnde ziekenhuis	Vhaar iss het **dikst**-baiy-zaiyn-duh **zee**-kuh-hows

Communication Essentials

Yes	Ja	yaa
No	Nee	nay
Please	Alstublieft	ahls-tew-**bleeft**
Thank you	Dank u	dhank-ew
Excuse me	Pardon	pahr-**don**
Hello	Goed dag	ghoot dahgh
Goodbye	Tot ziens	tot zins
Good night	Slaap lekker	slap **lek**-kah
morning	Morgen	**mor**-ghugh
afternoon	Middag	**mid**-dahgh
evening	Avond	**av**-vohnd
yesterday	Gisteren	**ghis**-tern
today	Vandaag	van-**daagh**
tomorrow	Morgen	**mor**-ghugh
here	Hier	heer
there	Daar	daar
What?	Wat?	vhat
When?	Wanneer?	vhan-**eer**
Why?	Waarom?	vhaar-**om**
Where?	Waar?	vhaar
How?	Hoe?	hoo

Useful Phrases

How are you?	Hoe gaat het ermee?	Hoo ghaat het er-**may**
Very well, thank you	Heel goed, dank u	Hayl ghoot, dhank ew
How do you do?	Hoe maakt u het?	Hoo maakt ew het
See you soon	Tot ziens	Tot zeens
That's fine	Prima	**Pree**-mah
Where is/are...?	Waar is/zijn...?	vhaar iss/zayn
How far is it to...?	Hoe ver is het naar...?	Hoo vehr iss het nar
How do I get to...?	Hoe kom ik naar...?	Hoo kom ik nar
Do you speak English?	Spreekt u engels?	Spraykt uw **eng**-uhls
I don't understand	Ik snap het niet	Ik snahp het neet
Could you speak slowly?	Kunt u langzamer praten?	Kuhnt ew lahng-zamer-praat-tuh
I'm sorry	Sorry	sorry

Useful Words

big	groot	ghroat
small	klein	klaiyn
hot	warm	vharm
cold	koud	khowt
good	goed	ghoot
bad	slecht	slekht
enough	genoeg	ghuh-**noohkh**
well	goed	ghoot
open	open	open
closed	gesloten	ghuh-**slow**-tuh
left	links	links
right	rechts	rekhts
straight on	rechtdoor	rehkht dohr
near	dichtbij	dikht baiy
far	ver weg	vehr vhekh
up	omhoog	om-**hoakh**
down	naar beneden	naar buh **nay**-duh
early	vroeg	vrookh

Making a Telephone Call

I'd like to place a long-distance telephone call	Ik wil graag interlokal telefoneren	ik vhil ghraakh **inter**-loh-kaal tay-luh-foh-**neh**-ruh
I'd like to call collect	Ik wil "collect call" bellen	ik vhil " collect call" **bel**-luh
I will try again later	Ik probeer het later nog wel eens	ik pro-**beer** het later laater nokh vhel ayns
Can I leave a message?	Kunt u een boodschap doorgeven?	kuhnt ew uhn **boat**-skhahp **dohr**-ghay-vuh
Could you speak up a little please?	Wilt u wat harder praten?	vhilt ew vhat hahr-der **praat**-ew
Local call	Lokaal gesprek	low-**kaahl** ghuh-sprek

Shopping

How much does this cost?	Hoeveel kost dit?	hoo-**vayl** kost dit
I would like...	Ik wil graag...	ik vhil ghraakh
Do you have...?	Heeft u...?	hayft ew
I'm just looking	Ik kijk alleen even	ik kaiyk alleyn ay-vuh
Do you take credit cards?	Neemt u credit cards?	naymt ew credit cards aan?
Do you take travellers' cheques?	Neemt u reischeques aan?	naymt ew **raiys**-sheks aan
What time do you open?	Hoe laat gaat u open?	hoo laat ghaat ew opuh
What time do you close?	Hoe laat gaat u dicht?	hoo laat ghaat ew dikht
This one	Deze	**day**-zuh
That one	Die	dee
expensive	duur	dewr
cheap	goedkoop	ghoot-**koap**
size	maat	maat
white	wit	vhit
black	zwart	zvhahrt
red	rood	roat
yellow	geel	ghayl
green	groen	ghroon
blue	blauw	blah-ew

Types of Shops

antique shop	antiekwinkel	ahn **teek** vhin kul
bakery	bakker	**bah**-ker-aiy
bank	bank	bahnk
bookshop	boekwinkel	**book**-vhin-kul
butcher	slager	slaakh-er-aiy
cake shop	banketbakkerij	bahnk-**et**-bahk-er-aiy
chip stop/stand	patatzaak	pah-**taht**-zak
chemist/drugstore	apotheek	ah-poe-**taiyk**
delicatessen	delicatessen	daylee-kah-**tes**-suh
department store	warenhuis	**vhaah**-uh-houws
fishmonger	viswinkel	**viss**-vhin-kul
greengrocer	groenteboer	**ghroon** tuh boor
hairdresser	kapper	**kah**-per
market	markt	mahrkt
newsagent	krantenwinkel	**krahn**-tuh-vhin-kul
post office	postkantoor	**pohst**-kahn-tor
supermarket	supermarkt	**sew**-per-mahrkt
tobacconist	sigarenwinkel	see-**ghaa**-ruh-vhin-kul
travel agent	reisburo	**raiys**-bew-roa

Sightseeing

art gallery	gallerie	ghaller-ee
bus station	busstation	**buhs**-stah-shown
bus ticket	strippenkaart	**strip**-puh-kaart
cathedral	kathedraal	kah-tuh-**draal**
church	kerk	kehrk
closed on public holidays	op feestdagen gesloten	op **fayst**-daa-ghuh ghuh-slow-**tuh**
day return	dagretour	**dahgh**-ruh-tour
garden	tuin	touwn
library	bibliotheek	bee-bee-yo-**tayk**
museum	museum	mew-**zay**-um

railway station	station	stah-**shown**
return ticket	retourtje	ruh-**tour**-tyuh
single journey	enkeltje	eng-**kuhl**-tyuh
tourist information	dienst voor tourisme	deenst vor tor-ism
town hall	stadhuis	staht-houws
train	trein	traiyn

Staying in a Hotel

Do you have a vacant room?	Zijn er nog kamers vrij?	zaiyn er nokh kaa-mers vray
double room with double bed	een twees persoons-kamer met een twee persoonsbed	uhn tvhay per-**soans**-ka-mer met uhn tvhay per-**soans** beht
twin room	een kamer met een lits-jumeaux	uhn kaa-mer met uhn lee-zjoo-**moh**
single room	eenpersoons-kamer	ayn-per-**soans** kaa-mer
room with a bath/shower	kaamer met bad/ douche	kaa-mer met baht/doosh
I have a reservation	Ik heb gereserveerd	ik hehp ghuh-ray-sehr-**veert**

Eating Out

Have you got table?	Is er een tafel vrij?	iss ehr uhn **tah**-fuhl vraiy
I would like to reserve a table	Ik wil een tafel reserveren	ik vhil uhn **tah**-fel ray sehr-**veer**-uh
The bill, please	Mag ik afrekenen	muhk ik **ahf**-ray-kuh-nuh
I am a vegetarian	Ik ben vegetariër	ik ben fay-ghuh-**taahr**-ee-er
waitress/waiter	serveerster/ober	sehr-**veer**-ster/**oh**-ber
menu	de kaart	duh kaahrt
cover charge	het couvert	het koo-**vehr**
wine list	de wijnkaart	duh **vhaiyn**-kart
glass	het glass	het ghlahss
bottle	de fles	duh fless
knife	het mes	het mess
fork	de vork	duh fohrk
spoon	de lepel	duh **lay**-pul
breakfast	het ontbijt	het ont-**baiyt**
lunch	de lunch	duh lernsh
dinner	het diner	het dee-**nay**
main course	het hoofdgerecht	het **hoaft**-ghuh-rekht
starter, first course	het voorgerecht	het **vhor**-ghuh-rekht
dessert	het nagerecht	het **naa**-ghuh-rekht
dish of the day	het dagmenu	het **dahg**-munh-ew
bar	het cafe	het kaa-**fay**
café	het eetcafe	het **ayt**-kaa-**fay**
rare	rare	'rare'
medium	medium	'medium'
well done	doorbakken	door-**bah**-kuh

Numbers

1	een	ayn
2	twee	tvhay
3	drie	dree
4	vier	feer
5	vijf	faiyf
6	zes	zess
7	zeven	**zay**-vuh
8	acht	ahkht
9	negen	**nay**-guh
10	tien	teen
11	elf	elf
12	twaalf	tvhaalf
13	dertien	**dehr**-teen
14	veertien	**feer**-teen
15	vijftien	**faiyf**-teen
16	zestien	**zess**-teen
17	zeventien	**zayvuh**-teen
18	achtien	**ahkh**-teen
19	negentien	**nay-ghuh**-tien
20	twintig	**tvhin**-tukh
21	eenentwintig	aynuh-tvhin-tukh
30	dertig	**dehr**-tukh
40	veertig	**feer**-tukh
50	vijftig	**faiyf**-tukh
60	zestig	**zess**-tukh
70	zeventig	**zay**-vuh-tukh
80	tachtig	**tahkh**-tukh
90	negentig	**nayguh**-tukh

100	honderd	hohn-durt
1000	duizend	douw-zuhnt
1,000,000	miljoen	mill-**yoon**

Time

one minute	een minuut	uhn meen-**ewt**
one hour	een uur	uhn ewr
half an hour	een half uur	een hahlf uhr
half past one	half twee	hahlf twee
a day	een dag	uhn dahgh
a week	een week	uhn vhayk
a month	een maand	uhn maant
a year	een jaar	uhn jaar
Monday	maandag	**maan**-dahgh
Tuesday	dinsdag	**dins**-dahgh
Wednesday	woensdag	**vhoons**-dahgh
Thursday	donderdag	**donder**-dahgh
Friday	vrijdag	**vraiy**-dahgh
Saturday	zaterdag	**zaater**-dahgh
Sunday	zondag	**zon**-dahgh

Belgian Beer and Food

Fish

Fish	vis	fiss
bass	zeebars	see-buhr
herring	haring	**haa**-ring
lobster	kreeft	krayft
monkfish	lotte/zeeduivel	lot/seafuhdul
mussel	mossel	moss-uhl
oyster	oester	**ouhs**-tuh
pike	snoek	snook
prawn	garnaal	gar-nall
salmon	zalm	sahlm
scallop	Sint-Jacoboester/ Jacobsschelp	**sind**-yakob-ouhs-tuh/yakob-scuhlp
sea bream	dorade/zeebrasem	doh-rard
skate	rog	rog
trout	forel	foh-ruhl
tuna	tonijn	tuhn-een

Meat

meat	vlees	flayss
beef	rundvlees	**ruhnt**-flayss
chicken	kip	kip
duck	eend	aynt
lamb	lamsvlees	**lahms**-flayss
pheasant	fazant	**fay**-zanh
pork	varkensvlees	**vahr**-kuhns-flayss
veal	kalfsvlees	**karfs**-flayss
venison	ree (bok)	ray

Vegetables

vegetables	groenten	**ghroon**-tuh
asparagus	asperges	as-puhj
Belgian endive/ chicory	witloof	vit-lurf
Brussels sprouts	spruitjes	spruhr-tyuhs
garlic	knoflook	**knoff**-loak
green beans	princesbonen	prins-ess-buh-nun
haricot beans	snijbonen	snee-buh-nun
potatoes	aardappels	**aard**-uppuhls
spinach	spinazie	spin-a-jee
truffle	truffel	truh-fuhl

Desserts

fruit	fruit/vruchten	vroot/vrooh-tuh
pancake	pannekoek	**pah**-nuh-kook
waffle	wafel	vaff-uhl

Drinks

beer	bier	beeh
coffee	koffie	coffee
fresh orange juice	verse jus	**vehr**-suh zjhew
hot chocolate	chocola	sho-koh-**laa**
mineral water	mineraalwater	meener-**aahl**-vhaater
tea	thee	tay
water	water	vhaa-ter
wine	wijn	vhaiyn

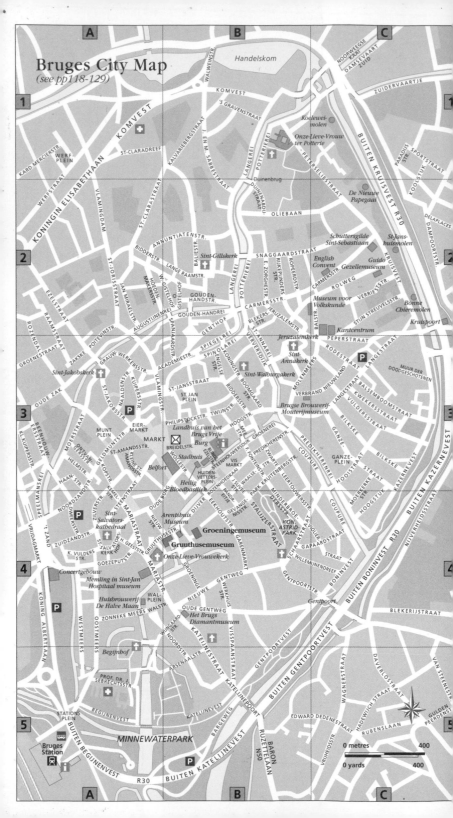